KT-574-283

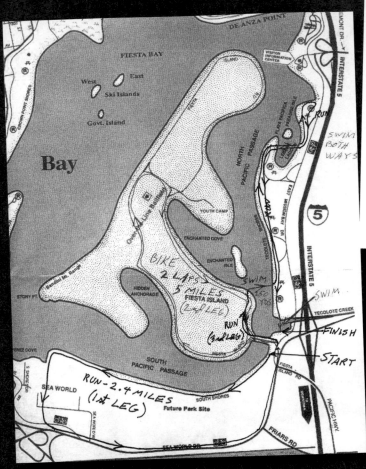

Jack Johnstone,
the Godfather
and founder of
modern-day triathlon,
exiting the water
after a hard swim.

Map of first triathlon –
September 25, 1974.

Induction into Triathlete Magazine Hall of
Fame – 1998. Bill Phillips (winner of the first
triathlon), Dave Pain (founder of Dave Pain
Birthday Biathlon), Don Shanahan and Jack
Johnstone (founders of the first triathlon).

H

n

First published in January 2013

British Library Cataloguing in Publication Data
A catalogue record for this book is available from the British Library.

ISBN 978 0 85733 302 5

Library of Congress catalog card no. 2012944800

Published by Haynes Publishing,
Sparkford, Yeovil, Somerset BA22 7JJ, UK
Tel: 01963 442030 Fax: 01963 440001
Int. tel: +44 1963 442030 Int. fax: +44 1963 440001
E-mail: sales@haynes.co.uk
Website: www.haynes.co.uk

Haynes North America Inc.
861 Lawrence Drive, Newbury Park,
California 91320, USA

Printed and bound in the USA

Author:	Sean Lerwill (Twitter @seanlerwill)
Project Manager:	Louise McIntyre
Copy editor:	Ian Heath
Design:	Rod Teasdale
Photography:	Guy Harrop, Bill Gidda, Kevin Winebold, Jonathan Josephs
Stock photos:	Shutterstock

Contents

Foreword by Jack Johnstone

In 1971 aged 35 I joined millions of other Americans in the jogging craze. One thing led to another, and before I knew it I was competing in road races, which at that time were relatively small and inexpensive affairs. My previous athletic career had consisted of eight years as a high school and college swimmer, being named to the 1957 collegiate and AAU All-American teams in the 100-yard breaststroke.

I conceived the idea of a run/swim biathlon with equal emphasis on the two disciplines and several alternate legs to the race. The initial run could be done in racing shoes, but subsequent sections would have to be barefoot on grass or sand. The Fiesta Island area of Mission Bay was almost perfect. I designed a course and asked for it to be put on the San Diego Track Club calendar, and it was suggested that someone called Don Shanahan and I combine our ideas so there wouldn't be too many 'weird' races on the schedule. After all, this was a running club. I called Don and learnt that he wanted to stage a race with a cycling leg.

We decided to call the event the Mission Bay Triathlon and I think the entry fee was one dollar. The flyers stated that participants needed to bring their own bike. It seems strange now that we thought it necessary to include a requirement about bringing bikes but someone had asked me if they'd be provided.

When ordering the award trophies the shop owner asked how to spell 'triathlon'. He hadn't found it in any dictionary. I thought; if it's not in any dictionary, the word must not exist, so I should decide how to spell it. Given the spellings 'pentathlon', 'heptathlon' and 'decathlon' I guess it was the obvious choice, but it seemed like I had a lot of power at the time.

On race day, 25 September 1974, 46 eager contenders toed the line, which significantly exceeded our expectations for a never-before-staged race held on a weekday evening. An injury kept Don Shanahan from competing but I had to do it. We shared the pre-race responsibilities but he was the director once the event began.

The winner was expected to finish in under an hour but we predicted that some competitors would take twice that long. Darkness could conceivably be a problem, so we arranged for a few cars to have their headlights directed on the last swimming segment. It was well after dark when the last of the first triathletes made their way across the inlet to the finish line.

These people were not known as 'triathletes' and none were into 'cross-training'. Neither word existed at the time. Most didn't own racing bikes and some were marginal swimmers at best, yet they had the adventuresome spirit to come out after a day of work to participate in a new athletic event. Few of the names listed in the results will be familiar to today's triathletes, but one name most should recognize was listed in 35th place. John Collins – who four years later would found the Ironman – had just completed his first triathlon.

Most of the bikes were beach cruisers and three-speeds. Riding my son's primitive 10-speed Volkscycle I had one of the quality machines on the field. As I dismounted my bike and tried to run my legs felt like they didn't belong to my body. I let out a moan and remember someone yelling to me, 'Well, it was your idea!' After finishing in sixth place I helped Don with the finish line.

During the next few years the local events became more popular and saw the emergence of a few athletes who considered the triathlon their specialty. Among these were Tom Warren, winner of the second Ironman, and two-time Ironman champion Scott Tinley.

In October of 1998 I was proud to become one of the original inductees into *Triathlete* Magazine's Triathlon Hall of Fame, along with Dave Pain, Don Shanahan, Bill Phillips and Tom Warren.

It is most satisfying to me to know that from the humble beginning on Mission Bay in San Diego we now have an Olympic event and numerous triathlons are held around the world.

Jack Johnstone
Founder of the first triathlon

TRIATHLON MANUAL
INTRODUCTION

Although the sport has been around since the 70s, triathlon has only really become popular over the last few years. For a very long time it was seen as a sport for people with amazing endurance and, perhaps, an inability to feel pain. Thanks in part to its name, the ironman triathlon has consequently become the *real* test amongst endurance sports athletes, leaving marathons and ultra-running behind in the dust.

Over the last few years gyms, local councils and even schools have started introducing super sprint and sprint triathlons to their health programmes, thereby opening the sport up for everyone, and with the influx of professional/semi-professional sportspeople leaving their own sports to compete at triathlon, it has come on leaps and bounds. Dubbed by some a bit of a 'fashionable' pastime, it's become the thing to say you're training for (certainly in cities), and thus races, kit, coaches and, yes, books have all appeared. With the arrival of a new breed of professional athletes who have trained specifically for triathlon, the sport's popularity has rocketed even higher.

This book is aimed both at newcomers who have decided to give triathlon a go, and those who have already tried one or two triathlons and wish to improve. It's a compilation of all the tips and advice I've accumulated during my own training and racing, as well as while training other people. If you're a seasoned triathlete I can't promise you that there'll be anything here you don't already know, but I've drawn on my Royal Marine Commando background to provide a further angle on health, fitness and exercise regimes, so who knows? Even one new tip could make a difference! If not, then look upon the book instead as a valuable repository of consolidated triathlon information.

The history of triathlon

There are two theories regarding the origins of the triathlon – one from 1974 and the other from 1977. The former contest was the birth of what we now call the triathlon, while the latter led to the competition that we know as the Ironman.

On 25 September 1974, Jack Johnstone and Don Shanahan of the San Diego Track Club put together the first race involving a swim, a cycle and a run. This was in Mission Bay, San Diego. Distances were six miles for the run, five miles cycling and 500 yards swimming; much of the run was performed on grass and sand, so was completed barefoot. Jack not only organised

the event but raced too, finishing sixth overall behind Bill Philips (winning in 55 minutes 44 seconds), Greg Gillaspie and Dave Mitchell. Most of the competitors were either runners or swimmers, being relative novices at the other disciplines. Strangely, finishing 35th was John Collins, who, after taking part in Jack Johnstone's first triathlon, discussed it with some friends and in 1977 expanded the distances to create the first Ironman.

The question, then, is if today's most up-and-coming sport can be credited to Jack Johnstone, what gave him the idea? It was actually a birthday biathlon race for Dave Pain held on 28 July 1973. This gave Jack the idea of creating a biathlon event on Fiesta Island, where Dave Pain's race had been run. However, Don Shanahan convinced him that a cycle element should be added, and the triathlon location moved to Mission Bay. Having raced in the Dave Pain birthday event and other biathlons Jack also felt that at around 250 yards (though advertised as 440 yards) the swim was too short, and that biathlons were consequently too heavily weighted towards running, so he wanted his own event to incorporate a longer swim. Little did he know that the resulting three-discipline contest would become one of the most popular fitness pastimes in the world.

The Ironman triathlon had equally modest roots, arising from discussions between John Collins (a US Naval officer), runners from the Mid-Pacific Road Running Club and swimmers from the Waikiki Swim Club. As usual, the runners and swimmers were 'discussing' who were fitter, runners or swimmers, during the 1977 Perimeter Relays Awards Ceremony (a five-person team relay race). Their argument eventually resulted in the formation of what they considered to be the ultimate endurance test, combining Oahu's three toughest events: the 2.4-mile Waikiki Rough Water Swim; the 112-mile around Oahu Cycle Race; and the 26.2-mile Honolulu Marathon.

The first race was run, cycled and swum on 18 February 1977. There were 15 entrants, and the winner would be known as the 'Ironman'. Twelve completed the course, with Gerrard Haller winning in 11 hours 46 minutes 58 seconds. Considered crazy back then, these men created what's seen today as one of the ultimate tests of endurance, the Ironman being considered one of the world's most arduous and prestigious events.

Why tri?

Like any sport or fitness regime, there are benefits. If there weren't, we probably wouldn't get involved in the first place. Triathlon is no different. Whether you're a compete novice, a willing amateur or a seasoned veteran, there are still significant benefits to be had from training and competing in triathlon:

● **Less risk of overuse injury** – With many sports/fitness regimes, where the same type of training is undertaken regularly, even daily, there's a significant risk of overuse/overtraining injuries, plateaus and eventually lack of interest. But with three distinct elements there's less chance of boredom, far more variety and consequently less risk injury.

● **Similarly**, if you're training for something very specific (a 10km race, for example), your training sessions probably become very repetitive and eventually boring. There's a

The start of any triathlon event is both daunting and exhilarating but definitely an experience.

variety of programmes out there and it's possible to keep it fresh, but humans are creatures of habit and if results aren't seen and plateaus are hit, we tend to push harder with the current programme, eventually getting bored and maybe giving up.

● **Upper body and lower body training** – At the gym, most people either hit the cardiovascular area to run, cycle, cross-train or row, or hit the weights floor to work the biceps, chest, shoulders, back and, of course, abs. Look at the park: it's the same story, running around it or doing dips, pull-ups and press-ups in the outdoor exercise area. What's the common theme? Either legs/cardiovascular or upper body is exercised, rarely both. Women are notorious for just running or cardio training, neglecting the upper body and never using weights (an entirely different book, but if this is you please research why weight training is so important for women, especially if you're trying to lose weight). Men, meanwhile, are notorious for training the 'beach' muscles – the arms and upper body – and neglecting the legs (though ironically it's training the legs that releases the hormones that allow the beach body to become a reality). But triathlon training requires full body workouts. Yes, the running and cycling are very lower-body specific, but a good swim technique is almost entirely upper-body specific, hence a great all-round regime – not to mention the upper and lower body conditioning required to be a great competitor.

● **In-built cross-training** – This has been pretty much covered above, but cross-training is something that everyone should try to incorporate, no matter what your actual sport or goal. Cross-training ensures you don't overtrain one area and get overuse injuries; it helps alleviate boredom, helps stop plateaus and ensures overall physique improvement. In short, cross-training is a perfect way to train and to enjoy a fitness lifestyle.

● **Increased mobility** – Many fitness regimes concentrate on one movement pattern – running, for example, where the legs, torso and body are moving in one way – but triathlon training expects the body to be able to change the way it works, not just at the energy systems level but also at the movement level. Swimming in particular is a great way of mobilising the shoulders and muscles of the upper body, something that many guys neglect when weight training, and despite becoming strong and muscular often have joint pains, and a real lack of range of movement. Triathlon training should really help alleviate this.

● **Increased flexibility** – In a very similar vein, flexibility comes with cross-training rather than focusing on one area. However, it also relies on some stretching, something which should be done after every run, bike or swim and as a stretch session even on specific rest days.

● **Endorphin release** – Whether it be a hard training session, beating a personal best on a run, swim or cycle, or the thrill of competing or completing on race day, endorphin release can be really uplifting and makes you feel alive, so it's a real motivator to train and compete. But it can also become an addictive feeling, so you must ensure that you don't overtrain.

● **Learn new skills** – Whether you're a runner who needs to learn to swim and cycle properly, a swimmer who needs to learn to run properly, or whichever combination, very few people who take up triathlon have it all, so there are new challenges and new skills to be learned. Even if you can swim, bike or run already, can you take off a wet wetsuit while running to a transition area?

● **Improve fitness** – It goes without saying that if you set out on a triathlon regime your overall fitness should improve. It obviously depends on your starting point, but short of already being a top competing triathlete, and bearing in mind that there are seven components of fitness (see Chapter 4), your fitness level should improve – drastically in some cases.

● **Strengthen the heart** – There are a number of reasons to start and continue a fitness regime. Living longer is always a popular one, as are keeping healthy, strengthening the heart and keeping a trim figure and physique. Triathlon training makes your body exercise its various energy systems, and thus makes the heart work harder to ensure you have the necessary oxygen to continue training or racing. The more the heart is worked in this fashion (as long as it's fuelled correctly) the stronger it will become, and the lower your pulse will be.

● **Increase lung capacity** – The more you perform cardiovascular exercise (again with adequate fuel), the stronger you'll become cardiovascularly. As you breathe and exercise you'll strengthen the various muscles that allow the chest cavity to expand, forcing air into the lungs. The more you exercise, the stronger these will become. Swim training takes this even further, as it makes you work hypoxically (without oxygen), which makes you even more proficient at using oxygen, and also as 'the body becomes its function' it makes you become 'swim-fit', which again strengthens the lungs.

● **Meet new people and make new friends** – Triathlon is fast becoming a very popular pastime, and certainly one of the 'to-dos' of the fitness world. More people than ever are entering a local sprint triathlon and then becoming hooked. Therefore it's a great way to meet like-minded people – and meeting them at tri-club or a swim club means you'll always have a significant part of your lives in common. Not only can you learn from their experience, but instead of running, pedalling or swimming alone you can train with new friends and make gains faster.

- **Have a new aim/interest in life** – As much as we don't want to admit it, life can sometimes become a little stale, a little uninspiring. Whether it's the job, the family, the local football team, it doesn't matter. You need a change, and what bigger change could there be than to become a triathlete? Rather than drifting away watching movies on TV or sitting in the pub, use triathlon to give your life new direction and meaning.

- **Visit new places** – Whether those new places are the gym (if you're using triathlon as a way to start a fitness regime), the pool (if you're a runner who's decided to compete in tris) or you decide to race around the country (or, if you're lucky enough, the world), then triathlon training can take you to places you've never been before. It really can change your life.

- **Purchase new kit** – Whether male or female, we all like to treat ourselves. OK, it's often gadgets for guys and clothes for girls, but with triathlon these tend to merge, and the temptation to buy a few bits to help with training and racing seems to get to everyone!

Finishing an Ironman is said, by those who have succeeded, to be one of the most relieving and rewarding experiences of their lives. So much so that some repeat it multiple times!

- **Condition for a reason** – Many people don't train for any particular reason, but simply because it's become part of their life or because they want to look good for a beach holiday. Either way, having a more specific reason can make you feel really good about yourself.

- **Competition** – Human beings seem to crave competition. It's in our genes, probably from an instinct to impress each other to gain a mate, or as a result of our survival instincts, endorphins and other hormones. Whatever the reasons, we love to compete, either against others or against ourselves. It makes us feel alive. Triathlon is a great sport for this, as there are so many things to work on and improve that it's actually quite hard to become bored, and you'll continue to improve and improve.

- **Get outside** – Many gym-goers really do just hit the gym, training indoors throughout the year. There's no problem with this, but it's nice to be able to get out and enjoy the fresh air and (in some places!) the sunshine, and associated 'free' vitamin D. Whether running, swimming or cycling, these can all be done outside as well as inside, so take the opportunity when you can to enjoy training in the fresh air.

- **Train a weakness** – Too many people simply train their strengths; when they see improvements in a specific area they keep working on that area. When you only have one aspect to your sport (10km running being an example, with its key element of middle/long-distance speed) you don't have the chance to pick a weak area and focus on it. But with triathlon you always have something to focus on. Very few people can say they're complete triathletes – they always have something to re-focus on in order to instil new drive.

- **Test your mental endurance** – The most important thing to instil into Royal Marine Recruits in the first few months of training is mental strength, to let them see and feel that they can push themselves further than they ever believed possible. Well, the same is true for triathletes. You'll have training sessions, races and even sleepless nights where your mental strength will be the key to not giving up. And mental endurance will make you a better, stronger person too, not just a better athlete.

- **Challenge** – Some people love a challenge, others hate it. Sometimes you'll feel like you've had enough challenges already and just want a quiet life; at other times you'll feel that your life has become stale and you need something outside of your family, job and weight training. A triathlon provides the challenge that can put a spark back into your life.

Types of triathlon

Whatever your reasons for picking up this book, you've essentially made the first step to becoming a triathlete. You've shown interest. Now it's just a case of getting the first (and always hardest) session done, after that it's easy...ish!

The ITU (International Triathlon Union) was set up in 1989 when the first triathlon world championship took place in Avignon, France. This was the point at which the official triathlon distance was set, using official Olympic distances for the separate components that were already part of the Olympic programme.

The official distances are:
Swim: 1,500m (previously 1 mile)
Bike: 40km (previously 25 miles)
Run: 10km (previously 6 miles)

This is the distance as used in the Sydney, Athens and Beijing Olympics, Commonwealth Games and ITU cup series. However, other triathlon distances do exist and are raced over:

Super sprint	**Sprint**
Swim: 400–500m	Swim: 500–750m
Bike: 10km (up to 20km)	Bike: 20km
Run: 2–3km (up to 5km)	Run: 5km

Half-ironman (sometimes called a 'middle')
Swim: 1,900m (1.2 miles)
Bike: 90km (56 miles)
Run: 21.1km (13 miles)

Ironman (sometimes called a 'long')
Swim: 3,800m (2.4 miles)
Bike: 180km (112 miles)
Run: 42.2km (26 miles)

Even if you see yourself as a seasoned athlete at one of the individual elements, when you start out in triathlon you should start with the shorter distances. This allows you to build up fitness slowly but surely, and will allow you to learn from your mistakes over shorter distances. This could mean only having to put up with blisters and chafed toes throughout a 5km run rather than a half-marathon!

If you're a good runner or cyclist, but a bad swimmer, then take the time to learn a decent swim technique before racing triathlon, especially if it's an open water swim. If you don't, it can be an awfully long swim (believe me, I know this from experience)! On the other side of the coin, if you're a good swimmer but need to build run fitness, don't underestimate the need to condition your legs to cycle and swim, especially in terms of avoiding injury.

⏱ All-encompassing

So before we head off to explore the world of triathlon, a final word on it as a sport, and how it's encouraging people to go back to our roots as endurance animals (running our prey into the ground was how we used to hunt). The next Paralympic Games in Rio de Janeiro in 2016 will see the Paratriathlon make its debut. There will be six separate categories across the sport to allow people of all abilities to race fairly against others in their category. We British are already leading the way, however, with 2010 ITU Paratriathlon World Champion Jane Egan, World and European Champion Faye McClelland, 2009 European Champion David Cooke and hopeful Iain Dawson, also an ITU World Championship Grand Final Winner. So, follow their example and get out there to train tri!

I've tried to cover all three disciplines from a beginner's point of view, so if you're literally new to all three you should be able to get up and going. If you're accomplished at one, but lack experience in the others, my advice would still be to read all three sections. I've trained a number of individuals who have said 'Oh no, my swimming's fine, I just need run training' or 'I'm a very good runner, but I need to learn to swim', and 90% of the time when I've taken a look at their running/swimming technique I've been able to improve it, leading to far better times and far easier swim or runs.

⏱ Conclusion

Hopefully this chapter has inspired you to read on, whether you read from chapter to chapter or skip to specific sections you feel you can learn from. If you enjoy running, tell others. Inspire them to run with you. We human beings become unfit and overweight far too easily, but if we encourage each other to run we can combat this. Get out there and discover your surroundings, discover your running ability, discover which friends enjoy running, and most importantly discover yourself.

Junior triathlons

As was discussed earlier, the triathlon is one of the fastest growing sports in terms of popularity and the number of events being run – both in the UK and worldwide – and this popularity is set to increase. As with any popular sport, children will soon want to have a go.

On first thoughts this is a great thing: children interested in a physical sport rather than a computer game version. But a triathlon is a long, arduous and (often) painstaking endurance sport, and not only do children have low attention spans, they shouldn't push endurance too hard too young.

The bonus is that compared to a long run, a triathlon mixes various elements that will not only hold a child's attention, but will teach them the lifelong skills of swimming, running and cycling. On top of that, to a child, rushing out of the pool to change and jump on a bike is fun and the hustle and bustle of everyone doing it adds to the excitement.

From a parent's point of view, if you have the time and money then triathlon is a superb sport to get your child involved in. Not only will it get them out of the house three times as much, it means different school clubs can be joined which also means a wide social mix. As well as the skills mentioned above, triathlon will also give children a superb strength of mind that will carry them through school, university and wherever they end up. The only downside is the cost, but to begin with a swimming costume, goggles (optional in many events) running kit, a bike and tuition should be enough. For the young, it's not about the winning it's about taking part and having fun, so the top-level tri bike dad or mum has will not be important (yet!).

Events are obviously far shorter than adult versions, and most, if not all, take into consideration the distances of the PE National Curriculum targets for the individual Key Stages.

The website kidstriathlon.co.uk quotes the following:
- 7-8 yrs – 25m swim, 1km cycle, 500m run
- 9-12 yrs – 50m swim, 2km cycle, 1km run
- 13-16 yrs – 100m swim, 3km cycle, 1.5km run

At most events the children are set off at 20 second intervals, giving each child their own start time in the pool, avoiding mass starts and the panic and uncomfortable feelings this can produce (even in adults).

The bike and run sections are often performed on grass around playing fields, which obviously avoids closing roads, but equally avoids falls on concrete. Depending on the age group the child may be guided through transition and helped with their kit. As with most adult events, a completion medal is awarded to each child that completes all three sections and crosses the finishing line at the end of the run.

For beginners, visit www.triathlonengland.org for information about local events and contact details of local clubs.

The British Triathlon Youth & Junior Super Series is designed to bring together the best young triathletes from across the UK, so they can race head to head at venues across the country (visit www.britishtriathlon.org/take-part/events/youth-and-junior-series). They have also partnered with Tata Steel to offer free triathlons to schoolchildren between the ages of 8 and 13. Bikes, helmets and t-shirts are provided at all events, so children only need to bring their running shoes and swim kit. Visit www.britishtriathlon.org/take-part/events/tata-kids-of-steel for dates and venues all over the UK.

CHAPTER 1
MOTIVATION & PSYCHOLOGY

Why are you reading this book? Are you thinking of doing a triathlon? Have you already entered one? Do you already do triathlon events? Do you want to get better? So ask yourself again: why? To really understand yourself you should question why you are doing something. Know the reasons behind the things you do. This will make it easier to motivate yourself, or enable you to realise you are doing something for the wrong reasons.

Know yourself

If you know why you're doing something it makes it so much easier to assess how you can achieve it. It helps to know your motivation so that on those dark, lonely, wet mornings you can envisage it in order to keep yourself going. Whatever it is you want to achieve, you'll have specific motivations that have a huge psychological impact on you not only when you're training, but also when you're thinking about training. The beauty of these motivations is that they can be harnessed to ensure training occurs as much as possible to reach your desired goal – which is perfect for triathlons, as for the most part a lot of training is required.

We humans are all motivated by different things and in different ways. So knowing yourself means being honest with yourself and getting to know what makes you tick: what motivates you, what annoys you, and even what will stop you training. The more self-aware you are, the easier it'll be to see your weaknesses and your strengths, so that you can avoid or work with the former and harness the latter. The important thing is to know what your motivations are and always to keep them in mind, especially when times get trying or hard.

 Feel alive!

Psychologically speaking, racing and competing are really good for us. Maybe it's the warrior in us all that rarely gets a look in any more, or maybe it's the 'fight or flight' nervousness than finally get an outing before a triathlon. Whatever it is, triathlons make us feel alive, and whether that's your motivation or not, it may well end up being something you love.

Smart training

The acronym SMART is a fitness-industry-recognised way of putting your goals into effect. It ensures they're not only thought out properly and considered fully, but are realistic and achievable as well. Hence SMART stands for:

S – Specific
M – Measurable
A – Achievable
R – Realistic
T – Timed

Specific

Specific means that your goal (or goals) must be specific and not general. What I mean by this is not just saying 'I want to be able to complete a triathlon' or 'I want to use tri training to lose weight'. These aren't specific enough, so you'll lose track of them quickly or will get halfway to your goal and think 'That'll do'. (While we're on the subject, one of my favourite mantras is 'That'll do will *never* do'. Remember that, and apply it in your everyday life too!)

The key is to state which type of tri – sprint, Olympic, ironman – you want to compete and complete, how much weight you wish to lose, what dress size you want to get into. Then you have a real, specific goal, a tangible bullseye to aim for, one that, with hard work and dedication, you WILL reach, and will be proud of yourself for doing so.

Personal experience...

I have a client who I rehabbed back from an ankle operation. She learnt to midfoot strike, and loved running in barefoot-type running shoes. She entered a local 10km race and asked for a training programme. We used the one from my running book, and she went all guns into training, including strength and conditioning. Then she caught flu, was quite ill the week before the event and couldn't race. She still hasn't. But the important point is that if she'd been well she was fit enough to. Sometimes even if you don't achieve your goal, the journey there is still a great learning curve.

Measurable

This goes hand in hand with specific. By being specific regarding the number of miles you want to run, the time you want to achieve or the amount of weight you want to lose, these goals become measurable. For example, saying your goal is 'to be fitter by a certain date' isn't measurable, whereas saying you want to be able to do a local sprint triathlon on 1 July is measurable. So set yourself measurable goals, aim for them, and if you don't quite make them within the parameters you set, believe me, you'll have made far more progress than if you didn't set any parameters in the first place. Even if on 1 July you crumple from heat exhaustion during your tri, I bet you can still swim properly now, and run and cycle far further than you could before.

Achievable

Simple really: when setting a goal it must be achievable. For example, if you're new to triathlon and your goal is to complete an ironman but the race is in three weeks' time, I'd say that's unachievable for most people. So be sensible; be honest with yourself, but equally don't set the bar too low. There's a big difference between making life easy for yourself and setting achievable goals.

Realistic

Setting realistic goals goes hand in hand with setting achievable goals. For example, if I decided suddenly that my goal is to be a better triathlete than both the Brownlee brothers put together, I think everyone would agree that I'm kidding myself. Not only is that unachievable, but it's unrealistic. Simply put, there's no point having a goal if it's unrealistic. For example, not many of us could ever complete an ironman in under nine hours, so this wouldn't be a realistic aim. Nor would learning to fly by flapping your arms. You'd simply be wasting your time. So keep it realistic – it makes the process so much more enjoyable, especially when you finally achieve your goal!

Timed

Timing your goals is very important, but the timing must be realistic. Setting realistic time scales will ensure you achieve them, firstly because you'll have something to aim for (without any pressure to improve you might let other things come between you and your training), and secondly because you won't get disheartened by not attaining your goal, despite training as hard as you could. Set timed goals as realistically as possible, then even if the times have to be modified at least you've had something to work towards.

Milestones

If your goal is particularly big, or a considerable way off, it can be worthwhile setting a number of smaller 'milestones' (little goals) along the way. For example, let's say your goal is to complete an ironman but you've done little more than walk to the pub in the last five years. Your motivation is obviously the ironman itself (which you've hopefully given yourself at least a year to build up to), but it's a long way off in both time and fitness terms; so it would be sensible to add at least one milestone – for example, it might be a local Olympic tri in six months' time. This is far more achievable, but will still require significant training.

Personally I'd add a series of smaller milestones leading up to the Olympic tri. These could be a few specific length swim/bike/runs, to either mile or time markers – for example, milestones may be a 1-mile swim, a 25-mile bike and a 5-mile run, or something along those lines; or a 30-minute swim, an hour's cycle and a 40-minute run. Get the idea? As these milestones are reached it may be necessary to reassess at what point your final goal will be achievable (you may be ahead of or behind

⏱ **Goals and aims**

Always set yourself goals and aims. That way your training won't become stale and pointless. If you get bored, find a new goal, speak to friends and other triathletes. With four types of tri events there are always new goals to aim for. And as a swimmer, cyclist or runner you can always enter separate events in all or any of these disciplines.

schedule), and change your training accordingly. And you never know what unexpected things life might throw up, a baby, relocation for work, a promotion etc. So training may need to be adjusted to suit changes in your life.

Motivation

Not everyone is motivated by the same things. Some people are competitive, and if they know someone who's running the local sprint tri they have to try to beat them. Others are just addicted to challenges or exercise and need to train. So know yourself and what your own motivations are. Focus on them and use them for encouragement whenever you can't be bothered. If you're not sure what motivates you, the following list may help:

● **Goal orientated** – This is motivation from the desire to achieve or even surpass a goal. This may be a certain length triathlon, to lose an amount of weight, or even just beating your friend who always wins when you train together! Whatever your goal, it's the goal itself that's the motivation to train.

● **Group orientated** – Group motivation revolves around our nature as social animals. Humans don't like to feel left out; we want to be accepted as part of 'the group'. This desire to be part of and to achieve with a group is great motivation. Within triathlon, swimming, cycling and running clubs, the group members feed off each other's positive energy and motivation. This doesn't mean all your training needs to be done within the group, far from it. For many members, training will purposely happen outside of the group, to try to improve fitness and become more highly regarded within the group. The obvious benefits from training with friends or as part of clubs can be seen in group orientated motivation.

● **People orientated** – This relates to the desire to have an impact on those around you. This may mean your fitness must improve to enable you to set a good example to your family, or maybe even so that you can stay around longer in order

to see them grow old. It could be that your new partner is an avid triathlete and you wish to join in that part of their life. Conversely, it could be the vanity side of training, needing recognition for the goals you've achieved and physical stature you've attained. Although such vanity may be frowned upon, it's still motivation to be fit and healthy and better than being lazy and unhealthy.

● **Habit orientated** – This is motivation provided by the need for a training/exercise habit. Some would argue that this is an addiction – to the endorphins released when training hard, to the feeling of burning muscles, or even burning calories and excess fat, or perhaps to the never ending goal of personal improvement. The 'habit' usually develops during formative years, from being part of a sports team or training culture at school/college/university, which has made training become part of a lifestyle. The dangerous side of this motivation is when it becomes THE focus of life. It can also lead to a very controlled lifestyle and eating habits, and in some people eating disorders. Nevertheless, a good habitual attitude towards training is a great one to achieve – just be very careful if it starts to become everything to you.

● **Challenge orientated** – Some people love a challenge. They need something to be focused on. Training for training's sake isn't good enough – they need an event, a competition. Such people often start with a local 10km, then a marathon, then an Olympic tri, then an ironman, then five ironman events in one year. These challenges are great, especially if they bring in other people too, or raise money for charity. Just be aware that they can become life-encompassing!

Motivation by others

Whether the session is hard or not, most people find that when they train with a partner or have a personal trainer the motivation to do well is somehow increased. This seems to be true whether the partner or trainer actively gives encouragement or not. The beauty of this is that the level of achievement is far greater than can usually be attained when working individually.

Although it's very important to have the ability to self-motivate, generally by the goal-focused methods discussed in this chapter, it still helps if others encourage or coerce you to deliver more to attain the goal you've set yourself. Let's take Olympians as an example. Although they're very self-motivated and disciplined when it comes to maintaining focus, everyone has a low point or a bad day, and this is when their teammates, coaches, partners etc really prove their worth by motivating, encouraging and inspiring them to achieve the best they're capable of. Furthermore, as a triathlete you can't see the way you swim, so you need a friend, coach or trainer to advise you. It's a mutually beneficial relationship – they help you, you help them.

Using others

Once you've identified your motivation, it's important to ensure you don't forget it. So tell people about it: tell your spouse, your friends, your room-mate. If you're going to do a triathlon, especially an ironman event, get sponsorship and let people know – believe me, not wanting to let others down is a huge motivation in itself. By telling people you're going to complete an Olympic tri or that you're going to lose two kilos by the summer by training triathlon, you start to add a little healthy pressure, which in itself becomes a motivator. Furthermore, your real friends will ask you how it's going, are you on track, and those reminders will help you on your way. Lastly, you may well become an inspiration for them and they'll join you on your fitness quest. So, tell people, not only for your own inspiration, but to spread the word.

Habit and addiction
A healthy habit

For many people, myself included, training isn't a chore; it's not something to find time for, it's part of the daily routine. For us, a day without some sort of physical training (unless it's a specific rest day) is an uncomfortable feeling, and the necessity to ensure a session takes place the following day is heightened all the more. The fact that training is habitual means it's not dreaded but looked forward to, and is therefore self-motivational and something to be enjoyed. If you can get to this point by enjoying your tri training, be it for the thrill, the competition or the social side, then you'll always lead a fit and healthy lifestyle.

If you can get to the point of enjoying even the most dreaded sessions, like intervals and even race days, then you've joined training's elite. Even if it's for the relief afterwards, it's still a great place to be; you are truly motivated.

An unhealthy addiction

We've touched on this already. For some people, having training as such a high priority in their lives can be taken a little too far, especially when the day's other business is scheduled around the day's training. Slowly such a person's training starts to control their life. It's at this point that the person has probably become addicted.

A training addiction in itself isn't too severe a problem – unless one's health, social life and personal relationships start to suffer. At the point when two or even three sessions a day are ruling one's life and rest days are never taken the body starts to suffer and decline. The addiction has become more than a habit or motivation – it's become a problem. Again, know yourself. Be honest with yourself – discuss your training with friends and professionals and you'll keep on the right side of an addiction to being fit and healthy.

Lack of motivation

A lack of motivation and the following slump in training can affect us all, whether we're pro athletes or local gym-goers. We all have good days and bad days, and we can all lose motivation. But what about those of us who don't have coaches, teammates or training partners to revive our enthusiasm? What happens when slumps occur and we have to deal with them ourselves? It's not an easy problem to overcome. It's the point when you have to focus even more. The trouble is, even the most practised ironman champion still has demons of doubt sometimes, and no matter how much we concentrate on our training that doubt and lack of motivation remains.

To really understand how to get over a lack of motivation, and how to use the various methods I describe further on, it's worth understanding what causes these slumps in the first place. Again, knowing yourself means you can correct yourself.

Fatigue

This is the major cause of lack of motivation; if you've trained hard for days and then wake up early to go for a run with your body stiff and achy, it's very difficult to get motivated. If the body is very stiff and achy then it's probably already fatigued and you're possibly on the verge of overtraining. Although it might seem difficult to do, rest is the key. Fatigue has probably occurred due to lack of rest, perhaps the beginning of an illness or simply from training too hard. If intense sessions continue without rest the fatigue will continue and your goal will slip into the distance.

⏱ An iron woman

Paula Newby-Fraser could be considered one of the greatest athletes the world has ever seen. Agreed, that depends on your view of 'great', but if you consider Mike Tyson, David Beckham, Usain Bolt or Shawn Johnson to be amazing athletes in their unique ways, then Paula surely deserves to be a name you know. Between 1986 and 1996 she won the Iron World Championships eight times (a record). She held the course record of 8 hours 55 minutes 28 seconds from 1992 until Chrissie Wellington broke it in 2009. Paula collapsed in the 1995 race and only completed the course by sheer, gruelling determination, yet she came back to win in 1996. Imagine her motivational slump after the 1995 race! Considerable one would think. So her ability to 'get back in the saddle' and win just a year later is phenomenal.

⏱ Six to eight hours' sleep

Six to eight hours' sleep is vital every night, otherwise a hormone cascade is released that makes you store fat, feel hungry and not feel full. Furthermore sleep is where we repair and improve. Getting no sleep means that the body isn't ready to work hard again, and probably isn't reaping the rewards of the day's training.

Overtiredness

Some people (yes, guilty!) try to stick to their training programme even if they've had a very long day at work or, worse still, have been out for a night, come back in the early hours and woken up with a hangover. Believe it or not this isn't good for your body or long-term training goals. The problem with a hangover is that the body's full of toxins and needs rest to recuperate; by forcing it to work when it's in dire need of fuel and rest doesn't help fitness gains, it just puts pressure on the heart, causes the body to become catabolic (ie it breaks down its own muscles) and can lead to injury – not to mention pumping all that poison around the body while you train (yes, I call alcohol poison).

Lack of sleep is very similar. It usually means you feel laboured when exercising and can't perform at your best. Being awake for more hours than normal means the body requires more fuel, but by exercising you're probably doing the opposite, so will again become catabolic and reverse all those days of training. Know yourself, listen to your body and react accordingly.

Overtraining

Overtraining is a real problem if people set impractical goals but see them as achievable. They start training more often and more intensely for sustained periods of time. The problem with triathlon is that we know it's acceptable to perform more than one or even two sessions in a day, as there are different disciplines to cover. Equally, we know that it's difficult to fit all the training in. However, if you have work and a family then sometimes you just can't do it. Hard sessions and recovery sessions are needed, not to mention rest days. But people start ignoring rest days, and eventually overtraining-related fatigue sets in. When this occurs the body and mind will demand rest, often by causing injury or illness. A serious consequence of overtraining is the lowering of the immune system, meaning the body will eventually succumb to flu or something worse. The body then becomes susceptible to injuries such as torn muscles, and overuse injuries such as patella tendinitis.

Repetitive training

By repeating the same race-paced session or interval session again and again in the hope of seeing vast improvements, the body is never allowed to rest adequately and repair. The heart becomes stressed, and the pulse rate increases at rest. Effectively, repetitive training causes overtraining-type issues within those muscle groups (in a triathlete's case the heart) consistently exercised, which can ultimately lead to injury and illness. Vary the training; vary intense days, rest days and easy days. If something works well, give it a day or two, then repeat it and better it. Don't attempt it on successive days, as you'll never improve.

Illness

Illness or injury results in lack of motivation, simple. You've worked so hard to get where you are and being ill or pulling a muscle has stopped you progressing. Even worse, it's making you lose ground. You're getting more unfit and further from your goal by the day. So what do you do? You try to train while you're ill. *But please, don't be tempted to do this*. It's not wise to train when you're ill – the body is busy fighting off infection, and by training you put it under further stress which is bad for the heart. Rest until you're better; don't try to come back too early or the illness may also come back. First session back, be careful and take it easy. Don't stress about losing fitness when you're ill, it takes a lot longer than you think. However, try to figure out why you've become ill. Is it because your body is run down from overtraining, or because training has taken place when you were overtired? Sometimes illness and injury are signs that things need to change.

Injury

Injury is slightly different, but that's dependent on the injury, of course. For example a pulled muscle in the hamstring will mean no lower limb activity, but an upper body session could take place. Just be careful and take it easy. Use the PRICE programme (see Chapter 12) to look after the injury and ensure you take it easy for the first few sessions back, to avoid a relapse. Again, not that much fitness is lost from a minor injury. Full fitness can be regained even after severe injuries. Always rest and rehab properly and get back to full fitness rather than coming back too early and repeatedly re-injuring yourself.

Environment

It's something we never consider, but a drastic change in climate or environment has an adverse effect on motivation and training. This is because certain environments affect the body drastically until acclimatisation occurs, and thus can severely decrease performance; this is true for very hot or very cold climates. Rather than letting the heat or cold demotivate you, take a few days prior to any hard training to do very easy exercises, preferably in the mornings or evenings when the climate won't affect you as badly. This will help with acclimatisation and will keep your motivation high.

Remember, REST Recovery Equals Successful Training.

⏱ Pulled muscle

If you pull a muscle *stop immediately*. Get ice on it ASAP, rest it, ice it and take non-steroidal anti-inflammatories for 48 hours. Then (for a lower body injury) try light closed chain exercise (squats, lunges, perhaps light cycling), and get the injured site massaged. Then slowly try to come back. The severity of the pull will tell you how quickly you can return.

Cold months

People often lose motivation during the winter, when it's cold and raining. It's not easy to drag yourself outside before or after work, especially in the dark, wet and wind. Of course, the opposite is true in the summer when the good weather is often inspirational and makes you want to get out and train in the sun. In winter, try to focus on your goal and motivate yourself beyond that day's training; think of that ironman finish line and the elation of reaching it, or the extra calories you'll burn off during today's session as your body tries to stay warm. Furthermore, the

exercise-induced elation that follows a session in really adverse conditions is something to be experienced. As with interval or hill sessions, the exhilaration from knowing that you've trained really hard is incredible – even if it's only because the session is over for another day!

Alternatively get a gym membership, train on a treadmill, go to the local pool, or buy a turbotrainer and train at home.

Diet

Diet, energy, calories or just fuel is SO important. Think about your body as a car. A car can't go anywhere if it has no petrol in the tank, and your body is the same – it will also come to a halt without fuel. If you're struggling for motivation ensure you've eaten well and aren't lacking energy. Training when energy levels are low is bad for both the heart and body, and can lead to injury. Certain environments, especially the very hot, suppress the appetite, so it may be necessary to work really hard on getting the calories in. There are lots of ways of achieving the right calorie intake. Remember, food is fuel, and unless you're training triathlon specifically for weight-loss purposes it should be seen as that.

Reaching a plateau

At some point most triathletes reach a point where no more improvements can be made. They've either peaked too early or have reached a plateau. They can't seem to add another interval at the same speed, they can't quite beat that 1,500m swim time or add another mile at the same speed to their long run of the week. If your goal(s) have been reached this isn't a problem, and you can be content just training to stay at this level of fitness. However, if your goal is still some way off motivation will drop dramatically. If nothing obvious is causing this plateau (*ie* overtraining, diet or illness) then the best method of overcoming it is to change your regime and vary the sessions. Don't keep banging your head against the same wall – mix things up, surprise your body and see if it adapts as you hoped. Changing your path to a specific goal isn't a problem as long as it still leads to success.

Psychological factors

As you'll have noticed by now, my philosophy comes down to the importance of knowing yourself – the importance of being self-critical, of being able to see that you're training too hard or have lost motivation, to see that there's something in your life taking your focus away from your training, such as family problems or a love interest, leading to a lack of focus and drive. Whatever it is, reassess your life, refocus and continue.

However, it's important to consider what the true goal of your tri training is. It may be that the family or love interest should be put above fitness, priority-wise. It may be that you were originally training to lose weight to help you find a love interest, yet if it's a new love interest that's causing your lack of motivation then surely that isn't actually a bad thing?

Triathlete psychology

Certain sports that we take part in as children and pursue into later life develop and change our psychology and mental strength when it comes to physical and sporting potential, either because of some link to our ability to overcome our central governor (see below) or because they create a different understanding of the work ethic required in sport. I was a cross-country runner at school as well as a track runner. I believe the hours of running training and races, especially in the depths of winter, helped me develop a mental strength that has enabled me to approach difficult and challenging events with a relative

⏱ Strength of mind

Over the first nine weeks of a Marine Recruit's training they do the same fitness test at week one and at week nine. They need to show improvement. Most do. But in reality it's only partly physical improvement. Most have simply learnt to push themselves. They've learnt that pain (or perceived pain) doesn't mean you have to stop: you just have to control it. Any good triathlete needs to develop this attitude to be in with a shot of achieving a good time.

sense of ease, in the knowledge that I have the mental capability to complete whatever I start.

I also played a lot of football when I was young, to a relatively high level, but I don't feel that I developed the same 'endurance psychology' from it. It can, of course, all be coach/mentor-specific, and depend on how hard you were pushed. For example, my girlfriend was an ice skater from a young age, and believes the same psychology to be true of her sport: training before (5:00am) and after school every day, and on both days at weekends, meant that she developed a similar mental toughness in relation to sporting activities. She sees this more as an appreciation of hard work and where it gets you, that without the early starts and late finishes she wouldn't have *achieved*, and that knowing this from a young age has helped her attain her health and fitness goals in later life. Personally, I believe I learned more than just a work ethic; I learned how to push myself, how to suppress my central governor, how to cope with the pressure and pain associated with endurance sports, and the ability to 'carry on regardless'.

So if you didn't develop this 'sportsperson's psychology' at a young age, from running, rugby, swimming, ice skating, gymnastic, rowing or the many other sports I've omitted, then try to understand and develop it now, in line with your motivation and chosen goals. That strength of mind could be the key to achieving the success you want.

Lack of progress

Sometimes, for reasons we can't necessarily pinpoint, despite seemingly doing everything else correctly, we fail to improve or progress. This can be very disheartening and a real setback. However, all is not lost. There are a few techniques that can help you to get over these little mountains.

Visualisation

Visualisation is a method adopted by top sportsmen all over the world. Bruce Lee also used it extensively when he was trying to master a new skill or better a previous one. Visualisation is simply going through the sequence of events in the mind and 'seeing' yourself perform them successfully. It can be used to overcome constant failure at something (like learning a tumble turn) or to perfect a technique (like your swim stroke). For triathletes, visualisation might be seeing yourself cross the finish line in first place, or simply swimming with perfect technique.

Self-study

This is perfectly suited for swimming technique. It involves recording yourself performing a technique and watching and analysing the performance. Not only does this allow you to review your technique and note where improvements can be made, it also allows you to reinforce the technique by watching it. 'Mirror neurones' exist within our brains that fire up the correct pathways when we watch others perform activities, so watching yourself provides the same stimulus and allows analysis to take place. It can be very helpful to record yourself running, cycling and swimming – maybe even removing your wetsuit or doing a T1 and T2 change – and then see where you could improve, be it serious faults or simple improvements.

Rest

This has already been mentioned, but is so important that I'm mentioning it again. If your body needs rest, listen to it. Don't overtrain or you'll become injured or ill. Above all, be sensible.

New angle

Often when a goal is out of reach we get so fixated on it that we can't see the other options. A varied training programme is always better for the body and general fitness, which makes triathlon a great choice for someone new to physical fitness. However, when a goal becomes so specific that the training is too focused on it all-round fitness can get neglected. If rest has been tried and no other option seems viable, then take a few weeks or even a month off and try another type of training. For example, rowing will maintain heart and cardiovascular fitness.

♥ Personal experience...

Before I became a Royal Marine PTI, a PTI friend of mine could see I was struggling to reach a personal goal. I wanted to be able to run a certain number of miles in an hour, and although I could run at the required speed, with the correct cadence, I would always overheat and have to slow down about 30–40 minutes in. I was consistently trying the run, maybe every other day; trying to add a mile each time to eventually reach the goal, pushing my body harder and harder, tipping water over my head to cool down, but I just couldn't do it. He advised me to buy a heart-rate monitor and only look at my heart rate – no speeds or distances – and just run for set time periods at set heart rates. He said I'd find it slow and boring, but it would work. He was right, it was slow and boring, but within a couple of months of 'heart-rate training' I was rested, stronger and fitter, and managed to complete my goal, not once but on numerous occasions. This new angle really worked for me, so I advocate not only trying new angles but also the use of heart-rate monitors.

The 'central governor' theory

Fitness professionals, doctors and athletes have always believed that our muscles become fatigued because they reach their limit of physical ability, be that because they run out of fuel (energy) or because they're overwhelmed by toxic by-products such as lactic acid (see Chapter 2), and we've never thought to question this.

However, two scientists – Tim Noakes and Alan St Clair Gibson – have recently questioned this belief, as they don't agree that fatigue is as simple as a car running out of petrol. Instead, Noakes and Gibson believe that fatigue is an emotional response that actually begins in the brain. (A similar idea was suggested in 1924 by Archibald Hill.) They postulate that what they call a 'central governor' in the brain constantly paces our muscles to stop them reaching exhaustion. Basically, high intensity exercise could threaten the homeostasis (general standing/heart rate/temperature etc) of our bodies and thus cause damage to the heart; consequently the central governor limits the intensity of exercise that can be performed by reducing the recruitment of muscle fibres. Less available fibres is felt as fatigue. Simply put, the output of the muscles during exercise is continuously adjusted as per calculations made by the brain in regard to a safe level of exertion for the heart and body – in other words our brains control our level of intensity to protect the body from damage. It's also thought that the brain factors in previous experience of strenuous exercise, so effectively the central governor can be trained to accept more intense exercise over a period of time.

Reserves

Just like any new theory, without concrete proof the 'central governor' theory remains controversial. But when everything is considered it does make sense. The body should really always keep a reserve in case of an emergency, such as a predator or an enemy trying to kill you. To be so fatigued that you can't escape would be a big mistake in evolutionary terms, which makes the central governor theory more sensible than it might at first seem.

It also makes sense when you realise that fatigued muscles don't actually run out of anything critical, as despite excessive exercise the glycogen levels (energy stores) in the muscles and liver never actually reach zero. Again, it seems as if the body stops us before we hit zero to ensure an emergency reserve is maintained. Furthermore, the central governor theory poses a huge question regarding the build-up of lactic acid as a supposed cause of fatigue, because if this was the sole cause then athletes wouldn't become fatigued so quickly when exercising at altitude, as the slower paces that have to be taken due to lack of oxygen mean that lactic acid levels remain low, and we should be able to run for far longer; yet we know that altitude training still sees fatigue set in. This too would seem to be explained by the existence of a central governor, measuring the levels of blood-oxygen saturation in order to protect the heart and body and maintain homeostasis.

Lastly, the central governor also makes more sense of medical conditions such as chronic fatigue syndrome, which see individuals experiencing fatigue even at rest, something that can't be put down to lack of glycogen in the muscles. Therefore psychological and motivational factors, ie the brain, must be considered the real reason for such conditions. Again, the central governor seems to make more sense in such instances.

Overriding the central governor

In a scientific sense the central governor theory isn't that different from what was believed previously, it's just a bit 'chicken and egg'. It was thought that the muscles tell the brain when they're fatigued and hence the body stops. However, it seems to be the case that what's happening in the muscles is irrelevant. In fact the governor constantly monitors physiological factors and signals, even though they're not the direct cause of fatigue; instead they're the signals the governor takes into account to make its judgement of when to signal fatigue.

The question, then, is if the central governor is really on the case, how is it that the world's top endurance athletes carry on at the paces they do? In the past we assumed they had some genetic gift that meant their muscles didn't fatigue like the rest of us, or the years of training meant they could work longer and harder despite the influx of lactic acid. The answer could be simple: all of us might have a degree of ability to override the central governor, despite the feeling of discomfort produced by the intensive exercise. This is, of course, dangerous, as continuing at the same intensity can/will cause damage to the body and heart. Consequently for most of us the override results in a natural slowing of the pace and intensity; but it's thought that top athletes can override the central governor completely. But if that's possible, how do they do it?

One possible answer is they're blessed with incredibly strong minds, strong willpower if you will, which fits in very well with my thoughts on the psychology developed by certain sportspeople at an early age. These top athletes can literally ignore their bodies. However, this suggests the central governor is more an emotional than a physiological mechanism, which isn't quite true. However, it would help to explain why shouting, music or other forms of distraction can allow someone to keep training at a higher intensity and for longer, by distracting the mind and preventing the brain's messages to stop from getting through to the body. A perfect example of this is marathon runner Paula Radcliffe. Watch her as she runs, a very strange head-and-neck thrust every step. Some Kenyans constantly tap their thumbs and forefingers together. Both these traits could be learned methods of occupying the brain to override their central governors and deal with the 'pain' of doing so.

Set goals for your training. In fact, set goals for your life – just make sure that you abide by the SMART acronym. If you struggle to complete your goal, set milestones to help you, or take a look at the lists above and, by knowing yourself, try to overcome your problems and then reach for that goal yet again. Goals may not be to everyone's taste, especially for those who are content and happy with their lives and have no real desires. Personally I think everyone can improve some part of their life, even if it's only beneficial to their spouse, family or children. For most of us, however, it's human nature to want to improve. We all want to be better, so set yourself a goal or challenge to make yourself feel alive. Set yourself a time frame and make it happen.

CHAPTER 2
ENERGY SYSTEMS

In simple terms our bodies need energy to do things. It doesn't matter if that's walking to the shop, washing up or completing a triathlon. We need energy for literally everything we do; movement, growth, repair and even keeping our heart beating. We also burn energy when our muscles are at rest, even when we're sitting at a desk or asleep in bed. It's important for triathletes to understand this at both ends of the scale.

For someone taking up tris to lose weight it's important to improve muscle tone by using weights exercises, and not by relying only on cardiovascular exercise such as swimming, cycling and running. Increased muscle tone will ensure you use energy when resting, not just when performing your swim, bike or run training. For a seasoned triathlete it's important to understand that you MUST feed your body consistently, so that it utilises the energy you provide rather than obtaining it by breaking the body itself down for fuel.

So, from the above I'm assuming that you're in one of two groups: either someone using tri training/racing to get fit and lose weight, or a triathlete trying to ensure you're in peak condition. Either way, understanding your energy systems is important.

Energy and therefore calories are burnt during and after exercise. The amount of energy expended by the muscles at rest or during exercise varies with size, gender and age. However, it will aid with weight loss and fitness regardless. All of our energy comes from the food we ingest (unless we're forced to break down our bodies by not ingesting enough). This is covered more fully in Chapter 3. We can get all our energy requirements from a good all-round diet containing the 'macros' we require, ie carbohydrates, fats and proteins. Once ingested and broken down our bodies can store this energy in a number of different ways until it's required. For someone using tris to lose weight or get fit, this is almost all you need to worry about food-wise, although the more you understand the more you can use what and when you eat in order to train and compete harder. For seasoned triathletes, however, matters are far more technical, from supplementation to number of meals per day, to pre-, during and post-session nutrition. Food is crucial!

Energy

To understand how your body works, how it utilises energy and therefore how you can get it to run, bike and swim for anywhere between 30 minutes and 12 hours, may not seem necessary. It does it, so why do you need to know how? Well, comprehending how your body does what you ask of it, and how the body's various energy systems function, may help you understand why you get tired at certain points, why you're slow at the start of the swim, and more importantly how you can improve.

ATP

Regardless of where it comes from, the energy we need can only be used when it's in the form of a chemical compound called ATP (adenosine tri-phosphate). Despite its molecular size, our muscles can only store very small amounts of ATP at a time, meaning our bodies have to produce it continuously. If the level of activities being undertaken means our muscles use up ATP faster than it can be made, then we'll get tired and have to slow down or stop what we're doing. In simple terms, if you're trying to train/race faster than your body can provide ATP to make your muscles work, you'll either have to slow down until you can produce ATP at a matching rate or, worse, have to stop entirely to let your body replenish its supply.

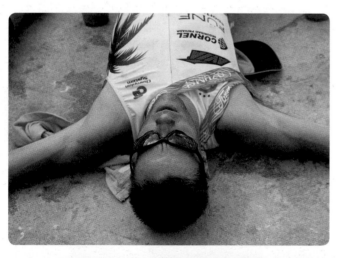

⏱ Complete training

As with anything, try to train every element to ensure that you leave nothing untrained or to chance. You wouldn't just swim and bike and never run, so think about training every element of your energy systems: perform short sprints, longer intervals and long continuous sessions in order to cover all three.

The three energy systems

So, we know that our muscles have a certain amount of ATP stored in them to give us immediate energy, that we can replace this as our bodies synthesise more, and that this process isn't immediate and often forces us to slow down or stop. In order to provide our bodies with more energy (ATP) as we use it, we have three different energy systems, each there to provide the muscles with ATP and allow sustained racing/training/movement. These are:

1 **The PCr or creatine phosphate system**, for 0–30 seconds of hard/explosive work. This system is the body's immediate supply source, providing energy far more quickly than the other systems. However, due to the way it works it can only provide energy for very short periods.

2 **The anaerobic glycolysis/lactic acid system**, for one to two minutes' hard work. This system can provide energy relatively quickly, but isn't long-lasting, so the muscles fatigue quickly, signified by a burning 'pain' as water products build up.

3 **The aerobic glycolysis system**. This can provide energy indefinitely (provided sufficient fuel is available). However, it must have oxygen to work and therefore requires energy expenditure not to exceed a certain level.

The three systems work together to maintain the muscles' energy (in the form of ATP) at all times. It's very important for triathletes to understand these energy systems, as we really do cover all the bases when training, depending on whether we're training hypoxically (without oxygen) in the pool, sprinting during interval training, or performing a long, slow cycle or run (and everything in between).

Energy systems interaction

It may seem that when performing a triathlon the majority, if not all, of your race will depend on the aerobic system. However, the systems don't work like that. What if you're halfway through the cycle stage and decide to put in a burst to overtake a few people before the next hill? You were using aerobic glycolysis, but you just sprinted for 20 seconds and are now breathing hard. Did your body sneak in some anaerobic glycolysis? Or did you even just nip into the PCr system? The key thing to remember is that the body doesn't use the three systems completely independently, and that all three will be used in conjunction with each other throughout your training and races. The amount each system is used will depend on the intensity of activity at that point, as well as how long the intensity needs to last.

The three systems in slightly more detail

The creatine phosphate system

ATP ➜ energy + ADP + P

ADP + CP (creatine phosphate) + energy ➜ ATP + creatine

(ADP = adenosine diphospate, P = phosphate,
   ATP = adenosine triosphate)

This system provides immediate energy by using energy stored in our muscles. This allows for an immediate explosive response, perfect for a sprint start or finish (even a tri still often comes down to this!). Unfortunately the ATP stored in muscles only allows for 8–10 seconds of hard work, and once these initial stores are depleted more must be created to allow activity to continue, and this is where creatine phosphate (often taken as a supplement) comes into play.

Along with ATP stores, creatine phosphate is also stored in the muscles. In simple terms, it's a high-energy source that can be broken down to create more energy for the working muscles. The amount stored in the muscles gives us, on average, another 20 seconds of hard work before stores are depleted.

⏱ Training intervals

Following a full out sprint most people need to rest for several minutes to allow the body to replenish its creatine phosphate stores, otherwise we simply can't repeat the sprint. Hence the importance of training intervals to ensure the system is used to replenishing these stores quickly, for every sprint overtake you want to do during your race.

The lactic acid (anaerobic glycolysis) system

ATP ➜ energy + ADP

ADP + glycogen to ATP + Pyruvic acid ➜ Lactic Acid
   (insufficient oxygen)

This system provides short-term energy beyond that provided by the ATP and creatine phosphate stores. When we exercise hard for longer than 10–15 seconds we start to breathe heavily and deeply, simply because our muscles need more oxygen. Due to the times it takes for this oxygen to get into the bloodstream and to the muscles, any ATP or creatine phosphate stores will have been exhausted. It's then that the lactic acid system provides energy until the required amounts of oxygen arrive.

The lactic acid system uses glycogen as an energy source. Glycogen is produced from the breakdown of carbohydrates. It's then stored in the muscles and the liver. However, when glycogen is broken down (without oxygen) to produce the demanded energy (allowing the muscles to continue working), lactic acid (lactate) is also produced as a waste product. As more and more of this waste is produced the muscles begin to feel tired and fatigued, eventually forcing us to slow or stop.

The lactic acid system can't be sustained for long. The length of time is dependent on the person, gender, age and, of course, fitness level. However, the 'lactic threshold' can be trained, to increase it, meaning the individual can continue for longer and longer with lactic acid building in the muscles. Top athletes will have far greater lactic thresholds than the rest of us.

The lactic acid system is incredibly important if maximum effort is needed for longer than ten seconds when the creatine phosphate system is exhausted. This is paramount to a triathlete if pushing hard over the last kilometre of a run, or working hard up a hill to overtake or stay in front.

Oxygen deficit

When the creatine phosphate or lactic acid systems are used, an 'oxygen deficit' is created: this means that more oxygen is needed than it's possible to take in. When the activity is finished it's therefore necessary to take in more oxygen to make up for and counteract this deficit. This is known as the 'oxygen debt'. By replacing this oxygen we restore the body's natural levels, allowing the removal of lactic acid, the replacement of oxygen stores in the body, and the restoration of ATP and creatine phosphate stores in the muscles

As a triathlete it's important that you can train your body to work hard utilising aerobic glycolysis, thus creating an oxygen debt but then recovering while still racing. Picture a big hill-sprint to overtake the competitors in your sights, then flattening out, hugely out of breath and needing to stop to recover the oxygen debt. You need to be able to slow the pace to aerobic glycolysis, but still keep going in order to prevent those you've just overtaken from doing the same to you.

The aerobic system

ATP ➜ energy + ADP

ADP + glycogen ➜ ATP + Pyruvic acid

Pyruvic acid + oxygen ➜ carbon dioxide + water

Due to the fact that the aerobic system provides energy far slower than the other systems, it's the one we use for the majority of our daily activities. However, the drawback is that it provides energy far too slowly for intensive activity, hence the need for the other systems. The aerobic system's energy supplies are almost limitless, dependent on the individual, body type, length of activity and the availability of fuel, but in general, for triathletes' purposes (perhaps ironman competitors aside), they won't run out. The aerobic system is essential for long training/racing periods.

Simply put, this system works by using oxygen in the breakdown of carbohydrate and fat to produce energy, but without any waste products that stop the process reoccurring (as in the lactic acid system). However, the aerobic system can only sustain its energy production when enough oxygen is being supplied to the muscles – otherwise the body drifts into anaerobic glycolysis and an oxygen debt is created (see boxout).

The aerobic system can be improved drastically simply by performing activities that use it. By doing so it becomes more efficient, the heart becomes stronger and therefore provides the muscles with more oxygen, keeping the onset of glycolysis and the anaerobic system at bay.

Your body knows

In reality, whether running, cycling or swimming, the body drifts between aerobic and anaerobic glycolysis throughout the course of a race or session. We obviously don't notice as we continually push ourselves, and our bodies allow us to do what we can with the fuel we have and from the training we've done.

Conclusion

It makes sense to have an understanding of how your energy system works, and its individual elements, to help you understand where your strengths/weaknesses are. Having said that, it makes very little difference to you as a triathlete which energy system you're using at a specific point in a race. But a little knowledge will at least help you understand why you're struggling or having to slow down during a race or a training session. The main thing to understand is the need for food and nutrition. Without adequate fuelling your body won't be able to complete your training or races. Always eat before and after training, and, if you're doing a long brick-style session (ie a session in which you train more than one discipline), maybe eat in the middle as well, to ensure your body has energy to burn and food to replace that expended energy when you've finished.

CHAPTER 3
NUTRITION & HYDRATION

Although I've called food 'nutrition' in this chapter heading, it should really be called 'fuel', as that's all you're really concerned about as a triathlete – that whether training or racing you have enough fuel to complete what it is you're trying to do. My aim in this section is to explain the various elements of a varied diet and how best to approach food for triathlon training and racing.

Although a varied diet isn't necessarily balanced, a truly balanced diet should consist of ALL of the following:

- → **Carbohydrates**
- → **Protein**
- → **Fats**
- → **Fibre**
- → **Fruit and vegetables**
- → **Dairy**
- → **Fluids**
- → **Vitamins and minerals**

Thankfully it isn't necessary to eat all of these every day, let alone at every meal. Where possible, though, an adequate quantity of the main foodstuffs should be consumed every day – that's protein, carbohydrate and fats, plus fruit and vegetables in some form or other. Furthermore it's also important to drink plenty of fluids to help with digestion.

As a triathlete you certainly shouldn't be following a faddy diet – the way you train should help you achieve weight management goals. Having said that, triathlon isn't an excuse to eat badly just because you're burning lots of calories.

A balanced diet

Protein

All the muscles of the body are made from protein, from the facial ones that allow us to smile to the heart that circulates blood around the body. To remain healthy, to grow and to repair, our bodies need protein.

Proteins themselves are made up of differing arrangements of amino acids, the individual building blocks that make up all our peptides, which in turn make our proteins. Unfortunately we humans, unlike some animals, can't synthesise all the amino acids required to make our body's necessary proteins, so we have to ingest them from elsewhere. The proteins and therefore amino acids needed for normal functioning of the human body can be sourced easily by eating meat, fish, eggs or chicken. Triathletes require proteins even more than other humans, because they're needed to repair damaged muscles, maintain a healthy immune system, and produce hormones, enzymes and blood cells.

Surprisingly, in long endurance events protein actually becomes a fuel, so for triathletes it serves an additional amazing purpose. It also helps in the stimulation of glucagon, which allows the body to use fat as a fuel more efficiently.

It's actually not necessary to eat protein with every meal, but as a triathlete it's advisable to try to. Failing that, at least one or two meals a day should contain protein. Unlike carbohydrate and fat your body can't store protein, it just takes what it needs, but

Vegetarians

Despite eating no meat or fish, vegetarians can still be endurance athletes/triathletes. I was a vegetarian for two years and still performed well. However, protein can become a problem. Animal protein is better than plant protein, as it not only provides all the necessary amino acids in correct ratios but also provides vitamins and minerals like iron and zinc, and is more readily digested. So it's important for a vegetarian to take protein supplements to ensure their body gets everything it needs.

it needs regular amounts – hence the importance of supplying it regularly. It's therefore better to have slightly too much protein in your diet than too little. Studies over the years have concluded that athletes such as triathletes should ideally consume 1.2–1.4g of protein per kilo of body weight per day.

There are several physical signs that your protein level is deficient, such as colds and a sore throat (low immune system), irritability, slow fingernail growth, thinning/loss of hair, sugar cravings, fatigue, failure to recover from workouts and little response to training stimuli. If you suffer from several of these you should try to up your protein intake. If you're worried about excess protein consumption, don't be. Very, very few people actually manage to ingest too much protein, and any excess will be excreted or converted to glycogen and stored. But always drink lots of water as well to help remove nitrogen, which gets produced when protein is metabolised.

Try to avoid fatty protein sources like cheese, whole milk, burgers, sausages etc, as these are high in saturated fats that are linked to health problems, even in those who exercise frequently.

Recommended sources of protein
- → **Beef (lean)**
- → **Turkey**
- → **Chicken**
- → **Tuna**
- → **White fish**
- → **Salmon**
- → **Eggs**
- → **Egg whites in a carton**
- → **Lean cuts of pork**
- → **Greek yogurt (Total 0% is my favourite)**
- → **Cottage cheese**
- → **Protein powders, eg whey, hemp, casein, soy etc**

Protein supplements

Protein supplements do have their place for triathletes, especially if you're struggling to ingest enough protein from your diet, either because you're vegetarian, work silly hours or just can't physically eat another egg! This can apply equally to new sprint triathletes who require protein supplements before and after training (and perhaps even amino acids during a session) to reduce the breakdown of their own muscle mass and support the repair of their body post-training, and seasoned ironman competitors who need to ingest a protein supplement immediately following, or during, a long training session.

Protein supplements aren't necessarily required if a healthy diet of protein is ingested naturally. However, I personally encourage my clients to use them in conjunction with a balanced diet (never instead of), simply because they absorb rapidly, which means that pre- and post-workout their benefits can be felt and seen far more quickly. Again, it depends on whether we're talking about a budding Olympian, a serious triathlete or a casual office super sprint first-timer. The differences are obvious and common sense should prevail.

Women often worry that taking 'bodybuilding' supplements will make them look like Arnie. First off, if taking protein supplements and swinging a 4kg dumbbell around made everyone look like Arnie then there's a lot of young men who spend hours in the gym trying to obtain a perfect beach body who'd love to know your secret! Sports nutrition brands like Maxifuel and SIS offer protein supplementation specific to endurance athletes, so look into their range, do some research and try/experiment for yourself. Hey, if the legs ache a little less tomorrow and you've got a bit more power in the muscles of the upper body for that 1,500m swim on Tuesday, surely it's worth a try?

♥ Personal experience...

Protein supplementation is something I've dabbled in myself over the years, but with a newfound understanding of sports nutrition I'm now a complete convert. Whenever I've found it difficult to get enough protein in my diet – especially when doing so much exercise on military courses that I was breaking down my own body for fuel – I turned to protein supplements to help me. These days I've tried training with and without them, and have seen such benefits from them that I now advise their use to a wide variety of my clients, big, small, male and female.

Carbohydrate

Humans are no different to their animal kingdom counterparts, and in terms of our energy sources we're exactly the same. Just like animals, we use carbohydrate as our main source of energy, whether it's ingested as 'simple' sugars or 'complex' carbohydrates. 'Carbs', as they're commonly known, are a must if we're to perform well in our everyday tasks. However, what this means is that uneducated, gung-ho triathletes eat a lot of carbohydrate, and some eat virtually nothing but carbohydrate, detrimental though that is.

It's absolutely true that for any triathlete, whether serious or casual, carbs are totally irreplaceable if an event/race/session is to be completed in good time and good form. To attempt to perform well with no carbs ingested that day will likely lead to a sluggish, slow and unresponsive body, and in turn bad form, which can lead to injury. Furthermore, by running without ingesting carbs the body is, surprisingly, more likely to break down its own muscle than any excess body fat, simply due to how the human body operates when in 'starvation mode'. Breaking down your own muscles rather than eating carbs is generally not what anyone's aiming for.

To attempt to perform well with no carbs ingested that day will likely lead to a sluggish, slow and unresponsive body, and in turn bad form, which can lead to injury.

It's nevertheless common within the endurance athlete world to overeat carbs, to have five or six small snack meals a day, ingesting bread, cereals, baked potatoes, cereal bars, juices, toast, pasta and rice – perhaps with some salad and fruit thrown in for good measure. These are all good sources of carbohydrate, BUT must be subsidised with healthy fats and proteins, for the reasons above and the reasons below. Furthermore, you're going to encourage your body to store fat. As a (very) brief explanation, when a high carbohydrate meal is eaten the pancreas releases insulin to regulate blood sugar levels. Insulin generally stays in the blood for around two hours. If another high carb meal is ingested, that insulin has an effect on the carbs, proteins and fats – such as converting carbohydrate and protein to body fat for usage later, moving fat ingested and in the blood to storage sites, and preventing the body utilising stored fat as fuel (because it doesn't need to – it has carbs, lots of them!). So, if you're using triathlon to lose weight, think about how you eat. If you're at the top level of your tri game you want your body to be good at utilising fat as a fuel source, as in a long race you're going to need it to do so, and do so efficiently. So a high, regular carb diet isn't going to help.

The problem with eating a lot of carbohydrate, as many endurance athletes do, is that they usually aim for the 'healthy' moderate to high glycaemic carbs, without any fat or protein to slow its absorption. This means their sugar levels remain high, meaning regular release of insulin and constant bouts of hunger – put down to being a triathlete and training harder than anyone else, so that more food is ingested. Consequently triathletes (at the intermediate level) often have issues with excess body fat. Unfortunately insulin not only messes up body fat and hunger; it has also been associated with high blood pressure, heart disease and diabetes. The answer, if you're hungry, is to reach for the protein, not the carbs – they only start the vicious (and possibly unhealthy) cycle all over again.

Having said all that, carbohydrate is still very important and must constitute a main (but not the only) constituent of any diet, especially that of a triathlete. It's particularly important pre-, during and post-exercise, when without it fatigue and an associated performance drop will be seen. It's therefore

> ### ⏱ High and low glycaemic
>
> Carbohydrate can be described as high or low glycaemic (see below). This basically let's us know how quickly it enters the bloodstream and thus affects insulin levels. High glycaemic foods do so very rapidly whereas low glycaemic foods do so slowly, which means that we're less likely to quickly crave sugar again.

imperative to replenish carbohydrate stores first thing in the morning (breakfast), before training and, very importantly, as soon as possible after training (ideally within an hour). Replenishing stores within that one-hour window allows the body to refuel its glycogen stores in the muscles and liver that much more efficiently for the next training session or event, which could be the difference between winning or losing the next race. Again, protein and high glycaemic foods at the end of a session are the most beneficial, promoting recovery both in preparation for the next session or race and in terms of repair and growth.

The glycaemic index

The glycaemic index (GI) is something that's hit the news over the last couple of years, mostly as 'the GI diet'. But it shouldn't be thought of in the same way as a 'celebrity' diet, such as the Atkins diet plan or the lemonade detox. Initially designed to help diabetics, the glycaemic index is a way of categorising foods according to how fast they release sugars/carbohydrates, by classifying them as red, amber or green:

Red = fast releasing
Amber = medium releasing
Green = slow releasing

Many supermarkets have now put these colours on their food packaging to let you know where they lie on the GI. Failing that, just look them up on the Internet or buy a pocket GI book.

However, it isn't as simple as something being high or low glycaemic, as the other food it's ingested with change its GI rating. For example, a normally very sugary, therefore high GI food eaten/prepared with a fat will significantly lower its GI rating. This means that adding protein, fat and fibre to a meal that contains a high GI carbohydrate will reduce the effect on blood sugar it would have had if it was eaten alone, thus making it lower GI and likely to release its 'energy' over a longer period, just as a normally low GI food would.

Any main meal should be eaten with a healthy portion of low GI carbohydrate; but as explained above, the foods ingested with it can actually change the given GI rating of that food. Examples are wholemeal brown pasta, brown rice, wholemeal bread, sweet potatoes, porridge and quinoa.

High GI foods for best effect

High GI foods shouldn't be avoided altogether. On the contrary, they can be used very effectively at specific times. As mentioned earlier, there's a 'window of opportunity' following exercise in which you should refuel the glycogen stores in your muscles. The faster this occurs the better, and the more efficient your muscles will be for the next session. So if speed of refuelling is important, it makes sense to ingest carbohydrates that release sugars quickly; therefore high GI foods are perfect for replenishing these stores.

High GI foods are also useful just prior to exercise, when a quick sugar spike is necessary to give an energy boost. However, it's imperative that a good balanced meal of proteins, fats and medium to low GI food has been eaten a couple of hours prior to the exercise sessions; then sufficient energy should still be within the body for the whole session once the quick-burning high GI snack has been used up.

Fats

Though the idea that all fats are bad and should be avoided is now widely understood to be a misconception, a lot of people who are into fitness still try to avoid them at all costs – to their detriment. The fact is we actually need some fat in our diet to stay healthy. However, that doesn't give us free licence to eat crisps, cream and butter with every meal. It needs to be the right fat, not the sort that will clog up our arteries. Furthermore, foods described as fat free are often very high in sugar, something which is arguably worse than fat for the insulin regulatory reasons described above.

So, there are 'good' fats and 'bad' fats. Good fats are monounsaturated fats, found in olive/canola oils, nuts, nut butters and avocados to name a few. Monounsaturated fats lower the total unhealthy LDL cholesterol that accumulates in and then clogs up artery walls. They also help maintain levels of healthy HDL cholesterol, which carries cholesterol from artery walls and delivers it to the liver for disposal.

Bad fats are saturated fats, which clog the heart and are found in butter, fatty red meats and full-fat dairy products. Very bad fats are man-made 'trans fatty acids' created when hydrogen gas reacts with oil, and consequently also known as 'hydrogenated fats'. These are found in a large number of packaged foods including margarine, cookies, cakes, icing, doughnuts, and crisps. Trans fats are even worse for us than saturated fats, damaging blood vessels and the nervous systems. They're also highly calorific.

So eat a diet rich in monosaturated fats, low in saturated fats, and if possible completely free of trans fats.

Now that you understand the difference between the three types of fat you can see that it's bad for any of us, and especially endurance athletes, to cut out fat altogether. The 'good' fats found in the food listed below not only form part of a balanced diet in terms of calorific value (9cal for every gram of fat compared to 4cal per gram of carb or protein!), but are also responsible for hormone production (testosterone and oestrogen), regular menstrual cycles, absorption and transport of vitamins and nerve/brain cell production, not to mention shiny hair and good skin.

The key is to limit the intake of fried and processed foods such as chips and burgers. These foods contain saturated fats, and it's best to stick to a diet that's low in these types of foods. Realistically they aren't too bad every now and then, but they certainly shouldn't be eaten multiple times a week. This may seem a little contrary to the paragraph above which stated the importance of protein in the diet, since burgers are a good source of protein. However, despite their high protein content they also have a very high bad fat content, so other less fatty forms of protein should be ingested instead. The simple answer is to limit your intake of fatty meats, processed meats and meat in pies surrounded by pastry.

The good fats, those that research has now proven have nothing to do with weight gain or heart problems, are found in oily fish (tuna, salmon, sardines and mackerel), nuts and seeds and their spreads, and olives. These are imperative to various functions of the body, specifically maintaining healthy skin and long-lasting, functioning joints (quite important to all athletes!), and they're therefore good for all-round health. Such fats can be eaten very regularly as the main protein constituent of any meal.

⏱ **Low fat to high carb**

Many triathletes find that they can train at a higher level and recover quicker if they change from a low fat high carb diet to a higher fat lower carb diet (good fats obviously!).

Fat choices

- ➔ Almonds
- ➔ Cashews
- ➔ Pecans
- ➔ Macadamia
- ➔ Olives
- ➔ Seeds
- ➔ Avocado

- ➔ Natural nut butters (no added sugar, and no or very little added salt)
- ➔ Coconut oil
- ➔ Oils in tuna, salmon, sardines and mackerel

Fruit and vegetables

There can't be anyone who doesn't appreciate the importance of fruit and vegetables to a balanced diet. We're constantly reminded by the media and supermarkets to eat our 'five a day'. Fruit and veg are said to improve our skin, help our digestive system and prolong our lives. They're good as a large constituent of any meal, and also make a perfect snack. Unfortunately, however, and despite being told how important they are, fruit and vegetables are still the main ingredient missing from the average diet. We still prefer our bread, rice, pasta and, worse still, chocolate, crisps and biscuits. Even the best triathletes will admit they don't eat the recommended dose of fresh fruit and veg daily.

Firstly, fruit and vegetables are superb sources of antioxidants. The thing is, although we get told about all these marvellous foods that are full of antioxidants, most of us haven't a clue what antioxidants are or what they do, which kind of makes us less inclined to source them. Well, in simple terms antioxidants help combat free radicals (oxidants), which are produced from general bodily functions, such as hard exercise sessions (like tri training), or ingested from certain foods. Free radicals can cause cancer and premature ageing, so anything that helps combat them can only be of benefit. A simple yet compelling reason to eat fruit and veg.

Fruit and vegetables are also a great provider of vitamins and minerals, and most of us will have heard of them! Yet once again, we probably don't know exactly what they do. In simple terms, they perform a wide range of functions from enabling our blood to carry oxygen, to preventing us from getting common colds. Compelling reasons to source both. (On the next page there's a table of vitamins and minerals showing exactly what they do.)

In addition fruit and vegetables are a great source of fibre, which keeps the digestive system running smoothly. For athletes this is very important: for a start it isn't nice to start a training session without having your daily bowel movement, and it's even worse if that bowel movement wants to take place while you're training – as often happens, as the blood is redirected to the muscles of the arms and legs and away from the muscles controlling the bowels.

In a nutshell, a diet plentiful in fruit and vegetables could help enhance your training/racing performance, reduce the chances of illness and injury, improve wound healing, improve long-term health and prevent constipation. And all you need to do to achieve all this is to eat five portions of fruit and veg a day.

Having said all that, let's now consider fruit consumption in terms of what I've told you about carbohydrate consumption.

Confusing, right? First, fruit is relatively high GI across the board, so try to have it with some fats and proteins. Second, have your fruit before or after a session so that it's utilised during glycogen replenishment after training, or energy pre-training. Last, don't have five snacks of fruit while training, just to meet your quota. Try spreading your fruit and veg through the day: a handful of berries at breakfast, some broccoli with lunch, an apple with cottage cheese as a snack, a banana post-training and a mix of vegetables with the evening meal.

Vitamins and minerals

Let's get the definition out of the way: a vitamin or mineral is a compound that can't be synthesised in the necessary amount by an organism (animal) itself (this doesn't include essential amino acids).

The majority of the essential vitamins and minerals required by the human body are provided by a healthy diet, especially if five pieces of fruit and veg a day are ingested.

Vitamin supplements are big business and sell themselves by claiming they'll prevent colds and flu, improve skin health and relieve joint pains. Although this is true, the same is of fruit and veg. However, vitamin supplements aren't expensive, and if there's some reason why you can't eat enough fruit and veg they're advisable. Multi-vitamins ensure that the body is supplied with everything it needs to function correctly, including ensuring that the immune system works. However, don't exceed the daily dosage. This is set at a safe level for medical reasons: too much can mess with the body's homeostasis and lead to illness, dehydration or sickness.

Essential vitamins, their scientific names and examples of where they can be found

Vitamin A	Retinol	Cod liver oil
Vitamin B1	Thiamine	Rice bran
Vitamin B2	Riboflavin	Eggs
Vitamin B3	Niacin	Liver
Vitamin B5	Pantothenic acid	Liver
Vitamin B6	Pyridoxine	Rice bran
Vitamin B7	Biotin	Liver
Vitamin B9	Folic acid	Liver
Vitamin B12	Cyanocobalamin	Liver
Vitamin C	Ascorbic acid	Citrus fruit
Vitamin D	Calciferol	Cod liver oil
Vitamin E	Tocopherol	Wheat germ oil, liver
Vitamin K	Phylloquinone	Alfalfa

Fibre

Fibre helps with digestion, and as we already know from eating our fruit and veg, it keeps the stomach healthy and prevents constipation. Eating fibre also helps reduce some forms of cancer, which is again hugely beneficial and possibly a good enough reason on its own. Beyond fruit and vegetables, fibre is sourced from wholegrain cereals such as bran flakes, porridge and muesli, or from wholemeal bread, brown rice or wholemeal pasta. It's important to stick to wholemeal, wholegrain (brown) variants of bread, rice and pasta and to avoid the 'white' versions, as these highly processed 'high glycaemic' versions aren't good for the body.

Sugar

Eating a balanced diet doesn't just mean ingesting enough of each nutrient, it also means avoiding too much of certain foodstuffs. Sugar, like saturated fats, is another prime example. Our ancestors only got their sugar from foods providing it, such as fruits and berries, but today it's a very different story, as almost every foodstuff we produce contains sugar. Not only does that mean we're ingesting too much sugar in general, but it is not even 'good' sugar from natural sources – most of it is refined and processed.

As already mentioned, things that are labelled 'fat-free' usually contain large amounts of sugar, so fat-free yogurt, for instance, may contain a very high level of sugar. So look at foodstuff labels when you're shopping: the closer something is to the top of the ingredients list, the higher the percentage of that ingredient the food contains. Sugar is often the second or third thing listed on processed foods, salt being its closest rival.

Sugars may not be ideal all the time, but they can actually serve a good use pre- or during training or a race. This is especially true if you're a seasoned athlete, as you're likely to need energy gels/drinks containing sugar pre-, during and post-races and events. Nevertheless, sugars are still just empty calories – basic energy but no nutrients; there are far better foods to get energy from that will also provide nutrients and minerals for your everyday life. Fruit is a great example.

Salt

Like sugar, salt seems to be added to everything we eat, especially processed foods. Despite this we all reach for the salt at mealtimes, often before we've even tasted our food. Yet our ancestors didn't put vast amounts of salt on their food – they acquired it naturally from their diet. Certainly some salt is required for normal homeostasis and body functioning, but most of us don't need the quantity we're getting. Having said that, tri training does cause us to sweat and therefore lose salt more readily than non-triathletes, so the body is consequently able to cope with a little more salt than normal. However, this isn't an excuse to eat junk like crisps and processed foods, just because you train a lot.

Dairy

The ingestion of dairy products remains controversial. Despite the fact that we've been drinking milk produced by other animals for years, we've finally begun to appreciate that many adult humans are in fact lactose intolerant, and that milk, cream and cheese doesn't do such people much good. In fact it gives them wind at best and allergic reactions, such as blocked sinuses, at worst. If you're in any doubt, see your doctor and get tested. Failing that, cut out the dairy for a few weeks and see if you feel better.

As babies we all drink milk (or should). The advantages of breastfeeding are far too great to warrant me listing them here; yet it may not be necessary for us to continue drinking milk – especially from another species – beyond infancy. Yes, drinking milk does have some advantages for growing children, and it may still be advisable for them to eat two to three portions of dairy food per day specifically for the calcium, which is important for healthy bones. However, humans don't have all the correct enzymes for breaking down dairy products and hence many of us are lactose intolerant, a high percentage of us without even realising it.

Nevertheless, dairy may still be beneficial for anyone taking part in extensive training, because it helps in avoiding skeletal issues, particularly stress fractures, by providing the calcium to repair and improve bones. However, remember that calcium can be found in other foodstuffs, such as fish, eggs and substitutes such as soya milk (which can be used instead of regular milk and comes with added calcium), which have most of the same benefits. Furthermore, some bottled water manufacturers have also started to add calcium to their products.

Eventually it comes down to personal choice. There's nothing wrong with having dairy, but like anything it shouldn't be overdone, and where possible healthy variants should be chosen (avoid the full fat versions, to avoid those bad fats); but in short, unless you think you're lactose intolerant or that dairy is doing you harm, a little of what you enjoy is good for you as long as it doesn't affect your goal.

⏱ Electrolyte, not salt!

Unless the day's activities have caused profuse sweating or muscular cramps are occurring, the addition of salt to food is unnecessary and should generally be avoided. An electrolyte drink sachet or tablet such as Emergen-C or MaxiTabs is far more beneficial – I've had a few clients who cramped whenever we swam (one in particular, who insisted on a 60–90-minute bike session before our 60-minute swim), and they've found such electrolyte supplements work well.

Supplements

Supplements are a huge business, from the cornerstone American bodybuilding companies to the smaller British companies recently bought out by huge pharmaceutical companies to realise the profits of this lucrative end of the market. The sports, fitness and health industries now receive sponsorship from supplement companies such as MaxiNutrition, PhD, Reflex, USN, SIS, Lucozade, Powerade and even Nestlé's PowerBar, to name but a few. As a triathlete, you're pushing the boundaries of what your body was designed for, and my advice is to provide it with all the necessary energy requirements and recovery building blocks it needs. I'm therefore an advocate of sports nutrition and supplementation. Studies have shown that athletes who use supplementation and ingest the right kinds of macronutrients at the right times perform better than those who don't. I've personally found this with my own training.

Protein

The average person (around 95% of the population) is said to need 0.8g of protein per kilogram of body weight per day, ie an average male of 80kg requires 64g of protein every day (0.8 x 80 = 64). An average female of 50kg requires 40g of protein per day (0.8 x 50 = 40).

If a chicken breast or a tin of tuna is around 20–24g, then the man needs three and the woman needs two. Great, but that's for sedentary people. But due to the high intensity of their training an active triathlete needs additional protein – research suggests around 1.2g per kilo of body weight per day. This can either come from food like fish, chicken and eggs, or from a protein supplement.

In simple terms, instead of cooking and eating more fish, eggs, chicken etc (many people find this difficult), a protein supplement drink or bars can provide what's needed. Such drinks and bars are packed with other nutrients, vitamins and minerals too, so can be a great addition to anyone's diet – especially a triathlete's – to enable high intensity training with aided recovery.

Carbohydrate

This leads nicely on to the other branch of supplementation that's huge business: carbohydrates. Whether we're discussing high energy sports drinks that supply sugars and help rehydrate, powdered forms of energy like 'Viper' from Maxinutrition and 'Go' from SIS, or 'energy gel' sachets, most of these are designed to help improve performance during training or a race, by pre-fuelling before, helping to stay fuelled during and refuelling after the session. Arguably these aren't necessary, and the same benefits can be gained from the foods discussed already. I'd encourage EVERY triathlete, whether doing their first super sprint or their 15th ironman, to utilise these drinks. Not only will they set your body up before a race, they also provide easy and scientifically enhanced fuelling during an event and an immediately ingestible source of energy to help you recover afterwards. Most of the post drinks like Recovermax or ReGo are also loaded with protein helping to repair niggles, aches and pains from the gruelling event.

❤ Personal experience...

When performing what can only be described as an ultra-running event in Wales, running up and down the Brecon Beacons with a heavy rucksack for between 5 and 18 hours at a time, consecutively for days on end, I had to make certain my supplementation was correct. This not only ensured I had the energy to complete the event, but also that I didn't lose all my body mass, which allowed me to carry the heavy rucksack. On top of my large breakfast and dinner before and after the daily runs, plus what can only be described as a packed lunch, I ensured I had:

1. A pre-start protein and carbohydrate mixed drink.
2. Carbohydrate supplements (carried in old film cases) sufficient for one per hour.
3. Energy gels (a couple of emergency ones with caffeine).
4. A film case containing a post-workout carbohydrate and protein mix.

I tried and tested these ideas before the event and found they worked very well, especially by ensuring I could be at my best for the next day's slog.

You may be thinking this is a little excessive, especially the protein supplementation. I can understand why, but the type of event and sheer physical nature of it meant that I was burning so many calories each hour that I was becoming 'catabolic' very quickly – my body was basically ready to break down my muscles and proteins to feed its energy needs. By drinking carbohydrate and protein drinks I was attempting to lower the negative effects of this. These days I'd take BCAAs (branch chain amino acids) as well, and I encourage my clients to do so, as the body can use these as a fuel (especially glutamine – which can also be taken separately) to avoid the body breaking its own muscles down in search of them. Protein supplementation can be just as important as carbohydrate supplementation for any athlete, especially before/after a long run, to help reduce the catabolic effects of exercise, and when the muscles need to repair after conditioning sessions.

Hydration

Simply put, water is more important to humans than food. Two-thirds of our body weight is composed of it. Water is required for almost every single occurrence and reaction in the body, from circulation to respiration and in the conversion of food to energy. Even without exercising we require around two to three litres of liquid per day, half to two-thirds of this from fluids and the rest from food.

Dehydration is the athlete's enemy, but for dehydration to occur more water must be lost (sweating, respiration, urine) than is taken in. Dehydration of just 2.5% of your body weight can lead to 25% loss in efficiency, with dehydration of only 1% affecting some people who aren't used to it just as badly. Water is therefore the second most necessary essential for the human body after oxygen. On average we lose over two litres per day to these functions alone. Now add in a swim, bike and run session or sessions in moderate heat and the loss can increase to eight litres! Think you drink enough water?

Although we lose water all the time simply by breathing and urinating, it's sweating during exercise that really causes us to dehydrate. It's said that around 75% of energy put into exercise is converted to heat and lost (which is why exercise makes us feel hot). To keep the body's temperature around its normal 37–38°C we sweat, and the fluid lost must then be replaced – otherwise the blood thickens which reduces the heart's efficiency and thus increases the heart rate, essentially slowing your speed and progress until you're forced to stop. So you can see how important it is, especially for an endurance athlete, not only to stay hydrated by drinking during an event, but also to ensure adequate hydration beforehand.

However, dehydration to some level is expected and deemed normal while exercising. It's nigh on impossible to drink enough while swimming or running to keep your hydration levels 'normal'. Cycling is a little different, hence the new-style bottles on bike handlebars that enable cyclists to drink without needing to change position. As long as we respond to our thirst – especially as soon as we finish exercising, when we all have an uncontrollable urge to drink – the body can return to its normal homeostatic level of hydration relatively quickly.

Always begin a training session or event hydrated. A good way to do this is to drink a half-litre bottle around two hours

⏱ Painkillers can kill!

Taking some painkillers such as aspirin and ibuprofen increases the risk of hyponatraemia, so you should be cautious about taking them when training or racing in hot climates.

before you start. Use the toilet just prior to the session, then drink another quarter of a litre just as you start. This will ensure you have enough water in your body and don't start off dehydrated, which will inevitably lead to a lower performance. Drink another half-litre bottle within 30 minutes of finishing, then keep drinking until you no longer have dark yellow/orange urine, or until you feel OK if you had a headache or nausea.

Bear in mind that when you train and race in hotter climates you'll sweat far more until acclimatised, but once acclimatised will need far less water than during the first few days.

⏱ At race drink stations...

Whether cycling or running, never skip a drink because there's a queue; instead, if there are drinks stations on both sides of the course go to the one on the left, as most people will go to the right because they're right-handed. If you're feeling hot and want to cool down by pouring the drink over your head and shoulders, check the contents first to ensure it's just water. Pouring a sticky sports drink over your head isn't recommended...

Over-hydration

It may seem counter-intuitive, but it's possible to over-hydrate – to literally drink too much. I've personally seen this during a summer 30-miler (one of the Commando tests for Royal Marines). During this example, the individual was so scared of becoming dehydrated that he drank too much and literally flushed the electrolytes out of his system, and keeled over at mile 24.

What occurs is actually known as hyponatraemia, which means low blood salt, as the excess water causes a massive lowering of the concentration of sodium in the blood. Hyponatraemia is generally relatively harmless, causing bloating and perhaps nausea, but in serious cases brain seizure and death can occur.

Despite my personal experience while training Marine recruits, it's actually (percentage-wise) women who suffer from this more than men. This is generally because they're smaller and less muscular than men and as a consequence sweat less so therefore need to drink less. On average women should drink around a third less than men.

For ironman competitors or anyone training for times in excess of three hours it's advisable to avoid drinking large amounts of water and instead only drink when you're thirsty. Electrolyte-containing sports drinks that also contain sodium may be the best choice, as these help hydrate and replace lost salt. Despite all this it's important to remember that for most triathletes it's dehydration rather than over-hydration that's the worry.

The simplest way to stay hydrated for training and races is just to drink throughout the day, every day. Dehydration was quite common amongst recruits in the Marines, so we instructed them to carry a water bottle at all times and take sips throughout the day. This is a good tip in any walk of life, but isn't always practical. Fortunately the colour of your urine is a good indication of whether you need to drink more. Basically, pale yellow or clear urine indicates you're hydrated; dark yellow or orange indicates you're dehydrated and need to drink; dark orange or brown means you're seriously dehydrated and should stop exercising, get into a cool place to stop sweating, and drink until your urine is pale yellow.

What to drink

The easy answer is water, it really is most important. However, personally, if I'm training really hard for long periods, I find I need both water and a sports drink to rehydrate and re-energise me. If you're training for less than an hour plain water (and perhaps BCAAs) is the best choice. However, if you're training for over an hour or feel that on subsequent sessions you've been lacking in energy, then drinks containing sugar or maltodextrin (a slow-release carbohydrate) may be more suitable.

Tap water?

A lot of people worry about tap water and buy bottled, but unless racing abroad, where I worry about stomach bugs, I'm personally happy to drink tap water. You can get a filter for your kitchen tap, or even a 'WaterBobble' bottle that filters the water as you drink it while training. Certainly in the UK and US we should have no worries about drinking tap water.

Hypotonic, isotonic and hypertonic drinks

There are a number of different types of drink that can be used when racing or exercising, from diluted fruit juice and squash to sports drinks like Lucozade. Whatever they're made up of, these drinks are of three types:

➔ Hypotonic

These contain a greater proportion of water and a lesser proportion of carbohydrate than the human body. As the drink is less concentrated than body fluids it's claimed that they're absorbed by the body faster than plain water, thus preventing or alleviating dehydration. Good examples are squash (not sugar-free, though) diluted at least one part to eight parts water, or fruit juice diluted one part juice to three parts water.

➔ Isotonic

These contain proportions of water and other nutrients similar to the human body, and are typically about 6% to 8% carbohydrate. As the drink is the same concentration as body fluids, it's absorbed at the same rate as water. Furthermore, these drinks are a perfect balance of rehydration and refuelling. Good examples are Lucozade Sport, fruit juice diluted half and half with water, and even squash (again not sugar-free) diluted one part to four with water.

➔ Hypertonic

These contain a lesser proportion of water and a greater proportion of carbohydrate than the human body. As it's more concentrated than body fluids it's absorbed more slowly, meaning the energy will be released over a long period of time. It's therefore claimed that these drinks can give an energy boost and also replace lost energy over the entire session.

All energy drinks are a good form of energy boost and rehydration. However, they should still be used with caution. Always ensure that plain water is also at hand just in case that energy drink causes dehydration or, worse, an adverse reaction. It's always worth testing an energy drink is compatible with your own body prior to using it in a specific race, where an adverse reaction could have dire results.

Conclusion

Food and water are fuel, and if you view them as that you can't really go wrong. You wouldn't drive your car without filling it up with fuel, so don't train without checking (putting in) the water and topping up the fuel tank (eating). Some fuels are better than others, so avoid the rubbish (bad fats) and avoid eating the same food (carbs) all the time. Appreciate the importance of protein and that when you're low on energy between refuelling, protein is far better for you than carbs, whether you're a triathlete or not.

CHAPTER 4
TRAINING

The most difficult thing for most non-professional triathletes is fitting the training in. For a first-time sprint novice triathlete this may only involve fitting in a couple of swims and runs after work each week and a long cycle at the weekend. You'll never break any records, but if you give yourself a good two-month lead-in you should at least be able to complete the course without needing a walking stick at the finish line.

Issues only arise when you want to go for a personal best or compete at a higher level over Olympic distance or in ironman events. Either way your training hours would need to increase, and increase drastically! Fitting it in with working, sleeping, eating and family routine is tough, but not impossible.

Considerations

● **Weakness** – Are you particularly weaker at one event? If so, does this need one-on-one coaching? Do you need to spend considerably more time on this aspect of things? If so this will be the main focus around which you need to build your training. If you need a swim coach, for example, and they're only available at 7:00pm in the evening, then you have to stick to that and work your cycling and running around it.

● **Same day** – Is it OK to train all three events on one day? Well you race them all on one day, so realistically yes! However, will you get the best out of your run home after an hour's swim? Probably not. Will your morning swim be any good after cycling six miles to the pool? Probably not as good as if you hadn't. However, if the only way to get the training in is to do this on some days, then so be it. However, remember that in many circumstances overtraining is more detrimental than undertraining.

● **How much training?** – This is like asking how long is a piece of string. It depends on so many variables – current fitness, current ability at various events, event being trained for etc. Later in this book there are some example training programmes for the various length tris; these are based on you being able to complete the previous distance before moving up to the next, hence a certain level of fitness and ability is expected.

Fitting training in

In the 'real' world we generally work a nine-to-five job, five days a week, and fitting training in around this isn't actually that difficult. Just remember that it's a part of the day, not the main focus of the day. It's OK to look forward to it (equally to dread it!), but make sure you also have time for family and friends. Just like a good job, triathlon should be part of your life, not your entire life. Make sure you remain a well-rounded individual, and not an obsessive. Believe it or not it will actually make you a better athlete.

Working in time slots

Looking at a normal nine-to-five or eight-to-six five-day week there are certain time slots within it – before work, at lunchtime, straight after work, evenings and weekends – that can easily be used for training. Yes, they may require some extra organisation, they may even require you to get out of bed 30 minutes earlier to allow time to change etc, but if you really want something then you'll do it. If you don't, then you won't have the requisite commitment and dedication and triathlon is not for you.

As I learned in the Marines, we humans give up in our minds long before our bodies fail. You can endure anything for a few months, so an eight-week training programme, where you're a little busier and get out of bed a little earlier (especially in the spring/summer months), is nothing if it gets you that finisher's medal.

Before and after work

These periods are often used to travel to work. At these times you're usually just sat in a car/bus/train or, if you're lucky, walking.

Making sacrifices

'I don't have time' is something I hear a lot when writing training programmes for people or telling them what I need them to do in the seven days before I see them again. But making time is easy, as long as you're prepared to give up something else (TV programmes, football with the lads, shopping trips, nights out). It all comes down to how much you want it. A personal mantra is 'If it was easy everyone would be doing it. If everyone was doing it, you probably wouldn't want to do it any more.'

So why not use this 'travel time' to train? Obviously, I'm not suggesting you take the local river to work, but cycling a five- to six-mile route to work, or doing a 30-minute run to get there, and then doing the same home in the evening is a great way to get some training in without any real effort other than ensuring your clothes and shower kit are prepped and ready to go.

Preparation is key. Taking clothes and training kit to work and preparing yourself is vital to making this work. Running to work carrying a briefcase doesn't work, and screwing your suit up in a rucksack won't endear you to the boss. The best solutions are either to drop clothes off at the office on the weekend, or travel in normally on Monday morning and leave a week's worth of kit there, then travel home normally on Friday (a nice rest evening) and take it all back.

If you don't have a shower facility at work this can be a real problem. You have two choices: use the basin in the toilet and have a stand-up wash (not ideal, and not something I can do, but I have clients who do), or join a gym very close by – preferably with a pool – and use those facilities before heading to work.

Lunchtimes

The lunch hour (one of the busiest times in gyms) has long been a split between co-workers – half an office will sit at the desk eating, or if the weather's good sit in the park, while the other half scoot to the gym to work out and shower before hitting the desk to scoff some food prior to starting work again. For a triathlete trying to squeeze in a silly number of hours' training in a week, the lunch hour can be a golden opportunity, especially if there's a gym or pool close to the office.

Personally I always found that I was more awake and productive in the afternoon following a workout at lunchtime. Be it weight training, a run or a swim, it fired me up, so that instead of having a post-lunch crash I'd actually be raring to go. Maybe triathlon training at midday could actually make you more successful at work.

Weekends

The beauty of weekends is that you have a decent amount of time available without having to worry about starting work, getting to bed etc. They're perfect for the longer sessions – those exceeding an hour or so – that you can't do before or after work, especially if you still want to have a life.

This certainly isn't the only way to plan things. Some people don't like using their commutes as part of their training, feeling that they can't concentrate on it properly, and that simply performing a run or cycle isn't really training at all. These people often feel they'd rather commute normally, perhaps getting some work done, thinking through the day's meetings or eating breakfast on the train while reading a triathlon magazine.

Individuals that dislike commuting by train often feel they'd rather set the alarm, get out for a good hard training swim, cycle or run, and then come home, shower, eat and head to work. In the same vein, some people can't stand the idea of using their lunch break to train, feeling it's rushed and just not long enough to warm up, train, stretch, relax, shower and eat before getting their work head back on. Equally, if you're anything like me you can't stop sweating for a good 30–60 minutes after a hard session, so probably won't want to put the suit back on!

Many other people prefer to get the day's work over and done with and then head out on the bike, off to the pool or gym, or out on the road. Work is done, the mind is clear, and training is an enjoyable and separate pastime. Combining the two doesn't work for them, and they prefer to keep their training and working lives apart.

However, one good thing about using commutes and lunch hours for training is that it often forces 'easier' sessions. The varying intensity of tri training sessions is very important to seeing gains, so can be more helpful than might be thought.

Routine

As with most things, I believe it is important to 'know yourself' – if utilising your commutes works for you, great, do that; if it doesn't and it stresses you out, don't, just use your evenings and weekends. Alternatively if you have family obligations in the evenings and at weekends then use your lunch breaks and commutes. The thing to do is to decide what works best for you and make it a routine. Humans are creatures of habit, so become habitual – then it's a hell of a lot easier to stick to.

However, if you're away a lot on business then the likelihood is that you don't commute the same way as most people and will find it hard to establish a good routine. This is where discipline comes in and planning has to become impeccable. Try to get booked into hotels with a pool or near a pool. Use the time before/after work to go for a swim and perform a run, either one in the morning or evening as suits you best. That takes care of your running and swimming and means all you need to take on the business trip is a swimsuit, goggles, trainers and running kit. All these can be rinsed in your room shower. Obviously you can't take your bike with you, so you'll need to either use an exercise bike or wait until you're home and then get on your bike and hit the roads.

One-week training plan

This schedule utilises time slots mentioned:

Day	Time	Session
Monday	AM commute	Take clothes to work
	Lunch	Swim
	PM commute	Run home
Tuesday	AM commute	Cycle to work
	Lunch	Swim
	PM commute	Cycle home
Wednesday	AM commute	Swim before work (run to pool?)
	Lunch	Rest
	PM commute	Run home
Thursday	AM commute	Cycle to work
	Lunch	Swim
	PM commute	Cycle home
Friday	AM commute	Run to work
	Lunch	Rest (so can finish early?)
	PM commute	Take clothes home
Saturday	AM	Rest
	PM	Long cycle
Sunday	AM	Rest
	PM	Long run or swim

Utilising commutes may be the only way to fit your training in as your tri distances lengthen. For a sprint or Olympic triathlon your runs need only be 5km and 10km respectively, so even a slow endurance run needn't be longer than 45 minutes. However, as you push into half and full ironman events you need to cover far greater distances across all three events, and more distance equals more time, so you have to find somewhere for the time to train for them; and often that can only be found in your 'dead time' if you want to avoid severely affecting your social and home lives.

On the next page is an example of a 'weekly training plan' chart. Each weekend, or at the beginning of a set period of training, you should use this to plan the week(s) ahead. It will enable you to plan am/pm sessions, length of sessions, intensity/heart rate and brick sessions, and there's a space for any notes you may need to make regarding what club it's at, or which track, or whether it's a commuting session, etc.

Weekly Planner

	Session	Time/Distance	Intensity/HR	Brick	Notes
Monday					
Tuesday					
Wednesday					
Thursday					
Friday					
Saturday					
Sunday					

Training considerations

Although Michael Phelps and Paula Radcliffe are both incredibly fit, it's unlikely that Michael would be as successful as a marathon runner, and Paula would be the first to admit that she's not built for swimming. Some of this is down to genetics, but more significantly both athletes train for their own specific events. They're what we called in the Marines 'fit for purpose'. Look at it this way: an Olympic athlete, a professional footballer and the World's Strongest Man are all very fit in their own specific areas, but they may be very 'unfit' in other ways.

The seven components of fitness

To be regarded as having all-round fitness someone must be fit across all seven components – flexibility, endurance, stamina, skill, strength, speed and power. Yes, someone can be fit without actually being fit across the board, but to avoid injury and to be at the top of their game it's important to at least train in each component to some degree. Depending on an individual's sport one component may be more important than another, but ignoring one or more because they don't seem applicable to your particular sport could potentially leave you open to injury and a lack of overall fitness.

Whether you're training for health, fitness or weight loss, triathlon is a great sport, as it ensures great breadth of training, or 'cross-training'. However, why not take it further than that? Design yourself a training programme that covers all seven components, to ensure that you really are fit.

Flexibility

Flexibility entails having the maximum range of movement around a joint allowed by the muscles, tendons and ligaments.

Every training session should involve a comprehensive warm-up (see Chapter 9), including mobility work and dynamic stretches. A post-exercise stretch is also very important – each session should end with a comprehensive cool-down and static stretch session. This will have a marked improvement on recovery time and help produce strong, healthy muscles. However, stretching doesn't have to occur only after exercise; separate stretching sessions are very beneficial in the evening after a hard session, or on a rest day. Watching TV in the evenings is a perfect time to sit on the floor and perform a stretch session. Always remember to warm the muscles first, though.

The following points are worth remembering:
- The type of joint – ie hinge (knee/elbow) or ball and socket (shoulder/hip) – determines joint mobility.
- A lack of flexibility can injure both muscles and tendons. Inflexibility can affect the curve of the spine, thus affecting the body's posture. Inflexibility can also lead to poor technique in specific movements (like swimming, cycling or running), which

can therefore injure those and supporting muscles, ligaments and tendons.
- It's really important to remain flexible, as being inflexible later in life can be very debilitating and really bring on the effects of ageing.
- Over-flexible joints can also be problematic, as they can become unstable and therefore cause injury to muscles, ligaments and tendons.

Flexibility training is particularly important in reducing the risk of injury and prompting recovery after exercise or following an injury. It should be incorporated into every triathlon session, even if it means cutting the session short by ten minutes to allow a stretch.

Endurance

Endurance is the body's ability to resist fatigue whilst performing relatively prolonged exercise of low to moderate intensity.

This type of fitness is probably more important to triathletes than any other, as having a good level of endurance will ensure you can keep swimming/cycling/running for long periods.

The easiest way to train endurance is to incorporate slow to medium-paced sessions. This is a gradual process, and either time or distance should be used as a marker and built on. For example, swimming 10 minutes one session, then 15 minutes the next, then 20 the next and so on. This progression is of utmost importance in any programme and thus is used in the programmes provided in Chapter 11.

As discussed earlier, a great way to train endurance is by using a heart-rate monitor, which will be covered in more detail at the end of this chapter. This is because it's the efficiency of the heart in pumping oxygen that's the limiting factor to your ability to perform well during endurance activities like long-distance swimming, cycling or running (let alone all three!). The heart is a muscle, and just like any other muscle it must be trained for it to strengthen and grow. My advice to anyone wanting to get into fitness would be that the heart is the most important muscle to train, so train it well and you should live a longer, more healthy life and, of course, be able to complete the type of triathlon for which you're specifically training (see 'Specificity' on page 56).

Skill

A skill is the ability to know when and where to use a specific technique that's required to complete an activity, and to be able to use it successfully.

Practice – does it make perfect?

Everyone reading this book has probably heard the phrase 'practice makes perfect'. Well, as I've now written in every one of my books and tell nearly everyone I train, practice does not make perfect! What practice does do is make permanent – ie if something is practised (repeated) over and over it's committed to muscle memory and becomes the way your body performs it. The problem is that if a bad technique is practised over and over then it too can become permanent. So when thinking about developing your skills, be it your swim stroke or your running technique, a far better phrase to use is 'perfect practice makes permanent', ie by repeating a technique correctly and perfectly, over and over, it will become permanent. It's always worth practising when you're fresh to ensure the correct technique is performed, since it's easier to slip into bad habits when you're fatigued. Take it from me, breaking bad habits and re-educating someone is far harder that starting with a 'clean slate'. If in doubt, get a professional to teach you.

There are many techniques a triathlete, especially a novice, needs to master – not just how to swim, cycle and run, but also transitions, removing wetsuits, turning in a pool, sighting a buoy in open water, changing a punctured tyre and how to refuel. And of course, any good triathlete also has a game plan for their race, and knowing how to implement it is also a skill.

Stamina

Stamina is the ability of the body to resist fatigue whilst performing repetitive high intensity work.

This type of training is important for a sprint triathlete, and perhaps even to an Olympic event. For a half and full ironman competitor endurance training and fitness is more important. Having said that, as we saw in Chapter 2 we drift in and out of different energy systems during a race, so stamina training certainly can't be ignored by any length triathlete.

The best way to train stamina is to perform repetitive sprints/intervals a set number of times. Training stamina is essential for all-round fitness and is an excellent way to lose weight, not only due to the level of work required, so that a lot of calories are burnt, but also because it raises the metabolism.

The added bonus of sprint-style training for triathletes is that it 'teaches' the body that it can perform faster than it usually does, thus over time speed is also increased – a huge benefit to cutting seconds and even minutes off your swim/bike/run time.

Strength

Strength is said to be the maximum force that specific muscles can generate against a resistance.

Strength training is often neglected by triathletes in favour of the road, track or pool. However, Michael Phelps did not get world records without strength training, and Chris Boardman's strength routine is something that would make most of us cry. If these swimmers and cyclists use weight training to make them better at their individual events, then all triathletes can surely see the benefits too. Every athlete requires strong muscles, ligaments and tendons, since good overall strength ensures you have the ability to compete with power and explosiveness.

Strength training and in particular resistance training strengthens tendons, ligaments and supporting muscles, with the added bonus of reducing the risk of injury. This is especially important for triathletes, as by the time the run stage has come around the leg muscles are already fatigued, so the huge amount of stress placed on them by running could cause problems if they haven't been 'injury-proofed' by some strength training.

Speed

Speed is said to be how fast the muscles can move given a set objective.

We all initially think of this as our sprint speed, but it could equally be our reaction time in ball sports or how quickly a triathlete can focus, spot the buoy and continue swimming. To train speed you need to do repetitive drills when not overly

fatigued. Doing so when fatigued will lead to bad technique, and even injury.

Speed training is usually similar to the sprint drills laid out for stamina work, but concentrating on technique and training only over shorter distances so that it doesn't become interval training. To a triathlete speed training may not seem important, yet speed can play a vital role in a race, not just in a sprint finish to the line but also in the race to be first to the swim buoy inside lane, or first out of transition when you were third in. Speed, in any part of a race, can be the difference between winning and losing.

Power

Power is the functional relationship between strength and speed. It's a key component to athletic performance, but especially over shorter distances in the context of triathlon. Having said that, endurance running is also greatly enhanced by increased power, as by improving power the efficiency and quickness of muscle movement is maximised, which in turn creates further efficiency and a greater VO2 max (maximal oxygen consumption, ie aerobic capacity) for endurance. Consequently all triathletes could benefit and achieve personal bests by the inclusion of power exercises.

To train for power properly you require some muscular strength beforehand. This means that prehab and conditioning is necessary. Increase your muscles, tendons and ligaments' strength levels with resistance exercises first, then increase your overall power with power training. Ideal for triathletes, power training itself requires a very strong core, so core exercises are imperative too.

Lastly, it's important to take up power exercises slowly, as they can easily cause injury if done incorrectly; therefore progress slowly, remember that genetics rather than power training can dictate your speed, and be realistic.

So there you have it: the seven components of fitness. More so for triathlon than most other sports, it's important to design a training programme that encompasses all-round fitness and doesn't concentrate too much on a specific event. Obviously, endurance training for swimming, cycling and running has to take place, but strength work, flexibility, skill and stamina sessions are all important too. Although it isn't necessary to train all seven components every day, or even to train them evenly, it's important that all get some attention to ensure all-round fitness and injury avoidance. For most novice triathletes a training programme that includes all seven components in some form or other is ideal. This is equally true even if your end goal is simply to lose weight.

Training order

Not all the components need to be trained in one session. They can be mixed together from one training session to the next. However, one type of training may interfere with another, so the following order should be kept to if performing them on the same day:

1. **Warm-up**
2. **Skill**
3. **Power/speed**
4. **Strength**
5. **Stamina**
6. **Endurance**
7. **Flexibility**

This order is quite obvious when you think about it – it wouldn't be sensible to try to concentrate on a specific skill if stamina training had been performed just prior.

Heart-rate training

The heart rate can be used as a guide to exercise intensity. Every individual has different abilities or fitness levels and therefore corresponding working heart rates (WHR). The traditional method of working out someone's heart rate zones can be inaccurate by plus or minus ten beats per minute or more. Consequently every triathlete should own a heart-rate monitor. It doesn't have to be a top-of-the-range GPS monitor – all you need is immediate feedback when training in different activities, conditions and terrain as to what the heart is doing, which will enable you to completely manage your training accordingly.

Heart-rate training zones for different activities

Believe it or not, your fitness and your body's ability will vary across the three disciplines, and not just because you may be a better swimmer than you are runner. Research has shown that with arm work alone, such as arms-only swimming, the same VO2 max cannot be obtained as is reached when running, even though the heart rate may reach its maximum in both cases. Therefore to gain maximum benefits for swimming you may need to run, as running will achieve a greater training effect since it uses a greater muscle mass and creates a greater load on the cardiovascular system than arms-only swimming at the same heart rate. So what does this mean? It means that even if you're a great runner but poor swimmer, you must keep up your run training, as once you've mastered the swim technique and gained some 'swim fitness' your actual fitness gains may come on the track/road, not at the pool.

Methods of measuring the pulse rate
➜ Manual pulse measuring
The heart rate can be measured by feeling the pulse in the wrist or the neck while timing using a watch. To minimise inaccuracies the count is taken over ten seconds and then multiplied by six, over 15 seconds and multiplied by four, or over 30 seconds and multiplied by two. Taking an average of two or three is often recommended, but remember that for those with a greater level of fitness the pulse will drop considerably over 30 seconds, or 60 seconds when resting post-exercise.

Misleading heart
The heart can be very misleading in its actual indication of exercise intensity, since it can be affected by the weather, climate, psychological state, hydration status, sleep patterns and other factors.

Resting pulse
Monitoring the resting pulse rate can be a good indication of recovery from previous training sessions, thus can help prevent overtraining.

➜ Heart-rate monitor (HRM)
A reliable heart-rate monitor is by far the best and most useful way of measuring the pulse. Many types exist (see Chapter 12), but in truth a simple no-nonsense version does the job.

➜ Estimated working heart rate equation
Our maximum heart rate decreases with age; hence we use this crude but workable equation to estimate our maximum and therefore working heart rate (WHR). Using this equation our 'estimated maximum heart rate' (EMHR) is derived. This can then be multiplied by the required percentage to estimate the working heart rate. (NB: This method is not individualistic and therefore not very accurate.)

Males 220 minus age (in years) x % = WHR
Females 226 minus age (in years) x % = WHR

➜ Karvonen working heart rate equation
This alternative is far more accurate, as it uses either a measured (MMHR) or estimated (EMHR) maximum heart rate. To use this equation, a measured maximal heart rate is first required, which can be obtained from an exercise stress test: to perform this test, after warming up thoroughly a best effort one-mile run is performed – the last half to quarter of a mile should be at absolutely maximum effort; the time and heart rate should be noted during the last ten seconds and at the finish.

Next the measured resting heart rate (MRHR) is needed. Immediately on waking from a good night's sleep, the pulse should be taken. This should be done on three consecutive mornings and an average taken. (Some people find a full bladder leads to a higher heart rate, so it may be necessary to empty the bladder and then return to bed for a few minutes before taking the pulse.)

Example: A 40-year-old male starts a triathlon programme and want to work out his 60%MHR –

Estimated maximum heart rate (EMHR)	220 minus 40	180bpm
Measured maximum heart rate (MRHR)		70bpm
Heart rate reserve (HRR)	180 minus 70	110bpm
Working heart rate (WHR)	(110 x 0.6) = 66 + 70	136bpm

Where possible use this equation to get the accuracy you need for training.

Finally it's necessary to establish the heart rate reserve (HRR). To find this deduct the measured resting heart rate from the measured maximum heart rate, ie MMHR – MRHR = HRR. However, it's also possible to find it by deducting the measured resting heart rate from the estimated maximum heart rate, ie EMHR – MRHR = HRR.

Once the HRR has been calculated it's possible to work out some very accurate working heart rates. To do this, multiply the HRR by the percentage wanted and then add the MRHR. This will give the working heart rate, ie (HRR x %) + MRHR = WHR.

→ Heart rate training zone adjustment for swimming and cycling

Research has also shown that compared to running, the heart rate will be a little lower when performing other activities such as swimming and cycling. So for accurate heart rate usage the following should be noted:

Cycling	**Subtract 10bpm**
Swimming	**Subtract 10–15bpm**

This is obviously very important for a triathlete, as you want to get the best from your training by considering the correct heart rate for the specific discipline being trained or performed.

Principles of training

When training for any event, getting better, improving and succeeding isn't just down to training more and more – this will lead to injury via overtraining. Instead, it's important that training should be carefully planned and tailored to suit your needs.

The principles of training, which can be explained by the acronym SPORTP, help explain how training for a triathlon should be undertaken in order to ensure improvement without overtraining. SPORTP stands for:

- Specificity
- Progression
- Overload
- Reversibility
- Tedium
- Periodisation

Specificity

Simply put, your training should be specific to triathlon events. If you're training for a marathon, constantly doing 100kg bench presses to strengthen your chest and arms won't be that beneficial. The majority of your training should be running-based, to increase your endurance and stamina. Having said that, some speed training and some strength training for the legs won't go amiss. In short you must do specific exercises to improve specific parts of the body in specific ways. Nevertheless, swimming sessions will also aid in long-distance running by enabling non-contact exercises to take place without the risk of injury or overtraining, and by making the body work hypoxically and thus help push the VO2 max.

For a triathlon you obviously need to train specifically for three events: swimming, cycling and running. So you need to develop:

- **Relevant muscles** – legs for cycling, core and legs for running, and upper body and core for swimming.
- **Relevant fitness** – endurance, stamina, speed and strength (or a combination thereof) depending on sprint, Olympic, half or full ironman.
- **Relevant technique** – the technique and then the skill to use it in order to swim, bike or run correctly.

Progression

Progression is exactly that: progressing. If you're new to triathlon you need to progress from the point you're at now to a point where you can complete a sprint tri. If you're a seasoned Olympic triathlete, but want to complete an ironman, you'll need to progress in all three disciplines to be able to cope with the added distances.

However, in terms of general exercise progression means gradually increasing the amount of exercise you do – 'gradually' being the key word, ie progressively improving, not jumping straight to 26 miles when 10km has been the length of your maximum run till now. If you increase any training too quickly your body won't have time to adapt and you're likely to fall foul of an injury. Slow and steady progress is the best way forward. Start training over a reduced and set time or distance, repeat this a few times a week, then after a couple of weeks increase by only a small, gradual amount – by one kilometre or five minutes, for example. Gradually increasing the frequency, intensity and duration of training sessions is the best way to gain fitness without risking injury.

As with anything in life, achieving a balance is very important. Without proper rest and recovery as you progress you may become too tired to train effectively. Then you'll become stressed and irritable and end up associating this with triathlon training, leading to you stopping it completely. The worst thing you can do is to overtrain.

Overload

The body and its systems must be 'overloaded' – muscular strength and cardiovascular fitness can only be improved by training. However, the training must be pushed – it must be made harder, it must overload the body. Simply put, unless the body is subjected to increased demands, improvements won't be made.

Any triathlon training programme should put specific demands on the body across all three disciplines, to ensure the body strengthens and fitness levels increase. If training levels remain the same, week in week out, then your level of fitness will simply be maintained, not improved.

→ **Overload can be achieved by means of the FITT principle, standing for:**

- **Frequency** – This is simply how often training is done. Increase the number of days a week or number of sessions a day to overload the body.
- **Intensity** – This relates to how hard the training is. If you usually do 10 intervals, and increase it to 12, or decrease rest from 90 seconds to 60 seconds, the intensity will increase.
- **Time (or duration)** – If you constantly do 30-minute swims you'll only be good for 30 minutes. By increasing to 40, 50 or 60 minutes you're increasing the duration, and so overloading the body.
- **Type** – Different types of training can be far more challenging than others. If you only ever do easy 20-minute runs, then try some interval training. This 'type' of training will be far harder, and will again overload the body.

Increased load

To see fitness increases and therefore improve your triathlon ability you must overload the body by making things harder in training sessions. However, beware of overtraining, which occurs when you push too hard or too fast or don,t allow for rest and recovery.

Frequency

The frequency of your triathlon training will depend on a number of factors: the time available, your overall goal, and the type of tri being trained for. In terms of maintaining general fitness it's suggested that you should do 30 minutes of moderate exercise five times a week. If you're attempting a sprint or Olympic tri for the first time and just wish to finish it, you may actually get away with this split across the three disciplines. However, if you wish to become an intermediate or elite competitor in any sport you'll need to train much more frequently. Elite and professional triathletes train twice a day, but then their lifestyle allows and their sport dictates that they do so. Remember, earlier in this chapter I showed how by utilising your travel time training twice or even three times a day is possible, even if you work a full-time job.

Increased frequency

Just remember that to increase fitness and ability you may need to increase frequency of training, and when increasing training doing so in a regular fashion is far better than ad hoc. Lastly, be aware of overtraining! Increase in small increments and constantly measure your progress.

Intensity

Intensity refers to how hard you work during your various training sessions, and as described earlier an excellent tool with which to do this is a heart-rate monitor.

In Chapter 2 we looked at the difference between training with oxygen (aerobic work) and without (anaerobic work). Aerobic work is less 'intense' than anaerobic, and we can use the measured heart rate to get a good idea of which energy system is being used.

As a basic rule for relatively fit individuals, to train the aerobic system their HR should be between 60% and 80% of maximum, and to train the anaerobic system it should be between 80% and 90% of maximum. However, when training at up to 90% of maximum heart rate, training time will have to decrease to allow more time for recovery.

Time

The duration of each training session can vary hugely depending on what needs to be achieved (and, of course, the intensity of the session). The length of a session may need to be extended to ensure overload if other factors stay constant, so rather than increasing the pace of a swim it may be necessary to increase the time in the water – maybe initially 15 minutes for a few sessions, then 20 minutes, then up to 25 or 30.

Bear in mind as well that the 'time' needed for training will depend on the chosen event. Training for a sprint triathlon will require far shorter sessions than training for an ironman, when to ensure the correct level of endurance, ability to complete race mileage and, of course, to overload will sometimes require hours of training at a time.

However, be wary of training too hard to try to see quick gains. If you have a weakness in strength or a bad technique, shorter sessions that are specific and intense are better than long 90-minute plus sessions that will just see fatigue creep in and encourage bad habits. Save these long sessions for endurance training on the weekend.

Type

This is more appropriate if someone is just training to get fit rather than for a specific event or sport. If fitness is sought, then the type of training is varied, but some sessions will obviously be tougher than others (intervals vs circuits vs an easy swim).

As we're training for triathlon the type of exercise completed is obviously very important. It's vital to cover all types of triathlon training: swimming, cycling, running and, of course, transition. However, these too can be split into 'types'. Take swimming, for example – we could do a long, slow endurance swim, we could do intervals, we could do drills; the 'type' chosen can make the session very easy or very challenging. This depends on the time and the intensity of the sessions as well, but it's important to keep three of the four components (frequency, intensity, time, type) constant, therefore changing only one component at a time.

Reversibility

As annoying as it is, nearly all adaptations that occur from training are reversible, certainly the physical ones, though some of the mental ones are perhaps more permanent. We therefore say that all training is reversible, meaning that any gains can just as easily be completely lost. Well, almost.

Fitness is lost if training is stopped, reduced, or in fact if overload isn't achieved. This is where injury can be so heartbreaking, as (depending on severity) training must cease following an injury to allow recovery, and this leads to loss of fitness.

This means, then, that even after a race at the end of the season, too much time off will lead to loss of any fitness gains made. Consequently where possible long periods of inactivity should be avoided. Aerobic fitness losses are said to be variable from person to person, the variation coming mainly from the level of fitness as opposed to a genetic predisposition. The fitter a person, the slower gains are lost, though a rough estimate is that three months of inactivity will result in about half of any aerobic fitness being 'lost'. Strength gains are said to decline more slowly; however, lack of exercise will soon be apparent as the atrophy (shrinking) of the muscles becomes visible.

The thing to remember as a triathlete is that if you've worked hard to gain fitness, don't give it all up for nothing. Keep things ticking over, even if it's just with maintenance-style sessions. Conversely, overtraining is a risk if you never rest through fear of losing fitness, and one of the most common outcomes of overtraining is an injury, which will force you to rest anyway so that all your fitness gains might disappear. Taking a week off every six to eight weeks is very advisable. So too is easing off training before a race – known as 'tapering' – which should occur before all serious events. Furthermore, resting after hard races, taking one to two weeks off for a summer holiday post-season and just generally listening to your body are all pieces of advice I'd stick to.

Tedium

Work, commuting, television and maybe even your diet may be tedious, but training shouldn't be. However, many people do get very bored with it, especially if they follow a poor training programme in which they do the same session day in and day out. Like everything, if your training is uninteresting and repetitive you'll get bored with it, lose your enthusiasm and motivation and eventually give up. But the beauty of triathlon training, compared to running or swimming or cycling as separate sports, is the sheer variety of its sessions, since these different activities are all intrinsic parts of the same sport.

However, many people who train triathlon still seem to make their sessions rather tedious, performing the same 10km runs twice a week, the same interval session every two weeks, the same one-mile swim twice a week and so on. They've obviously forgotten the principle of overload – that you need to overload the body to see gains, so repeating the same thing each week is pointless. Add more intervals, shorten the rest, lengthen the distance, change your swim drills, go to a swim class – try something new.

Personal experience...

I've had injuries that most probably resulted from overtraining, and they made me very depressed because I was unable to train or compete for months at a time. So I've learned not to push too hard. Give your body time to rest and recover, and just relax every now and then. In the long run – whether it's in a year's time when you get a personal best, or in 30 years' time when you don't need a walking stick to walk – you'll thank me!

⏱ Variety beats tedium

Some people argue that if you worry too much about ensuring training doesn't become tedious you often forget about specificity, and start training 13km runs because 10km runs each week are boring. I understand this concern – you must be specific. But how about doing one 10km run every one to two weeks and then taking the other run down to 5km to see how fast you can do it? After three weeks make this 6km and see how fast you can run that: try to beat that the next week and the week after that. Then increase it to 7km, then 8km etc. I bet that after three to four months your 10km time will have reduced.

Periodisation

No matter what type of training you do, no matter who you are, you can't maintain your top fitness indefinitely. If you try, you'll either burn out and suffer from overtraining, sustain an overuse injury (from overtraining) or plateau and possibly lose interest in your sport. To avoid these fates, periodise your training. What does this mean? Have you heard of the term 'off season'? Have you noticed that boxers often look very different between fights than on the day of a fight, and that footballers get three months off a year then have to do pre-season training? They've 'periodised' their training seasons, allowing them to lose some fitness, build on fitness, peak their fitness, complete the season, then recover. If, as a triathlete, you decide to do just one

triathlon, this isn't something to concern you; you just need a good build-up training programme to the event, a taper week and then a good rest after the event. But if you decide to do a season of triathlons, then periodisation is for you.

Periodisation explained

Think of an athlete's training as a lot of jigsaw pieces that need to be put together. The finished picture is how they look when they're ready to face the season, with no rough edges. But to achieve this each piece has been shaped, smoothed and coloured, sometimes one piece at a time, sometimes two or three at a time, and only when they're all ready can they be slotted together to create the final picture. That's essentially how all the training elements come together to make a top athlete.

A training programme can be a four, eight, ten or twelve-week build-up to an event. Such programmes are relatively easy to put together and to follow – there are examples in Chapter 11 – and they're great for a single event, or to prepare for the first event of the season and then just maintain your fitness for subsequent events. However, at the next level up from this a well thought-out periodisation programme would be over a 12-month period, looking at rest time, the season start, the season end and everything that needs training: technique, stamina, endurance, flexibility and so on. Admittedly this is at the upper end of competitions, but it's something of which all triathletes should be aware.

Even within an ordinary rather than a periodisation-style programme some sessions should be hard and some easier. This allows for recovery, planning for hard sessions and the overall bigger picture of what needs to be accomplished. If you consider this alongside the principles of training and overload it makes sense: we can't overload ALL the time – it must be progressive.

Periodisation seasonally

If we use the UK as an example, the triathlon season runs from May to September, so it's important to think of the season and training in relation to this time frame. Since the season ends in September the year looks something like this:

➜ Post-season

October/November for a period of 4–6 weeks:

- Complete rest for 1–2 weeks, perhaps coinciding with a holiday.
- Lower intensity exercise and 'active rest'. Perhaps other forms of exercise.
- Any rehab/prehab for old injuries; technique issues can be started at low level.

➜ Off season

November to February/March for 20+ weeks:

- Endurance training is the focus. Long sessions at easy pace to strengthen the heart and regain lost fitness.
- Technique work, especially in terms of correcting any flaws, should be high on the agenda.
- Any interval training is more low-key, focusing on endurance rather than stamina, so long exercise periods but not at high heart rate. Short recovery times, as no oxygen debt should be created by training.
- Strength and conditioning drills are vital here. Drills for swimming and gym-based conditioning for all three disciplines will pay dividends.
- Techniques like sighting, turning, transition skills etc, and any new kit and supplements, should be tried and tested.

➜ Pre-season

February/March to April/May for 8–12 weeks:

- A real focus on the first race of the season, with a good programme aiming for that.
- Endurance training is kept up and extended onwards.
- Strength and conditioning is continued, but perhaps reduced to allow more anaerobic training.
- Anaerobic intervals are introduced to push stamina fitness; short, hard bursts of exercise with longer recovery.
- Endurance work focuses on distances of the race, and race pace sessions are included towards the latter stages.

➜ Race season

May/June to August/September for 12–18 weeks:

- It's imperative to draw up a race calendar. Choose which races you're going to do (be realistic) and design training sessions around them allowing for taper and recovery. Don't be tempted to throw in extra races unless as 'training sessions'. Bar injury, stick to your calendar and plan.
- It's easy to lose fitness in the race season as your focus is on racing; but if too many races are included, with too much tapering and recovery time, then fitness will be lost or you'll fatigue. Chose wisely: it's better to race well over eight races than to be disappointed with all but the first two or three events of a 20-race season.
- Endurance training is key to maintaining fitness. Don't be tempted to throw in too many hard interval sessions – they take time to recover from.
- Keep the quality of your disciplines by maintaining drills and technique work, especially if weaknesses become apparent during races.

Proper planning prevents poor performance. Plan your training, your season and your time and you'll see the rewards in your races.

A final word on periodisation

Periodisation isn't for everyone. Some people, pro athletes included, don't like splitting their training in this way. As I've said repeatedly, 'know yourself'. By all means try things, experiment, listen to others, read books, magazines, articles and websites; but if you find something that works for you, use it – rely on it. Don't be afraid to look into other methods, but have an understanding of what works best for you and harness it to its full potential.

⏱ Easier the second time

Studies suggest that once a certain level of fitness is gained, if it's lost it's easier to get it back than it was to achieve it first time round.

Overtraining

Overtraining is one of the real problems faced by triathletes. If we don't achieve the times, results or body that we want we push harder and train more. This is true of professionals, amateurs and novices alike – even fitness industry professionals such as myself who should know better. I hold up my hand and admit that I'm an exercise addict, and that I've been guilty of overtraining – and more importantly that I've paid the price for it. So I can't stress enough the importance of being aware of overtraining.

What is overtraining?

Wikipedia defines overtraining as 'a physical, behavioural and emotional condition that occurs when the volume and intensity of an individual's exercise exceeds their recovery capacity'. Simply put, it's attempting to complete more exercise than the body can tolerate. The downside to overtraining is that is doesn't just halt progress, it can also cause a loss of strength and fitness.

Rest

The most effective weapon against overtraining is rest, and the acronym REST will help you remember why:

→ **Recovery**
→ **Ensures**
→ **Successful**
→ **Training**

Basically, to stop overtraining be sensible and listen to your body: if you feel overtired and fatigued you probably are, so combat this fatigue with a day's rest and appropriate nutritional intake. If you think of rest as a tool to aid your training and help you improve then you'll use it effectively and appropriately. Bodybuilders are told that the hard work happens in the gym, but growth happens when resting; if they train again immediately, the body can't grow. The same might be said for triathletes. Your training involves kicking your body into improving, into getting fitter, and when resting it makes the necessary adaptations. Even if you end up doing easy sessions or drills/techniques instead of hard endurance or interval sessions, that can be what the body needs.

Allowing your body to recover from exercise fatigue is so important. To push on not only degrades the body, but doesn't allow the little aches and pains – or DOMS (delayed onset muscle soreness) as they're known – to recover, and can therefore lead to injury. For triathletes, not allowing the body to recover adequately will lead to slower times, which leads to frustration and a feeling of needing to train harder; a vicious circle will ensue and possibly a downward spiral of continued fatigue and overtraining, leading to short-term or possibly long-term injuries.

If you always feel like training on a rest day, then train really hard the day before. Then you can rest assured that you trained thoroughly yesterday and couldn't have done more; that way you deserve your rest day – and need it!

☉ Symptoms of overtraining

The following are all indications of overtraining:

- Loss of performance.
- Inability to progress.
- Increased difficultly of easy sessions.
- Lack of enthusiasm.
- Increased recovery time.
- Muscular atrophy and associated weight loss.
- Heart rates (working and resting) higher.
- Blood pressure higher.
- Lowered immune system (leads to colds, infections and allergic reactions).
- Nausea.
- Loss of appetite.
- Emotional and psychological effects (lethargy, listlessness, procrastination, fear of failure, unrealistic high goals).
- Disturbed sleep patterns.
- Loss of libido.

Pushing the boundaries

The fitter you get, the more intensely you'll be able to train. Furthermore, your rate of recovery may be greatly increased, and therefore training can be done for longer or more frequently without as much rest. This isn't an excuse to start overtraining, but you must be aware that your individual rate of adaptation to exercise is different from the next person's, so whereas your training partner needs a rest today you may not need one until tomorrow, or vice versa. Just remember, we all have a limit at some point.

No one can force their body to adapt and improve when there's no capacity left, and this is where training with a group or partner can backfire. If your partner is a little fitter, or their body is adapting and improving faster, they may be able to cope with the excessive intensity and frequent sessions while you can't. Although it goes against your competitive nature and may hurt your pride, it's important to take the rest your body craves, even if your swim club coach or training partner is raring you to go. Remember that only you have to cope with the consequences of overtraining.

Overtraining is something pretty much all fit healthy people will border on occasionally. It sometimes takes a friend or loved one to point it out. Don't fall into this trap. Write your sessions down on a calendar, look at the number of rests days you take over a month (especially when race season has started) and self-evaluate. Remember, training and racing triathlon is to be enjoyed: no one wins races or achieves personal beats by hating their daily training grind and turning themselves into an injury-ridden, rest-craving mess.

Peaking and tapering

Before wrapping up this chapter I want to mention peaking and tapering, which go hand in hand with periodisation and the basic principles of training. Furthermore, understanding them now will make things easier when you go on to create your own training programme.

Peaking isn't easy. It's getting all your training and nutrition and every element right so that you're in the perfect and best fitness for a specific event or race. No one can remain in peak physical fitness at all times, all year round. You need to have an off season, then rest, train and peak.

→ Signs of a peak are:
- Increased power in the body.
- Less lactic burn than normally felt.
- Greater red blood cell concentration.
- Better fuel storage.

You also 'feel' good, and are therefore more confident and more motivated, and have better concentration so that little mistakes don't get made. In short, you're as close to a superhero as you're going to be!

To get the best out of your peak you need to ensure you taper leading up to your important event. If you get this right all your signs of peak fitness will marry up with great technique and form, as well as a rested, non-fatigued body. It's not easy to time it right, though, and you probably won't get it perfect every time, but it's worth trying, if only to have a more enjoyable race.

It's actually possible to peak two or three times during a season, but this requires very structured training with specific sessions of specific intensity situated in the training programme to prepare you for particularly important races. These races are therefore preceded by 7–21 days (depending on sprint, Olympic or ironman) of specific sessions to achieve the required peak. Rather than go into that here we're going to look at a general taper before racing.

☉ Tapering near the race

The more unfit you are approaching a race, the more important it is to keep training hard to get your fitness level up. If you're less fit you don't need to taper as much, as you won't be as fatigued. However, if you're really fit your session intensities will have been high, so you'll be very fatigued and require a bigger taper to rest. However, it's difficult to gauge fitness, and all triathletes therefore push on thinking 'I'm not fit enough'. But it's better to taper too much than not enough.

Tapering considerations

Deciding how long you should taper for is actually quite a scientific process, and not just a 'one size fits all' operation. It depends on:

- Point in the season (if later, perhaps with more rest).
- Length of race (if longer, with more rest).
- Fitness level (if very fit, with more rest).
- Injuries (if carrying any, with more rest).
- Age (if older, with more rest).

How to taper

→ **Ironman/half-ironman**

Taper over three weeks and cut training volume across all three disciplines by 20% per week.

→ **Half-ironman/Olympic**

Taper over two weeks and cut training by 30% per week.

→ **Olympic/sprint**

Taper over one week, cut training by 50% for entire week.

Keep your frequency of training the same, ie the same number of workouts – just slash their duration. This means you don't break your routine and feel unfit, you just aren't training as hard.

Intensity and rest are key

As we all know, training stimulus is what makes us fitter, and it's also what keeps us focused, so intense training is still important. Perform race pace workouts once or twice a week during the taper. These should be of race intensity; either swim/bike/run but for a shorter distance than the race itself, or concentrate on your weakest area but still at race intensity.

Take everything else easy. Work on running and cycling at low recovery heart rates, swim technique/drills only, work towards

resting for the intensity of the race pace sessions and the race itself. Above all maintain focus, but don't train into the ground!

You should have a complete rest the day before the day before race day, not the day before race day itself. Otherwise you may feel sluggish on race day. So rest completely two days before the event, then the next day perform a short session(s), but include each element and take them up to race pace for a few minutes to ensure you're comfortable and focused.

⏱ Conclusion

A training programme goes hand in hand with your goals and aims. Without a goal you're training for nothing in particular and will soon skip sessions, lose interest and become unfit. With a dedicated and chosen goal, however, you'll be focused and crave improvement. To ensure you satisfy this craving get a training programme that will help you reach your goal. Not only will it make you train properly and regularly, it will also prevent overtraining, which can occur when you keep adding bits here and there. The programmes in this book (see Chapter 11) are simple and easy to use – no difficult formulas, no complicated sessions; they should allow anyone to go from novice non-triathlete to being able to complete all elements of a sprint tri, getting a good sprint tri or Olympic tri time, a decent half-ironman time, and even completing an ironman. But you don't have to do all of them. Just take your time, 'know yourself' and set realistic goals.

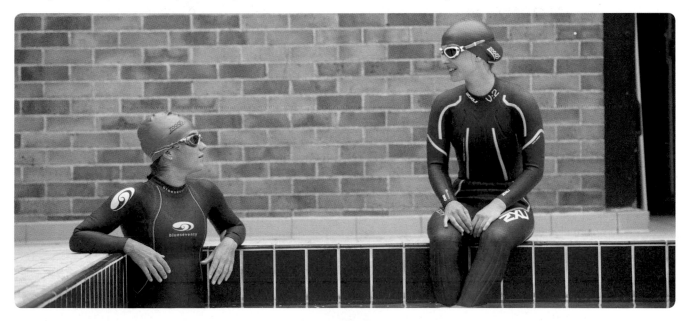

CHAPTER 5
SWIMMING

Swimming is perhaps the most difficult of the triathlon disciplines, in terms of both planning sessions and, if you're not a proficient swimmer, learning. Most of us can run and most of us can ride a bike, but swimming is a different matter. Many people simply can't perform a front crawl properly, and don't even know how to. This chapter will teach you the basics, but in some circumstances a coach will help.

Once you decide to tri train, planning swim sessions is made easier by the fact that most public pools appreciate that people need to use them outside normal working hours. Consequently many open early in the morning (around 6:00am) and some stay open until around 10:00pm. Furthermore, even when they're busy with families and children in the middle of the day, pools usually have one, two or three lanes separated off to allow swimmers to train. Weekend opening times are often shorter, so these lane systems prove invaluable if you're planning to swim on a Saturday or Sunday but still want to enjoy a lie-in and an evening in or out on both days.

Where to swim

We saw how to plan your training sessions around your everyday life in the previous chapter, and in Chapter 11 you'll find some example training programmes where we've put together all three disciplines to determine a workable run, swim and bike training programme. But where do you do your swim training?

Local pool

Convenient and easy to use before or after work and at lunchtime. Changing is easy, and as they're indoors and often heated, pools are far more preferable than lakes or reservoirs in the winter. If you race in pools, turns (see pages 84–87) must be mastered, as these can shave minutes off a time.

Lakes and reservoirs

Perfect for amateurs wanting open-water experience, as currents and tides are non-existent, and in a sense the whole experience is very controlled, especially as land is usually visible on all sides. The major downside is the cold temperature, so a good wetsuit is a must (see pages 66–67).

Docklands

Many docklands now organise swim sessions, especially if a triathlon is started or run from their location. They're great for specificity (see previous chapter) prior to a race, or just for gaining open-water experience if pool sessions are your normal venue.

Rivers

On the whole these should be avoided due to their hazardous nature. In general only swim in rivers as part of an organised session, as depths, widths and currents vary. Pollution, driftwood and river traffic can also be dangerous.

Having said that, swimming with or even better against a strong current can be an excellent training session.

The sea

This is the most popular place to train or race in the UK, as most of us are no more than a couple of hours from the coast. Always read weather reports and get to know the area where you choose to swim, otherwise tides and currents can cause problems for even the best swimmers. Acquire good knowledge of how to escape a strong current, and where possible swim in pairs or groups for safety.

As a brief idea of how to escape a current, don't swim against it – you'll only tire yourself out. Instead, let it take you in its direction, and swim at right angles to it to try to get out of its way. Once you're free swim back to the shore.

Swim kit

Swimsuit or trunks

Your swimsuit is something you'll be wearing a lot. Whether for training sessions or races, it needs to be well-fitting, hard-wearing and comfortable. It's one of the few bits of kit where it's worth purchasing a decent brand. Personally I always use Speedo or Adidas swim kit, but Zoggs and Arena are also very reputable.

● Never buy a costume that's too small, thinking it'll sag over time and will then fit properly. It'll ride up your backside and be really uncomfortable, especially under a wetsuit during a race.
● Avoid 'racing suits' – these are for 50m sprint swimmers and won't be hardwearing enough for tri training.
● Rinse them and wash them regularly. As they start to sag, either throw them away or wear two costumes on top of one another, similar to wearing a slightly larger than needed costume (as some pro swimmers do for training). This adds more drag, so on race day when you wear a well-fitted new costume you're more hydrodynamic and will feel faster and tighter.
● When swimming in new kit have some Vaseline/petroleum jelly in your bag to add to rough spots or rubs to prevent sore areas becoming blistered or raw.

Drag trunks

ABOVE Worn over a normal swimsuit, these add 'drag' to make the swim harder, thus simulating open water swimming more readily.

Tri suits

RIGHT Designed for purpose, and so you don't feel quite so 'on display' as you do when you run or cycle in a swimsuit. Train in a swimsuit, but race and do your periodic brick or race pace sessions in your tri suit.

Wetsuits

Forget warmth, buoyancy and streamlining – the most important characteristic for a wetsuit is that it fits. In addition wetsuits aren't an option in many triathlons (especially in the UK), they're compulsory, since due to local water temperatures they're worn for safety reasons. Triathlon wetsuits are allowed to be up to 5mm thick, and for that you'll pay between £100 and £200.

All wetsuits need to be tight enough to ensure they provide decent insulation and avoid drag, but not so tight as to impede movement, especially around the shoulders. A tight wetsuit can also restrict breathing, so it's imperative to get one that fits while also ensuring that as you either lose weight or put on muscle it will still fit and allow you to swim. Among top athletes this is achieved by having their suits custom made, and as you get more into triathlon this is perhaps something to consider. However, for most of us it's a case of just finding one that fits as well as possible. Try on a variety of brands as sizes vary and a medium in one brand can be very different to the medium in another.

If you're aiming to buy via the Internet to save a few pounds (of which I'm a huge advocate), make sure you try wetsuits on in a shop first to get the right fit, then search for the best price online.

The correct fit

1 Pull the legs on all the way up to the crotch before putting the top half on. Treat the bottoms as a pair of running tights, put them fully on, crotch tight, and see how far down the legs they go.
2 Once the top is done up, take some large, deep breaths and rotate the arms through the shoulders. The arms should move freely without too much resistance, and breathing in and out should be unrestricted.
3 Ensure there are no excess folds of material anywhere. Problem areas are usually at the base of the spine and under the arms.

So it fits, but can you swim in it?

Swimming in a wetsuit feels different to swimming normally. A good wetsuit will be tight, to give support and buoyancy, especially around the core of the body, but will equally be flexible to allow a decent full stroke around the joints, especially the shoulders.

Although it can feel weird, a wetsuit will actually make most people better swimmers, especially if your swim coach says you have a good stroke but need to work on your core or kick. The wetsuit adds buoyancy to everyone, so makes them sit a little higher in the water, seemingly making the core control and leg kick more effective. Swim times just over 10% faster with a wetsuit than without one are commonplace.

Wetsuit stroke

Overall a wetsuit swim stroke is very little different to a normal stroke, with perhaps these marginal differences:

1 Reach slightly longer than normal and roll the body a little more than normal. This will help maintain the glide from the extra buoyancy of the suit.
2 Utilise a slightly wider arm recovery phase as this will reduce difficulty in movement around the shoulders if the wetsuit is particularly tight.

Lube

Ideally you should use wetsuit lubricant from surf shops or tri shops around the cuffs and neck to stop chafing and facilitate rapid removal. Avoid Vaseline or any type of petroleum jelly as it can speed up the breakdown of the suit itself.

Goggles

Goggles come in all shapes and sizes, with different extras and methods of adjustment, not to mention lenses for different waters and weathers. The problem is that bad goggles can literally sabotage your swim! A simple leak can either have you putting up with bad vision for the best part of 30 minutes or trying to fix it every five!

Lenses

The lenses are made of polycarbonate, which not only provides good clarity but also can have impact resistance up to bulletproof level, which helps to avoid breaking them during transition or in a backpack while running.

If you wear glasses or contact lenses, goggles can be made up to match your prescription requirements. Some brands just sell interchangeable lenses from their top-of-the-line goggles, while others can be bought in the +8 to -8 range (Speedo and Zoggs are good examples). Unfortunately it can be difficult if you have differing prescriptions in each eye, when your only real option is to purchase two sets of prescription lenses for interchangeable lens goggles, unless you buy a pair suited to your worse eye.

Having said that, if you want to get a perfect set, fall outside of the +8 to -8 range or have astigmatism, then optical specialists can make up any prescription, but expect to pay around £50 – again not a huge sum considering how important your eyes are and how important your sport is to you.

Tints

In open water lens tints can be hugely advantageous. The different colour lenses offer different benefits to a swimmer, and thus at the top level interchangeable-lens goggles may come with a variety of lenses to suit the conditions on a particular day. The varieties most commonly available include:

● Polarised lenses – Filter out light of a certain wavelength and thus minimise the glare reflecting off water.

⏱ Diving in goggles

If you find your goggles fall off when you dive in, tuck your chin to your chest. They should stay put that way.

- Grey, mirrored lenses – Reduce the amount of overall light transmitted, while keeping all colours even.
- Blue lenses – Used as a contrast lens; the blue reduces the glare of white light as it bounces off water.
- Yellow, brown and amber lenses – Used on overcast days, to enhance contrast, sharpness and depth perception, as well as reducing glare. Photochromic versions exist that adapt to the light conditions as they change.

Anti-fogging solutions

The first step in preventing fogging is to look after your kit. Don't just throw your goggles in with your wetsuit or into a trainer for safe keeping – if they come with a little bag or box, keep them in that. Most are scratch-resistant to a point, and furthermore most are treated with an anti-fogging coat, but as this gets handled and rubbed it deteriorates, so touch the inside of the lenses as little as possible. However, you can buy anti-fogging treatment from good swim and triathlon suppliers, so it may be worth reapplying rather than replacing the goggles.

There are dozens of old wives' tales as to how to prevent fogging, including washing-up liquid, spitting on them and immersing them in the water to be swum in. At the end of the day, if you find something that works for you, do it.

The seal

Most goggles come with a flexible seal that secures the lens to the face. However, some goggles – known as 'Swedish style' – don't have one and rely on the skin and face to form a seal. These work for some people and not for others. Personally I find they're OK for a short swim but become uncomfortable after some time; a flexible seal, by contrast, allows the face to relax.

The type of seal on goggles depends on their price. At the bottom end of the market it's made of foam. These tend to disintegrate over time, and aren't very durable.

Skin irritation from both Swedish goggles and foam goggles is common, so the most popular type is that with moulded TPR or silicon seals. These don't cause irritation to the skin and are incredibly flexible, meaning that unlike the other two they literally fit any face.

Fitting goggles

To fit a pair of goggles, lightly press the seal on to your eye sockets; a small vacuum should be felt if the fit is good, so much so that it should hold the goggles to your face for a few seconds. If the goggles feel right and fit well there's no need to over-tighten the head strap, a common mistake among swimmers and triathletes.

Swim hat

Swim hats serve three purposes in triathlon:

1 They allow race organisers to spot people in the water clearly (many will actually issue you with a swim hat).
2 They can lower water resistance for people with long hair and thus save you time.
3 Because around 40% of body heat is lost through the head one or even two swim hats add insulation that can keep you warmer, even if swimming in near minus temperatures.

They also provide some protection from the sun, flailing arms and heart-rate monitor watches, which can cause abrasions if they hit you.

You can buy special neoprene swim hats that offer added warmth, and other insulated styles. They aren't expensive, so perhaps buy a normal swim hat for pool sessions and an insulated version for open water swims if you feel you need it.

Even if you don't think you need one, training in a swim hat is a good idea whether in open water or a pool. It offers some protection and also gets you used to the feel of swimming in one and how it affects your goggles etc.

After use, rinse your swim cap, turn it inside out and sprinkle it with talc. It'll feel far better putting it on next time than if it's still damp.

Bands

A simple rubber physio-type band is used to tie the legs together so that you can focus on your arm pull.

Drink bottles

Too many people swim, either training or racing, and fail to rehydrate adequately if at all. I advise all swimmers/triathletes to have two drink bottles ready at the end of the pool or in their bag, one containing just water and the other containing some form of sports fuel or electrolytes.

Pool buoys

These are excellent for 'switching off' the legs and concentrating on the arms and upper body. The pool buoy fits between the legs, just above the knees, and keeps the legs afloat and thus the body streamlined without the need to kick.

Fins

Fins (often incorrectly called 'flippers') are great for a swimmer with a weak or 'incorrect' kick to learn how to kick correctly. They can be a great asset to both stroke correction and stroke development. They're also useful in training swimmers how to swim faster.

Paddles

Paddles can be really great for increasing power and strength in the shoulders and lats (the main muscles used while swimming) without having to spend extra time conditioning in the gym. However, make sure they're the right size. Too small and little gain will be made; too big and the stroke is impeded, and the shoulders and back muscles being worked can be overloaded and injured. See pages 79–80 for a few paddle swim training drills.

Kickboard

A kickboard is simply a float that's held out in front when training your kick on the front or side and can be held across the chest when training the kick on your back.

Swim stroke (front crawl)

It isn't wrong to swim breaststroke, doggy paddle or even backstroke in many triathlons. However, front crawl or 'freestyle' is the recognised most efficient stroke to compete with in terms of speed and ability to cycle and run afterwards. I'm therefore only going to discuss the front crawl.

Use a swim coach

If you want to take your triathlon seriously, then do a 30-minute or hour session with a decent triathlon or swim coach. Not only will this bring any weaknesses to your attention, it will give you areas to work on instead of just training your strengths and then hitting a plateau, as we all tend to do.

When I teach front crawl I like to split the stroke into several parts. This makes it easier for a new swimmer to learn, and makes it easier for me to see where the swimmer is going wrong, as different parts are learned and practised separately. I like to use the analogy of driving a car, where the different elements seem so difficult to a learner when all done together – steering, gears, accelerator, brakes, mirror, indicator etc – but when each individual action is taken separately they're all very simple. Swimming is exactly the same: individual steps practised and learned separately that when put together make for a strong, fast, elegant stroke.

Swim stroke elements

Many people starting triathlon tend to swim like they remember being taught as a child – fast and furious, kicking as hard as they can and moving their arms like a cog through the water. However, though this may have won the 25m sprint in your school summer sports day at the age of 12 you can't keep it up for a mile or more. Like running, there's an economic (aerobic) pace that can be held for long distances which is far different from a full-out 100m (anaerobic) sprint pace. The techniques of the two 'styles' of swimming are as different as those of a long-distance runner compared to a sprinter.

To help you to learn, many swim teachers use the acronym **BLABT**, which stands for body, legs, arms, breathing and timing. Anyone wishing to become a competent swimmer will need to master all of these elements. Personally I don't always teach them in that order, but change it around depending on the particular student and their specific weaknesses and strengths.

Film your stroke

Unlike weight training or running, where you can perform in front of a mirror to check your technique, swimming isn't something that you can ever check for yourself, is it? Yes, it is! Get a friend to grab your smartphone, switch it to video camera mode and film your stroke. It's surprising to see what you actually do as opposed to what you think you do. (Be sure to ask permission to film at the club/centre you're using, especially if women and children are around.)

Body

1 The body should be parallel with the water's surface and as flat as possible. If your legs or lower body are low it creates drag and slows you down.

2 The body should rotate lengthways, rolling slightly from side to side, allowing an extend and reach by engaging your back muscles and 'gliding' into the front, non-working arm.

3 The body has a slight slope down to the hips to keep the leg kick underwater.
➜ Stomach flat, core tight to support your lower back.
➜ Head position and leg kick are key to flat body position.
➜ Head should be in line with the body, with eyes looking forward and down. Water level should come between your eyebrows and hairline.

4 Face should be straight down, but eyes at 45°.
➜ Keep your head and spine as still and relaxed as possible. Rotate your hips and shoulders to generate momentum through the water. Your head should only join the rotation when breathing.

5 Your shoulder should come out of the water as your arm exits while the other begins the propulsive phase under the water.
➜ The hips should not rotate as much as the shoulders.

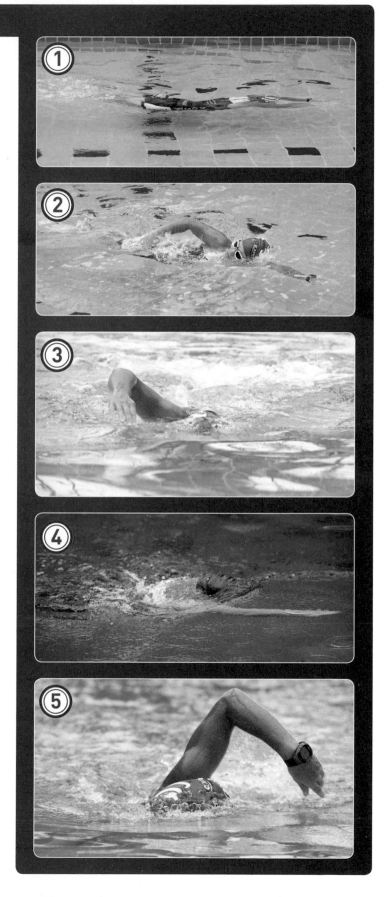

Legs (the kick)

1 Your legs should be close together, ankles relaxed and loose.

2 Keep movements small and under the surface.

3 Kick from the hip and move your whole legs.
→ Keep legs as straight as possible, with only a little knee-bend between the end of the upbeat and beginning of the downbeat.
→ The straighter your legs, the more efficient and powerful the kick.
→ The more kicks per cycle, the more energy used, so 'kick, kick' as the arm strokes to ensure fewer kicks.
→ The legs move alternately, with one leg kicking downward while the other leg moves upward.
→ Kicking is done for stabilisation and balance in the water, not for propulsion.
→ 'Kick, kick' every time one arm does its stoke. It's therefore like pulling the throttle all at once: 'arm pull/kick, kick'.
→ Feet shouldn't really leave the water but should kick to the depth of the body.

Arms – Entry

1 With the elbow pointed towards the ceiling and the lower arm hanging loose, the hand is prepared to enter the water.

2 With hand held flat to the water or the palm turned away from the swimmer, the hand is then pushed forward into the water.

Arms – Entry (continued)

3 Entry is in the order fingers, then wrist, then elbow, to make a long stretch out of the arm.

4 Entry is between the centre line of the head and the shoulder, not across the head as this causes a barrier to the water that slows the swimmer down.

5 Entry of the hand is 30–60cm in front of the swimmer.

6 Reach forward under the water and lean into the stroke, rotating the shoulders to maximise the glide.

7 The arm entering should be fully extended for a moment before your hand moves into the catch.

Pulling

Some people teach to kick all the time, but I find that this lends itself to 'splaying' the legs when twisting to breathe. Better to kick when pulling, then be streamlined and relaxed when breathing, to stop any splaying and subsequent 'drag' this causes.

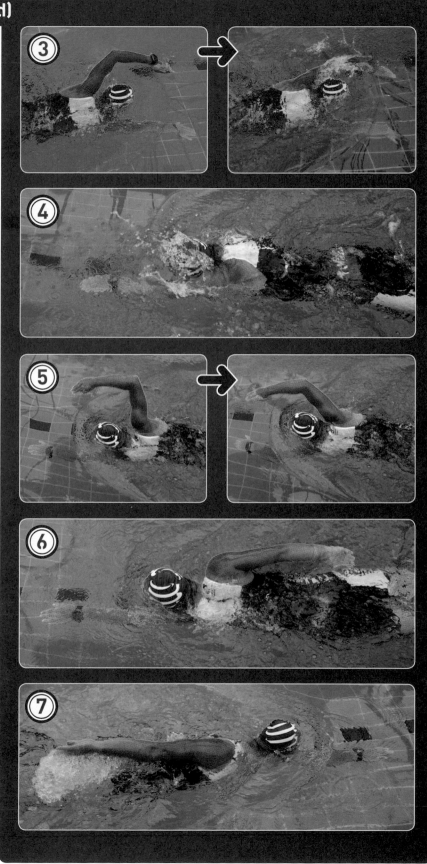

Arms – Catch

1 The catch or pull is an S-shaped movement (or backwards S for the right hand) from the outstretched position to midway between the ribs and hip.

2 The idea of the 'S' is to catch as much water as possible and to propel the body forward.

3 Initially the pull is down, then back.

4 With your elbow slightly bent, sweep outwards, then back towards the centre of the body, then back towards the thighs.

5 As you pull, keep the arm close to the body for streamlining and accelerating through the stroke.

 Look at ease

A good swimmer makes it look like they're not working at all. Everything above the surface is relaxed and easy (like the recovery arm), but underwater everything is power and hard work.

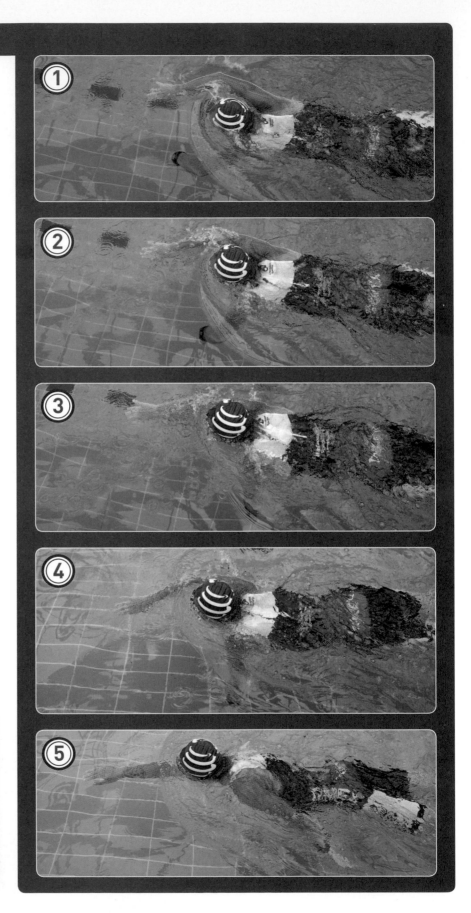

Arms – Push away

1 After the catch has propelled the body forward, the arm will now be alongside the body with a slightly bent elbow.

➜ Maximise the efficiency of your stroke by completing the whole arm action and not bringing your arm out of the water before it's completely straightened.

➜ This is the fastest and most powerful part of the stroke, just before the arm leaves the water.

➜ Although it's the strong muscles of the chest and lats that drive the stroke during the catch and 'S' curve (hence the rotation on to the side, to give these muscles maximum use), it's the

triceps that push the last bit to finish the stroke. Inexperienced swimmers miss this last part and cut the stroke short. Don't do this. Get some coaching and make sure you swim properly.

Arms – Recovery

1 The recovery moves the arm in the swimming direction to allow the hand to re-enter the water and the next stroke to take place.

2 This part of the stroke is reliant on good shoulder flexibility. Poor flexibility results in a wide arm, which will take you off target.

3 Many poor swimmers also 'flag' the arm. This is unnecessary: the lower arm and the hand should be completely relaxed and hang down from the elbow. It's very important to relax the arm during the recovery, as having your hand higher ('flagging') than your elbow results in drag and loss of balance.

4 The recovering hand moves forward, just above the surface of the water. I teach this one of two ways. One is finger tippling: the fingers literally tipple the surface all the way from the 'push' to the 'entry'; the other is thumb hip to armpit, literally running the thumb from the hip bone up to the armpit after 'the push'.

5 As part of the recovery, to maximise the glide of the stroke the shoulder is moved into the air by twisting the torso and extending into the opposite arm as it enters the water.

Breathing

➡️ Keep your face down in the water for the entirety of the stroke, except when breathing (or sighting – see below).

Breathing is done through the mouth by turning the head to the side of a recovering arm at the beginning of the recovery. The head is rotated back at the end of the recovery as the hand re-enters the water.

1 The head turn should be as smooth and as minimal as possible.
➡️ Head and spine should join the rotation of the natural swim stroke rotation of the shoulders.
➡️ To ensure the head isn't lifted, one side of the face remains in the water at all times.
➡️ Don't lift the head out of the water. This causes the legs to sink, creating drag.
➡️ After a sharp inhale, turn the face back into the water in time with the rotation of your shoulders.
➡️ Exhale underwater when the head is back to a neutral position as the hand that you're going to breathe with enters the water. It can be gradual or explosive. For triathletes I teach gradual to keep the stroke relaxed.
2 Triathletes tend to want to swim bilaterally, so take a breath every third arm recovery, alternating the sides for breathing. Some triathletes prefer to breathe one side only and either every other stroke or every fourth. This is dependent on swim fitness and ability, and, of course, what you prefer.

When breathing don't lift your head too high out of the water. It should be as smooth as possible, with minimal movement. Try to breathe every third stroke, breathing on alternate sides – it's better for body symmetry. Breathe as naturally and normally as possible.

Breathe each side

Any triathlete wanting to compete in open water must be able to breathe to each side. If you only ever breathe to your right and the waves are coming from that direction you'll find it hard to breathe at all! Breathing both sides also enables you to spot buoys, landmarks and other swimmers on either side. So learn to breathe both sides, even if you only use one most of the time.

Timing

As swimming is so specifically technique-based, timing is everything. This is the same for all strokes, not just front crawl. If you kick at the wrong time your legs will cause excess drag as you roll to the side to breathe. At first, like driving a car, your mind is overloaded with all the separate elements – hence the drills below that help to split them up – but once mastered individually they can be fitted together, and with good (or perfect!) timing can make swimming your strength in a triathlon, rather than just the dreaded first section.

Improvement test

In their first swim session I always get my clients to swim a length or two so I can assess their stroke. I also get them to count the number of strokes they take. This is usually in the region of 18–30 for a 20–25m pool. However, with good coaching I would expect to drop this to 12. This improvement shows the power they've generated with each stroke and the glide they're maximising, as well as the drag they've eliminated. Test your stroke numbers once every few weeks to check how much you've improved.

Glide to success

The more distance covered per stroke, the fewer strokes you'll need per length or race. Maximise your glide by rotating to the side to lower the drag from frontal resistance. Ensure your stroke is powerful enough to give you glide, and aim for a minimal number of strokes per length by achieving a good catch and push-away. Catch-up or three-quarter catch-up (see drills below) will lead to a really long stroke, meaning fewer strokes are needed. Finally, don't rely on your legs – a good swim stroke is all about the arms!

Swim drills

I generally use swim aids – floats, buoys, fins and so on – when I'm teaching a new swimmer or completely changing someone's stroke. I utilise them in particular to retrain a specific part of the stroke, by taking out one part of the stroke and enabling the client to concentrate on the part I'm aiming to train. The swim aids most often employed are the pool buoy, which is a foam float placed between the thighs to make the legs buoyant without the need to kick normally (or at all); fins, more often termed flippers, for the feet; the kickboard, a float held in the hands; and paddles, glove-type attachments for the hands. (For a full description of swim kit see pages 66–69.)

Swim aids are a great way to gain power and therefore speed over your chosen tri swim distance. They also add variety to swimming lengths and lengths of the local pool, and in addition can (and if used correctly should) improve your stroke. However, relying too heavily on swim aids, or using them solely or badly, can hinder your stroke; so read up on them or get a coach to steer you in the right direction! Use them, but don't rely on them.

Catch-up

The catch-up drill is my personal favourite. It's one of the most useful drills when teaching any level of swimmer since it helps perfect the stroke: it slows it down, makes it look smooth, maximises the glide and keeps the body elongated in the water. It also stops the swimmer using their arms like cogs and makes them realise they're independent.

Swim with a slow movement, catching as much water as possible as you stroke. One arm stays outstretched while the other arm strokes. The stroking arm must 'tag' or 'catch up' the stationary arm before that arm can stroke. If you find this too hard, perform with a kickboard first, passing it between the hands each stroke.

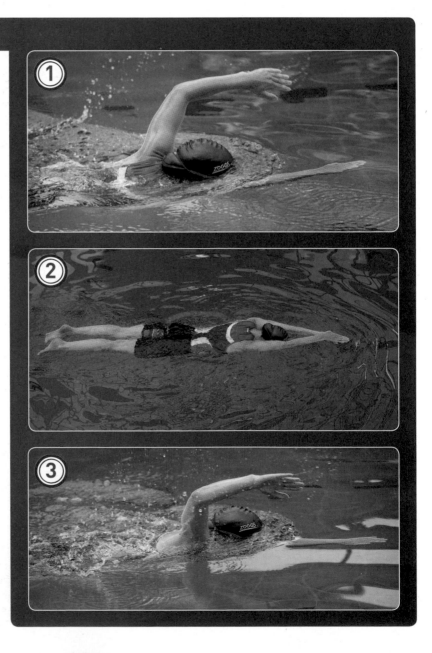

Catch-up with pool buoy in between legs

➡ Allows full concentration on the upper body, and the added instability works the core even harder.

Catch-up with kickboard passed between hands

➡ Can add confidence if you feel unable to perform the exercise without added buoyancy. It really slows the stroke down, and allows complete isolation of each arm to see if the power or stroke differs.

Catch-up with fins

➡ Allows for development of a full straight-leg kick with flexible ankles as it forces the stroke. Allows practice swimming at a higher speed, which can be beneficial.

Catch-up with paddles

➡ Accentuates the ability to pull and generate power from the lats.

Single-arm swimming

➡️ This is often the next drill after catch-up. Simply swim using one arm, keeping the other outstretched. It's great for slowing the stroke down and working on each arm independently to fix problems and maximise power and glide.

Variations

➜ With pool buoy
Adds instability to make the core work harder. Allows complete isolation to really see how the arm stroke is.

➜ With kickboard held in outstretched hand
Gives confidence and buoyancy if needed.

➜ With paddles
Accentuates the ability to pull and generate power from the lats.

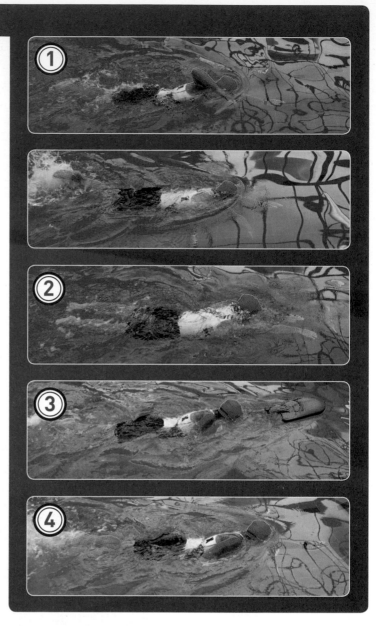

Dead leg swimming

➡️ Simply swim lengths as if you can't move from the waist down. Let the legs sag/drag in the water. Very hard work for the upper body, and forces powerful strokes. Great drill to do before pool buoy sessions to show their worth.

Variations

➜ With paddles
Accentuates the ability to pull and generate power from the lats.

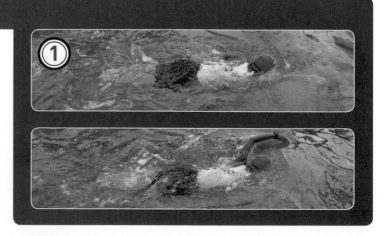

Finger tippling

➡ Swim with the fingers (below the knuckles) trailing through the water. This forces a high elbow during recovery, stopping any looping round of the arm (which messes recovery and causes imbalances in the water).

Variations

➔ **With pool buoy**
Allows complete isolation so that the legs needn't be worried about.

Side swimming

➡ Side swimming improves the body's balance and rotation in the water. It can be great for non-bilateral breathers as well, as it can help with breathing on both sides. Also a great way of testing the leg-kick to see if it's straight or from the knee, and for improving balance in the water. Perform with one arm outstretched and the other by the side or on the hip.

Variations

➔ **With kickboard held in outstretched hand**
Gives buoyancy and confidence.

➔ **With fins**
Allows for development of a full straight-leg kick with flexible ankles as it forces the stroke.

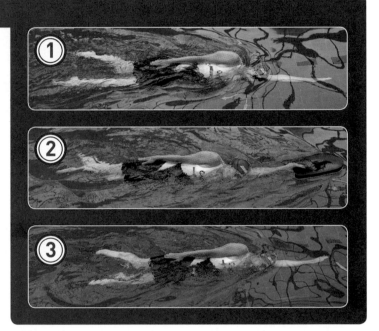

Clenched-fist swimming

➡ This forces you to use your forearms to propel you through the water, since it develops forearm 'feel' for the water so that they become part of the catch. Very good for teaching how to become more efficient without using the hands. A top tip is to point the fist toward the bottom of the pool so that the forearm can act like a paddle and propel you forward.

Variations

➔ **With pool buoy**
Allows complete concentration on drills without worrying about the legs.

Open-finger swimming

➡️ Good as a cool-down or warm-up, often used by pro triathletes in a lake swim warm-up, as helps get the blood flowing without too much fatigue.

Variations

→ **With pool buoy**
Allows complete concentration on upper body.

Just kicking on front

➡️ Concentrate on kicking from the hips and not the knees. Breathe every 5–10 seconds to minimise lifting the head.

Variations

→ **With kickboard held in outstretched hand**
The usual way to perform as it gives buoyancy and confidence, especially as the kick is being learned. The drill is achievable without a kickboard, however.

→ **With fins**
Allows for development of a full straight-leg kick with flexible ankles as it forces the stroke. Allows practice swimming at a higher speed, which can be beneficial.

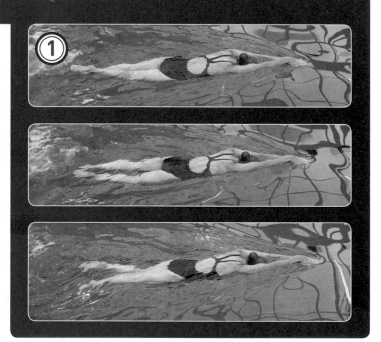

Just kicking on back

➡️ Backstroke kicking is my preference out of the kicking drills, as people can breathe all the time. It also leads to a better hip-kick than on the front.

Variations

→ **With kickboard held in outstretched hand**
Allows for development of a full straight-leg kick with flexible ankles as it forces the stroke.

→ **With fins**
As above.

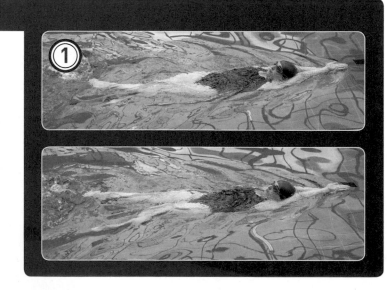

Power pulls

➡️ Once in the water walk a metre away from the edge of the pool and then start swimming without pushing off. Pulling away from a stationary position builds swim-specific strength. A good warm-up is essential to avoid pulling a muscle.

Variations

→ **With paddles**
Accentuates the ability to pull and generate power from the lats.

Tap/tap entry

➡️ The fingers of the recovering hand brush the top of your shoulder and then head before entering the water. Great for slowing the stroke and correcting bad high-elbow recovery.

Variations

→ **With pool buoy**
Adds instability to the core and allows full concentration on the upper body.

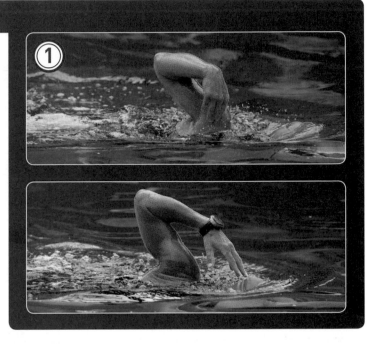

Thumb to armpit

➡️ Similar to tap/tap entry and finger tippling, thumb to armpit is designed to slow the stroke and concentrate the swimmer on high-elbow recovery, especially to stop flagging.

Variations

→ **With pool buoy**
Makes the core work due to instability, while the upper body can be fully concentrated on.

Mix-and-match and combinations

➡️ One of the major things to think about is where your stroke is lacking and which drills will benefit you most. Some sessions just perform two to eight lengths of each drill, while others concentrate on those drills that will improve your personal stroke. Sometimes it's also worth combining drills: try catch-up finger tippling passing a kickboard between your hands. These combinations relieve boredom and add another variation to stroke development.

Pool swim turns

Believe it or not, when you're racing in a pool the race can be won or lost by how you turn at the end of each length. A good, powerful, slick turn can shave minutes off a 1.5km swim.

There are two classically recognised ways to turn in the pool. Both will not only save you time but can also improve your technique. These are the touch turn and the tumble turn.

Before we look at the technique, or before you skip this section altogether as you want to be a 'real' triathlete and race in open water, bear in mind that in many places (the UK being a prime example) there are actually more pool-based races than open water, hence your ability to turn and push effectively off a wall should be a priority, especially considering how much of a difference it can make.

Push–off perfect

If someone comes to me to improve their swim only a few weeks before a pool-based triathlon, and their stroke is pretty credible, I will often concentrate on their push-offs, as it's a great way to shave minutes off a swim without hours and hours of practice in other areas.

The touch turn

For many people this isn't as quick and efficient as a good tumble turn, but equally it doesn't require hours of practice to perfect. The push-off should be as efficient, powerful and elegant as possible at the start of the swim and on every turn. This will maximise the glide, utilise the legs and ensure minimal strokes per length, thus lessening fatigue. The momentum from a good turn maintains the rhythm of the stroke and helps you keep your speed up.

1 Grab
As you approach the side of the pool take a last stroke and keep the hand/arm extended to grasp the side of the pool. Turn/swing the legs under you so that both feet are against the wall, one on top of the other, around 0.6m below the surface. The opposite arm is extended for balance, but both shoulders are as near to the waterline as possible. I call this the 'Spiderman position'. The legs are bent around 90°, ready to push with power back into another length.

2 Breathe
In the same position as before, ensure the head is clear of the water and take a deep breath, with a gentle pull from the hand holding the edge to ensure that your head is clear of the water. As you finish inhaling, release the edge and drop into the water, almost like a flop.

3 Drop
Let the body continue dropping naturally: relax and remain on your side with your head looking slightly back. The hand that was grasping the edge now starts moving forward so it'll be able to join the opposite hand in front of the body.

The touch turn (continued)

4 Submerge

The grasping hand enters the water over your head and joins the opposite hand. To ensure a linear position and lack of drag, the whole body must drop to the level of the feet. There should be no push-off until the head, hips, knees and feet are all aligned. The position should be finished with the body like a coiled spring and the hands together almost as if about to dive.

5 Push

Using the big muscles of the legs, the body is pushed forward through the water. It's important to push-off using both feet equally and not to favour either, otherwise an upward or downward drive can be caused instead of a straight one. It's really important to avoid surfacing yet, as disturbing the surface causes lots of excess drag and slows you down. The body remains sideways, head, hips, knees and ankles in line.

6 Extend

A full extension is something that comes easily to some people (gymnasts, dancers etc) but can seem really unfamiliar to others (cyclists are a prime example). If this includes you then lie down on a gym mat in front of a mirror and practise the 'extend' position out of the pool until you can see you've got it right. The body should be fully extended, arms straight, hands in 'diving' position, head tucked into the arms, the legs straight, feet pointed and – possibly the most neglected element – the core held tight to stop the hips dropping. The whole body is still on its side at this point and no stroke or kicking has been performed. Just relax and maximise the glide.

7 Subsurface glide

This is the point where it's important to relax and not do anything too early. Some coaches encourage a count in the head at this point (one mississippi, two mississippi, or one 1,000, two 1,000 etc). The important thing to do is to really wait before starting to kick, so as to maximise the glide and allow the body to get the underwater acceleration your powerful leg-thrust has earned. Slowly roll on to your front during this element before the kick. At the end of the glide your head should be looking straight down at the bottom of the pool. With practice and self-control underwater most people can push to at least the 5m mark of the length in under two seconds. Depending on the size of pool this could be a quarter of the length at each turn!

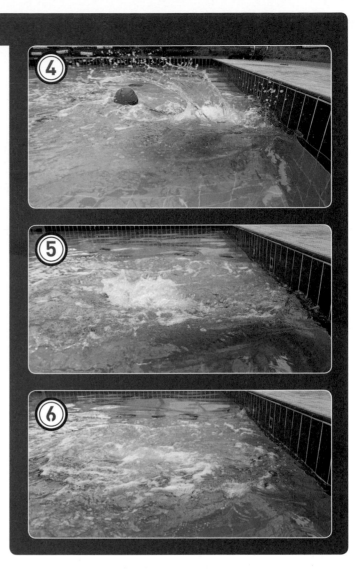

8 Holding the glide

Top coaches will tell you that the underwater speed achieved from a good push-off can be up to double the speed that most triathletes swim below the surface – another huge reason to maximise its use and potential. Hold the full extended position while looking at the bottom of the pool and then slightly angle the body to reach the surface. Again, relax and don't rush the first stroke. At this point some people like to take a 'dolphin-kick' to extend the glide prior to a real stroke. This is a personal preference and comes down to how good your glide and dolphin-kick are. New athletes should probably stick to just the push-off, but seasoned swimmers could try the dolphin-kick as well.

9 Stroke

Before the glide subsides, but ensuring maximum use of it, surface and begin to kick and perform an arm stroke, taking a breath as per a normal stroke. Continue swimming as normal, and ensure that the next turn is as good as the first.

Tumble turn

If you have time to perfect it, the tumble turn is the quickest way to turn at the end of each length. However, it's also difficult to perfect and needs time and energy spent in practising it that could be spent on your stroke if a power-push is used. A bad tumble can be slow and look messy. If you're going to learn the tumble, do so because your stroke is good enough and you can afford the time, not because you want to look good!

Many coaches believe that tumble turns are a must if you spend a lot of time training and perhaps racing in a pool. Having said that, many triathletes will argue that they race in open water, where tumble turns aren't used, so why waste the time learning? There are arguments in support of both viewpoints. Tumble turns will improve your confidence and spatial awareness, and will certainly help with swim fitness, speed and progression in the pool, and most likely in open water, but they shouldn't take priority over perfecting your actual swim stroke, as in an open water race this will be the real make or break factor.

If done correctly, confidently and with conviction a tumble turn will certainly make pool swimming far easier. It causes less drag than a touch turn, and in a sense provides more momentum

The tumble turn

→ As with any difficult technique, breaking it down into stages helps considerably. The tumble turn consists of five:

1 Approach

- Be quick and confident. Any hesitation and subsequent slowdown will result in a bad turn. It's imperative to use the speed of the approach to 'bounce' off the wall and therefore make the turn hard and fast. If the turn is too slow momentum isn't transferred off the wall and into the next length as it should be.
- Know your mark. Every pool should have a mark on the bottom that lets you know you're approaching the wall. Use this mark to initiate the correct timing of the turn. A usual (but due to varying pool sizes not universal) rule is one stroke past the mark then start the turn.
- During the final stroke, leave the non-stroking arm at the hip (the final point in a full stroke). To make the turn, pull the stroking arm to the same position and then initiate the turn.
- Just like a front somersault, pull the head down to the chest, tuck the chin in and start the turn.

2 Turn

- Complete the somersault. From above, complete the full rotation in a normal straight line. Don't attempt to twist until you're all the way over.
- Tuck up and stay tucked, with knees into chest, feet to backside and legs bent.
- As above, hands start by the hips, but as the rotation starts turn them palm downwards to push against the water and help the rotation.
- The head should come round so it ends up in line with the hands and should stay in line ready to shoot forward through the water once the push occurs.
- The feet should now be just off the wall around a foot below the surface, with the legs bent at around 90° and thighs parallel with the wall. Place the feet into

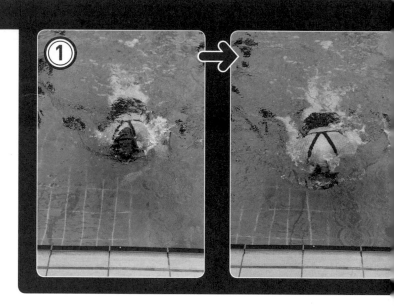

the wall, facing 1/8 towards the ceiling rather than directly upward.
- As soon as connection is made, extend the legs and arms to begin the push-off.

3 Push-off

- Push through your feet into the wall to explosively shoot yourself into the next length, but in a controlled manner.
- Due to foot placement at an angle, rotation should follow easily towards the front. This should feel natural.
- Extend the arms forward, and point the toes to really straighten the legs. Think streamlined (or 'become a torpedo', as I say to my clients).
- Ensure you propel in a straight line, not up or down. This is usually down to foot placement, which directs the angle of the push. Get it wrong and you won't push-off in a straight line!
- Rotate. Bring the top leg down and the bottom leg up to allow the body to finish rotating on to its front. Stay streamlined and maximise your acceleration.

to the next length by saving energy and effort. The thought process is that by changing from touch turns to tumble turns normal pool times will be beaten easily with seemingly less effort, giving the swimmer extra confidence which when transferred to race conditions in open water lead to better swims there too. I'm definitely a believer in 'tricking the mind' when it comes to physical performance. My time in the Marines taught me that belief and confidence can take a person far further than they ever believed possible. An athlete confident in his or her abilities is likely to do far better in a race than one who's lost a little self-confidence.

The turn itself isn't hard. People tend to get it wrong for one of two reasons. They either overcomplicate it, as it looks difficult, or they struggle with the timing and turn too far from the end of the pool and therefore don't get enough power from the turn to make it worthwhile.

There's an old mantra that timing is everything, and in the case of the tumble turn (and, to be honest, swimming in general) this is true – though practice is also important. The technique isn't hard – it's a simple forward somersault followed by a one-eighth twist so that you end up halfway between sideways and facing the ceiling as you push off the wall.

4 Glide
- Complete rotation to the front and into the streamlined position and maximise your glide time. Don't break the acceleration to stroke too soon, and equally don't wait so long that you stop gliding and lose all the momentum from the turn.
- As in the touch turn, count for two seconds before stroking (one 1,000, two 1,000, stroke).
- Kick. The kick actually takes place halfway through the glide, just to ensure the legs don't start sinking and cause drag. So, one 1,000 kick, two 1,000 stoke.

5 Stroke/breakout
- The first stroke is called the breakout, as it's a strong hard stroke that brings the head to the surface to break the waterline.
- Timing is crucial. Ideally the head should break to the surface halfway through the arm stroke.

Top advice I read in a magazine was that in a 20m pool you have 79 turns when swimming a mile, or 59 in a 25m pool. Take advantage of these to practise a tumble at every turn. Remember, 'perfect practice makes permanent'.

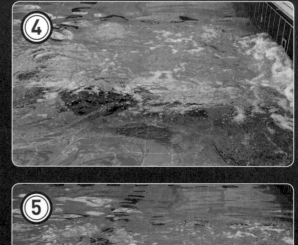

Open water swimming

With the exception of swimming about 50m and back when we're on holiday by the sea, open water swimming is something of a new experience for most of us. But as always, experience puts everything into perspective. If you've never raced in open water before it's nothing to be afraid of – either get out there and practise, or throw yourself in at the deep end (terrible pun) and race. In 30 minutes or less you'll have a wealth of experience!

There isn't really a great deal of difference to swimming in open water other than cold, disorientation and much less control (or at least a feeling that there is). A good tip is to make sure you can tread water confidently. As a warm-up one day, go to the deep end of your pool and tread water for ten minutes. It was part of a swim test for a course I did in the military after a 500m swim in clothes. Its actually quite hard, but a good skill to have.

Clothed training/wetsuit training

Ask your local pool manager or lifeguard if you can swim in a T-shirt and long shorts, then in your wetsuit. Get used to the restrictive nature of the wetsuit and the drag of the clothes. It'll give you more confidence in open water.

Swimming in a wetsuit is actually an advantage if you're a weaker swimmer. The neoprene adds buoyancy and brings you to the surface a little bit more, making you less likely to drag and more likely to glide. Fit is essential, as is using a tri-specific (not surf or sail) suit – see page 66. As the suit restricts you slightly around the shoulders you'll need to rotate and roll a little bit more to get the recovery and extension of the stroke in. This isn't a problem, as it means you glide further, so things should be less of an effort. As the legs are slightly higher a shallower kick may be needed, but again, the added buoyancy means the 'kick/kick' every arm stroke is all that's needed to keep the legs up.

Swimming straight

Theoretically you should already be able to swim straight, but most of us are physiologically unbalanced, with one side stronger than the other, and what this means is that we end up with a stronger catch, and therefore stronger propulsion, on one side. Over a series of strokes over a few hundred metres this pushes us off course, left or right, and the more strokes we do without sighting and realigning, the more we end up off course.

If you can't swim straight you may end up covering 25–30% extra distance than someone who can. Swimming straight is something that requires haste, not speed. Sometimes you're better coming up, sighting and ensuring you're on the right line than putting your head down and swimming in zigzags for the entire race, meaning you end up covering a far greater distance than intended.

A simple test you can do in a pool is to swim down the line on the bottom with your eyes closed. This is best done during quiet periods, to ensure the lane is free. Swim six to ten strokes and then open your eyes to see where you are. If you're right above the line, that's great. Repeat the process and if you're consistently straight you can rest assured that you can swim straight without undue effort.

Plan ahead

'Prior planning prevents poor performance.' Get to the race early, prepare you kit for the transition and then sight your swim line. Come the end of the race you'll be thankful you did.

Landmarks

Landmark sighting is the key to a successful open water swim, but choose your landmark wisely. It must be something as in-line with the buoy as possible, that you'll be able to see from the water, and that won't move. Remember, a boat can be moved, so just because it's moored in a good sighting position now doesn't mean it will still be in 30 minutes' time. Buildings, trees and solid immovable landmarks are best.

The best sighting landmarks are ones that no matter how rough the water gets, you'll still be able to see them. Pylons, cliffs, aerials and piers are the best. Choose the biggest, most visible immovable object that works, and then even when the sea state is bad you'll be able to spot it by a cursory glance upwards rather than needing to keep your head up for two or three strokes until you can see it.

Goggles

Goggles are covered in detail on pages 67–68, but it's worth emphasising here that it's imperative you get the right ones. When you're training or even racing in a pool it's possible to pull off a misted-up set of goggles, clear then and then continue (not ideal, but do-able). In an open water race, however, this should be avoided wherever possible, so it's very important to make sure your goggles aren't old (and therefore prone to sitting up) and are right for the conditions, ie suit the light. If you have the wrong goggle type, or goggles that are prone to misting or even leaking, sighting your landmark will be a real issue.

Another top goggle tip I read in a triathlon magazine is to splash your face with the water you'll be racing in prior to putting on your goggles. This cools the skin to a temperature closer to that of the goggles and prevents the huge difference between them that causes misting.

Swim strokes suited to sighting

There are two main ways to swim and sight your landmark or the swim buoy. Unfortunately the first impacts on speed and momentum significantly and thus makes the swim more tiring. The second, although impacting on the stroke significantly less, is more difficult to execute and requires practice.

Sighting and breathing combined

This technique allows you to look ahead while lifting the head to breathe. This is obviously completely counter to the way we're generally taught to swim (ie breathing to the side to maintain a low horizontal profile), and for good reason. As we know, when we lift the head the legs drop, creating a huge amount of drag and vastly slowing momentum. Well, that's exactly what happens during this technique. As the head's lifted to sight the landmark the legs drop, creating drag and losing a lot of momentum. The head is then dropped down again and a big effort made to regain the lost speed. This is really tiring, especially when it has to be done repeatedly. The added downside is that if it's timed badly (which is almost out of the swimmer's hands), just as the head is lifted to sight and take a breath a big wave crashes into your face and prevents both. Nevertheless, the sighting and breathing technique works well enough, especially in calm waters.

Sighting and breathing separately

This technique is more difficult at first, at it feels counter-intuitive (if you lift the head you should breathe!), but with a little self-control and practice it soon comes naturally, and the benefits are obvious. It allows sighting to take place yet maintains a low horizontal profile and high legs, so that the momentum and speed of the stroke is hardly disturbed.

Open water swim turn techniques

Picture this. You're doing well in your first tri. You've broken away from the little pack around you, but you're having a personal battle with one swimmer hot on your heels, or you feel like you're swimming really well and this tri is going to be your personal best so long as you keep up your momentum. Then you realise you're approaching the buoy and your race could be won or lost on your turn!

There are basically two 'correct' ways to negotiate this little obstacle: the sweep turn and the rollover turn. For both techniques, it's important not only to practise to ensure that you're comfortable with them, but also to approach the turn without hesitating or slowing. Approach at full race speed and keep a tight line with the buoy.

A huge amount of time can be lost on the turn if it isn't negotiated well. Like anything, if you don't practice before the event it'll haunt you afterwards!

Stay close to the buoy

Many beginners give the buoy a wide birth. Not only will this allow close competitors to overtake you on the inside, it will also add valuable seconds to your race time.

The sweep turn

The sweep turn involves 'sweeping' the arm out to the side instead of under the body as for the normal stroke. This is done using the arm on the outside of the turn, not the inside. By extending the arm forwards and then sweeping around to the side the body is pushed around the corner. It may take more than one sweeping stroke to complete the turn.

→ **Advantages**
- Easy to execute.
- Easy to learn.
- Allows a tight line to the buoy.
- Difficult to get wrong.
- Keeps 'overtakers' wide to avoid your arm.

→ **Disadvantages**
- Quite a lot of effort is required.
- Can be difficult in a pack.
- Not great for 180° turns.

→ **Performing a sweep turn**

1 Sweep the arm once your head is level with the buoy.

2 Continue to sweep for as many strokes as it takes to pass the buoy.

3 Once past the buoy correct your line if necessary and continue swimming as normal.

Rollover turn

➡️ This is a great turn that's both energy-efficient and fast, but it requires practice to ensure it's faster than your sweep turn.

➔ Advantages
- Energy-efficient.
- Perfect for 90° and 180° turns.
- Little effort required.
- Fast.

➔ Disadvantages
- Requires practice.
- An extra stroke past the buoy is required.
- Difficult in a pack if swimmers are tightly packed.
- Loss of momentum.

➔ Performing a rollover

1 Maintain a full-speed approach.
Check your line and maintain a tight approach.

2 Take a full stroke past the buoy.

3 Roll on to your back and perform a single backstroke with the arm closest to the buoy.

4 Bring outside arm across chest and roll back on to your front to change direction on to new line.

5 Swim hard to get back up to speed as fast as possible.

Drafting

Drafting is the equivalent of slipstreaming in motor racing. It can occur in swimming, cycling and running, but as swimming comes first we'll cover it here. I should start by emphasising that though it's allowed in swimming and running it isn't permitted (for the most part) in cycling; this is due to the much greater speeds attained in cycling, which would give the 'drafter' such a great advantage as to be deemed unfair.

1 Swimming behind another swimmer while they push through the water can make a huge difference to the amount of effort you have to put in, and can really improve swim times. Consequently it's well worth doing, and can save you energy for the bike and run stages.

2 Hip drafting (swimming alongside the hips of the competitor in front, rather than behind their feet) has a similar effect, though perhaps not quite as much. It also allows the drafter to see a little better, as there are no bubbles or feet in your face, there's a clearer line to sight by, and it's easier in packs.

Be sure to check that the swimmer you're swimming behind is headed in the right direction – if not you'll both end up in the wrong place!

Play chase in the club

Whether as part of a swim club, tri club, or just a group of friends, get together in the pool or open water and 'chase' each other as you swim, rotating the lead swimmer every so often. This allows you to feel what it's like to be the lead swimmer and to be drafting. It's invaluable training pre-race day. The leading swimmer can wear paddles or fins if it makes them quicker.

Conclusion

All of the above bits and pieces are fine – you can tumble turn, swim in a wetsuit, perform all manner of drills and can sight without breathing. However, can you really swim front crawl properly, because if at the end of the race it's your swim that's let you down that's where the big losses will be. So, we'll conclude with a swim technique checklist:

- Head still and down, eyes at 45°.
- Legs in line with the body, long and loose at the ankle, not kicking from the knee.
- With toes pointed, kick from the glutes/hip, not the knee.
- Body rotates to allow shoulder to leave the water and arms to stretch out. Equal both sides.
- Once you've entered the water, outstretched arm remains so for a spilt second until other arm has passed the head.
- Elbow bends to create a strong stable paddle.
- Once the paddle is created, an S-curve is performed to 'fix' the water and drive the body forward as the rotation into the opposite arm occurs.
- A straight arm with extended triceps finishes the movements of the stroke, fast and powerful at the end.
- A high elbow leads the recovering arm with the lower arm hanging relaxed. Recovery is along the side of the body – the fastest route.
- Finger, then wrist, then elbow, enter the water between head midline and shoulder, 30–60cm in front of head.

As I've said several times before, and will again, practice makes permanent, so ensure your stroke is correct before making it permanent!

CHAPTER 06
CYCLING

Cycling is perhaps the Marmite – you love it or you hate it – of the triathlon disciplines. It's the most expensive, the most time-consuming and the most heavily weighted in terms of distance. People either look forward to their long rides during training (perhaps more so in the summer than the winter...) or they dread the thought of being on a bike for that long.

People either get addicted to spending their hard-earned cash on all the kit and equipment, upgrading, replacing and really making the whole cycling side a hobby in itself, or they hate the thought of getting the bike serviced, let alone buying a new inner tube and practising changing a tyre. So, once again, 'know yourself': if you love it, acknowledge it and try to limit the amount you spend each month or year; if you hate it, then 'train your weakness' – practise cycling, practise changing an inner tube and spend money when you need to, as it could lead to much faster times and a far more comfortable session.

Cycling is actually the one event where equipment can make a real difference. Trainers and goggles do make some difference in running and swimming, but not a hugely significant one, whereas a good or bad bike can make a big difference to your cycling.

The bike

Although an expensive bike may be lighter, and possibly faster, it's not the expense of the bike that makes the difference. It needs to be the correct size, set up properly and most importantly, in mechanically sound condition. If these things are right, then the cycle stage of a race and general cycle training will be far more comfortable and enjoyable.

To fully understand how to set up a bike, you first need to know about its parts:

If you're doing just the one sprint triathlon and don't already have a bike, then borrow or hire one, don't buy one.

Tri bike vs road bike

One of the most difficult questions for any triathlete looking to buy a (new) bike is whether to go for a tri bike or a regular racing bike. Most tri bikes sell for over £1,000, so if you're just buying for the once-a-year local tri, for which you'll only train for two months each year, then a normal road bike is better. There are myriad options for road bikes under £1,000 – just ask at your local bike shop or check on the Internet. (When buying my last new bike I worked out which one I wanted, waited until a new colour scheme came out and bought one in the older colours for less than half price!)

When buying a road bike ensure it has a low front end and that a tri bar can be used easily. You can spend £1,000 or more on a normal road bike and will get a lot for your money. It will also be more comfortable and safer on long road-training sessions than a tri or time trial bike.

However, if cycling is simply something you do for tri races and you tend to train on the flat, put your money into a good tri bike and get used to the low aerodynamic position.

Carbon vs aluminium

Frames are usually either aluminium or carbon fibre; both have advantages and disadvantages. To start with, carbon fibre frames are far lighter than aluminium. But the price and brand does make a difference – a well-built lightweight aluminium frame can sometimes weigh less than an inexpensive carbon frame. How long the frame lasts can differ considerably between the two varieties. Many carbon fibre manufacturers offer lifetime guarantees whereas aluminium frames often come with five- to ten-year guarantees. Realistically, you'll probably be looking at upgrading to the new 'perfect' frame by that time anyway.

The main difference to remember is that aluminium frames are less 'comfortable' so all the bumps are felt along the way, whereas a carbon frame absorbs some of the shocks, making for a smoother ride. However, the 'stiffer' property of aluminium means the transfer of human power to forward motion is better, so aluminium frames are in some ways better for sprints and time trials.

However, a good carbon frame is built so that carbon weaves still provide stiffness, but lessen road vibrations leading to fast yet comfortable rides.

Turbo trainer

This is a supportive structure for the back wheel of your bike that has a roller underneath it, which turns your bike into a stationary exercise bike. Depending on what feedback you want and how portable you want your turbo trainer, basic models start at around £80, with the upper end being £800.

Wheels

Where possible get a set of racing wheels. The deeper the rim, the more aerodynamic, though you lose on handling and have to cope with more weight on hill climbs. If you have a tri bike, put them on that and save the normal 40–60mm wheels for your road bike.

Saddle pack/Bento pack

These little bags that go either under the saddle or on the top tube are great for your puncture kit, spare inner tube, tyre levers and fuel.

Pedal adaptors

For duathletes (competitors in run/bike/run or bike/run events) it's often not worth changing to cycling shoes, so pedal adaptors are often used. These allow trainers to be worn, but give a more solid base for cycling than normal pedals.

'Clipless' pedals

Choose suitable clipless pedals (SPDs) to allow cleats to clip in. Make sure you then get the right shoes/cleats to fit.

Drinking system

A drinks bottle mounted on the handlebars with a built-in straw. Ideal for race fuelling, and it also means you don't have to come out of your aerodynamic tuck position.

Tribars/aerobars

If you're thinking of making tris your sport aerobars are a necessity, unless you'll only be racing over the hilliest courses. The low tuck they encourage means time and energy will be saved.

Cycling cleats

If you're training for one triathlon only then a set of cycling shoes is probably a waste of money. Borrow some or cycle in your running shoes (which can save time in T2). However, if you've bought a nice bike and are planning on doing a few tris this year, then cleats are more of a necessity.

Like a decent set of running shoes or a good bike, it's worth asking about them in a reputable store. Make sure your shoes are compatible with your pedals. Make sure they're comfortable, and explain that you're a triathlete, not a cyclist, and therefore may be wearing the shoes with damp sock-less feet.

Attach the cleat to the shoe so that the 'centre of cleat marker' (a vertical line on the side and centre of most cleats) is approximately 0.5cm back from the ball of the foot. Once both cleats are attached, check that the toes are even on both so the cleats are positioned equally. Put your feet in the shoes and them attached to the pedal. Make sure that the ball of the foot is 0.5cm ahead of the pedal axle.

The lateral position (or 'Q-factor') is the distance the cleat can be adjusted towards or away from the crank arm. To get this right, there should be about 2cm between the heels of the shoes and the crankarm when the pedals are rotated. The width of the rider's hips will determine where this is.

Once set up, the ankles, knees and hips shouldn't be twisting. If they are, get someone to take a look and see if they can spot the mistake. Failing that, head to a cycle shop for expert advice.

Some cyclists move the cleat to the centre of the foot, not the ball, as it can give more power. This is fine for sprints or time trials but not ideal for long rides or triathlons.

Many modern road shoes are compatible with both the 'Shimano SPD' cleat standard and the more traditional 'Look' road cleats but you need to check before you buy.

Maintaining your bike

When cleaning your bike, check the following areas thoroughly:

→ Frame
Check for any breaks or cracks, particularly if it's been transported or you've had a fall. The area where the tubes meet each other is most important.

→ Wheels
● Listen to and check the hubs for grinding sounds that may mean damaged or dirty bearings.
● Check for buckled or dented wheel rims.
● Check spoke tightness and for any wear and tear.
● Take out and clean the quick release mechanism.
● Check the rear hub to make sure gear sprockets spin in line with wheel and hub.
● Check hubs for excessive play and adjust if necessary..

→ Freewheel and chain
● Clean off dirt and debris.
● Ensure chain is tight but not rigid tight.Chain length is a difficult topic to cover. My advice would be to learn from an expert at a bike shop or an experienced triathlete, and to service your bike regularly. But basically, there should be 3–5mm of clearance between the bottom run of the chain and the one directly above it as it moves into the derailleur. If there is more than 5mm clearance, the chain will probably be too tight, but less than 3mm and the chain may rub.
● Check chain for stiff links. Replace if necessary.
● Check chain for broken or cracked links. Replace if necessary.
● Check the freewheel spins freely and without noise.
● Clean debris from the teeth.
● Lightly oil.

→ Tyres
● Check for baldness, bulges and holes or cuts. If you find any, replace the tyre.
● Check undercord for fraying. Replace if major fraying is visible.
● Check pressures.

Further info

For more indepth information about bike maintenance have a look at the Haynes Bike Book.

The Bike BOOK
Complete bicycle maintenance
6th Edition

Two bikes

Top triathletes are likely to have two bikes: a cheaper road bike for commuting, long training sessions and general riding, and an expensive tri or time trial bike for racing and pre-race pace sessions. If you do this, make sure you train on your tri bike or you'll get to the race and be unable to use it properly.

→ Brakes
● Check brakes are working and respond immediately. Adjust if necessary.
● Check blocks are even, central and not overly worn.
● Check cables for fraying and then lightly oil them.

→ Headset, handlebars and stem
● Check that all bolts are tight and free of debris and rust.
● Ensure full range of movement for headset, without noise or sticking.
● Check if headset is overly loose or self-centres. Both indicate the bearings are worn and should be replaced.
● Check for play in headset and adjust if necessary.

→ Gears
● Check that gear change across all gears is smooth and debris-free, and that all gears are available.
● Check that the gear selected stays selected.
● Clean and lightly oil.

→ Chainwheel and bottom bracket
● Check for debris and wear.
● Ensure free running and that there's no tightness or lateral movement.

→ Pedals
● Ensure pedals are tightened to the cranks.
● Ensure they're free-spinning.
● Ensure cleats attach tightly, giving power and stability.
● Ensure cleats can be removed easily should they need to be.
● Ensure cleats engage correctly and that clean mechanism is correctly adjusted.

→ Cables
● Check brake and gear cables for damage, fraying and freedom of movement.

Tools

A good selection of tools will always be required. Every triathlete should start with a basic toolkit for on-the-road repairs. This should be carried at all times and contain enough tools to enable most basic repairs to be carried out.

A basic home toolkit will add some general hand tools and a few specialist bicycle tools. A bike-cleaning kit will be needed, as well as a selection of oils and lubricants. Some means of supporting the bike while carrying out repairs will also be useful.

An advanced home toolkit will contain many specialist and specific hand tools. A proper bike repair stand can be added, and for the serious home mechanic a wheel-truing stand will be essential.

1 Allen keys

A set of metric Allen keys in steel, sizes 2–10mm, will be more useful than you'd ever imagine. Some come on a key chain, others as a multi-tool.

2 Spanners

Adjustable spanners seem like a good idea, but they round the nuts and will cost you a lot in the long run. Get a set of spanners instead – it'll be worth it.

3 Lubricant

WD40 and motor oil aren't suitable. Buy specific cycle chain lube from a bike store.

4 Screwdriver

A 3mm Phillips screwdriver is all that's needed, but buy a good one so it doesn't ruin any of the screw heads.

5 Chain tool

Chain tools are easily broken, so spend about £10–£20 on a good one. Spare pins for chains are worth having too (the alternative is to use a chain with 'breakable' links).

6 Pump/CO2 canisters/tyre levers

Everything, except spare inner tubes, which you'll need to change a tyre or mend a puncture. Giant do a Quick-Fix Ultra Combo pack that covers the lot. Make sure not only that you have these, but also – just as importantly – that you know how to use them properly.

7 Cable cutters

Keep them sharp and clean and they'll ensure your cables are cut, not just frayed for you to snap!

8 Multi-tool

Multi-tools with various adaptors can substitute for many of the above.

9 Chain cleaning bath

A device that clips on to the chain which, after a few turns of the pedals, comes out sparkling, without even having to remove it from the bike.

Setting up a bike

When cycling, you're fighting against three main things, which your bike, your riding position and your output need to overcome as much as possible – that way you can maximise the bike phase of your race. The three hindrances to cycling quickly are:

1 **Wind resistance** – As you cycle you 'hit' the air. This acts as a barrier, and you constantly have to push through it. Reducing this barrier as much as possible is crucial to going faster, so the aerodynamics of your bike – and you – are really important. Hence the importance of your riding position.

2 **Friction** – Friction comes in the form of the tyres and the road surface. The worse the road surface, the more the friction. A good set of well-maintained tyres, fully inflated to the correct level for the road surface, the weather and the race conditions, is therefore vital.

3 **Gravity** – Most triathletes loathe hills. Fair enough – they're hard work, draining and anaerobic. However, imagine riding uphill on a toddler's bike with flat tyres and no seat, compared to riding uphill on a top-of-the-range carbon fibre road bike. Now I'm not saying go and buy a top-of-the-range bike, but a bike that's the right size, with a good riding position that fits you, will make cycling uphill far easier.

Bike size

As a general rule your bike frame should be two-thirds of the inside leg measurement you use for a pair of trousers, so for the average male with a 32in inside leg it would be a 54cm frame.

Riding position

There are a number of general guidelines that will ensure a 'correct' riding position. However, we're all different and will all have personal preferences that help us generate maximum force and power. So follow the general rules, but then try little adjustments to see if they actually make any difference.

There are three points at which you connect with your bike, and it's these areas that we need to set up correctly to ensure a perfect riding position: these are the saddle and buttocks; the handlebars and hands; and the pedals and feet.

➜ Saddle height

Even in a spin class at the local gym, the instructor will tell you to set up the bike (or should) so that you'll have a more enjoyable – yet still tough – workout. If they didn't, they know that people wouldn't just feel worn out, they'd possibly feel pain, and therefore not return to the class.

The seat height is the first thing to set up on your bike, and possibly the most vital in terms of getting the overall set-up correct:

1 Place the bike on an even piece of ground and ensure the saddle is parallel with it, ie straight.
2 Sit on the saddle.
3 Rotate the left crank around so that it points straight down in line with the seat post.
4 Ensuring you're wearing your cycling shoes, put the heel of your left foot on to the pedal.
5 Adjust the seat up or down so your leg is straight, but not overstretched.

→ Saddle position

With the height adjusted correctly, it's necessary to work out the position of the saddle in relation to the rest of the bike:

1 First, using a spirit level, make it parallel with the ground.
2 Sit back on the bike with cycle shoes clipped into the pedals.
3 Rotate the pedals so that they're horizontal (parallel with the ground).
4 Ensure the knees are directly over the balls of the feet as they're connected to the pedal. Adjust the saddle forwards or backwards until they are.
5 Occasionally, if a big change is made, the seat height may need to be readjusted, but this is rare.

→ Handlebar position

The handlebar position relies on the correct setting of the saddle, so ensure you do this first.

1 Lower/raise the handlebars so that the lower surface, parallel with the ground, is in line with the top tube.
2 Set the brake levers so that they're facing forwards, not up or down.
3 The handlebars should now be adjusted so that you're comfortable when riding, both in the drop position (bottom of the handlebars) and the top position. This means the top of the bars should be between saddle height and 2in lower.
4 As you grow in confidence and flexibility you'll most likely start to lower the handlebars to become more aerodynamic.

Gears

As we are talking about the bike, it seems sensible to mention the gears. A compact chain set has two chain rings:

● 50/34 – the number of teeth on the two cogs at the front of the bike.
● 12/25 cassette – on the back wheel, 12 teeth on the smallest cog and 25 on the largest.

There are many other chain ring set-ups and these vary depending on what and how you're racing: hilly course, time trial, road training, sprint distance or Ironman. As mentioned above, a 12/25 is the most common and will cover you for almost everything,

⏱ Mark the saddle height

Once you've adjusted your seat post to exactly the right height, wrap a band of hard-wearing electrical tape around the post, flush to the frame. This gives you a marker so that if at any time the height gets changed you can easily restore it to the correct position. This is useful when you have to remove the seat, or give the bike a good clean after a wet ride.

which is the main thing. A 12/23 would be better for a flat course and a 12/27 better for a hilly course, but a 12/25 is best for a changeable course and will generally cover all bases. This is also somewhat dependent on your cycling style and cadence.

Having said that, some Ironman tri riders prefer setups such as an 11/23 rear cassette with 39/53 front, or an 11/26 rear cassette and 39/53 front, as it allows for a higher cadence on hills, thus preventing the lactic burn. However, such riders may use a 12/27 or 12/28 rear cassette for a particularly hilly course, which leads me to my final piece of advice: KISS 'keep it simple stupid'. Stay with a 12/25 if this is new to you, and finally, if you're likely to attempt different gearing systems, select easier gearing if in doubt.

The left-hand shifter controls the gears at the front by the right-hand pedal: the bigger the chain ring is, the harder it is to pedal. This has a big effect on your cadence as it shifts. The right-hand shifter controls the cogs on the rear wheel, where the bigger the cog is, the easier it is to pedal. This has a smaller effect on your cadence.

When changing gears you need to be moving and pedalling, but pedal softly (you shouldn't lose much speed). If you pedal hard the derailleurs (which change the gears) may struggle, and grinding sounds will tell you you're not doing it right!

Try to avoid 'cross chaining'. This is where certain combinations of gears from front cog to back cog put the chain under a lot of pressure due to the angle. If you do this you risk the chain coming off and possibly getting damaged, which may end your race.

Clothing

Tops

For training it's nice to have something like a cycle jersey. Made of wicking material, these offer protection from the sun on the shoulders yet some warmth when it's cold. They also have pockets on the back for provisions.

Cycle jerseys aren't great for racing in though. A tri suit as described in the swim kit section is probably best, or a singlet that you can get on easily after the swim and cycle, and run in OK. Wicking material is best and buying two or three is always good for training, to alternate them.

Bottoms

Cycle shorts and leggings can be a real lifesaver if you decide to do some of the longer races and a fair bit of cycle training. The most important part of either is the 'chammy', the soft insert that gives your backside some comfort. Buy a decent brand and they should be long lasting and comfortable.

The similarity of cycling shorts to tri shorts means there may be a temptation to swim in cycling shorts under your wetsuit, but it isn't advisable as the chammy area fills up with water and acts as a drag.

Number belt

Most tri race organisers make you wear a number and once you buy a trisuit you might need a number belt. Left with your bike, it's worn on your back for the cycle and then your front for the run.

Sunglasses

These provide protection from grit and insects as well as glare – vital for avoiding crashes. They have to be comfortable on the nose and ears. Interchangeable lenses to suit the weather are almost standard and worth the extra cash.

Gloves

Not only important for keeping your hands warm, they will also save you from grazes and cuts. It's worth paying for a good, well-fitting wicking pair.

Hat

A skull cap that's windproof, insulated and can be worn under the helmet in adverse conditions is really worthwhile. Fleece inners or Merino wool mean prices can be up to £40, but a good version for £10 is often enough.

Base layer/bike jacket

In both cases fit is everything. Make sure they're long enough and they cover the wrists. Base layers should be worn next to the skin, so need to be wicking. Hard shell and soft shell jackets exist, though soft shells are often more comfortable and don't make you sweat as much.

Helmet

I'm starting with the helmet because it's the most important piece of your bike kit. Firstly, buy one. Wear it. Always. Whenever you cycle. You'd wear a seat belt in a car. You'd wear a helmet on a motorbike. So ALWAYS wear a helmet on your bicycle.

Helmets are compulsory for races anyway, so get a good streamlined one. Pay decent money for a well-made, legal, reputable crash hat. You want a thin aerodynamic one if you're going to race and train in it. Comfort is also key, so as ever try before you buy.

Old for new

If you crash and hit your helmet you must always replace it. Once hit, its internal structure is damaged, and won't react properly to another crash. But hey, £50 or brain damage. Easy choice. Oh, and never buy a second-hand helmet or lend yours to anyone.

Cycling technique

Pedalling

Strangely, pedalling is something most of us don't do properly. Because we've been cycling since we were kids we assume we can do it. The problem is we've been cycling in trainers, without toe-clips or cleats, and hence we only push. Even when cleats and toe-clips are added most people think of cycling as a piston (up and down) motion. It isn't.

Pedalling properly involves a circular action. Cycling this way allows a number of different muscles to work simultaneously, rather than just getting a few to do everything. This means more muscles are used, so you're able to go faster, and less work is required from a couple of large muscles, which keeps fatigue at bay longer. This will save energy for the run that's yet to come.

How to pedal

OK, so I've just said pedal in a circular motion. This is easy, right? Not quite – 100% effort isn't applied at all times throughout the circular motion.

The best and most effective way to describe how to pedal correctly is to use the 'clock-face method'. This relies on visualising a clock face as you pedal to determine where your pedal is in relation to it, and what you should be doing at that point:

The phases of pedalling

→ The power phase

The downward push (from 2 o'clock to 5 o'clock) is generally considered to be the power phase. However, this can be lengthened from 5 o'clock to 7 o'clock by 'scraping the shoes'. To do this, when you're at the 5 o'clock position angle your shoes as if you have chewing gum on the bottom and are trying to scrape it off. Keep the foot and ankle in this position until you're just past 7 o'clock. This should increase the power phase considerably.

→ The pull phase

Undertaken between the 6 and 12 o'clock positions. However, to make it more efficient towards the top, at the 11 o'clock point kick forward with the toes uppermost. Kicking your toes over the top of the clock allows more power to roll into the power phase and enables you to start the power push as soon as possible.

→ Dead spots

Many people who use a Wattbike find that it shows they have weak pedal cycles between 12 and 2 and 6 and 7 o'clock. This is common, but can be corrected. All that it takes is a little concentration at these points to ensure the legs aren't 'lazy' or resting. Performing drills and practising the entire revolution is key to making the correct technique part of your muscle memory.

- **12 o'clock** – Top of the pedal stroke. The pedal must be pushed FORWARD, not down.
- **2 o'clock** – Push the pedal slightly forwards and down at the same time.
- **3 o'clock** – Push directly down.

- **4 o'clock** – Push the pedal slightly backwards and down at the same time.
- **6 o'clock** – Pull the pedal backwards.
- **9 o'clock** – The foot should be dragged straight upwards preparing for a move forward towards the 12 o'clock position.

12 o'clock

7 o'clock

Improving your cycling
Single-leg pedalling

If you aren't lucky enough to have access to a Wattbike, then try single-leg pedalling. Just like one-arm swimming, it allows you to concentrate your attention on one side, meaning you can get to grips with the technique far better. It also means you won't compensate for dead spots in one leg by using the other leg.

The best ways to single-leg pedal are on an exercise bike or a turbo trainer. Sit on the bike as normal but rest one foot on the frame, or on a box or step alongside the bike. (I prefer the frame, as a box needs to be switched from side to side unless you have one each side.) Select a gear that isn't too easy for one leg, otherwise momentum rather than technique will carry your foot over. Equally, a gear that's too hard will fatigue the leg quickly, and this is a cycle technique, not fitness session.

Alternate between the legs every 30 seconds to 2 minutes dependent on your session, and repeat 5–10 times each leg. You'll notice how different lifting the pedal over the top feels without the opposite leg helping by driving downwards at the same time. However, if you can get over this difficulty it becomes natural and more efficient. You'll have upward and downward (opposite leg) momentum every revolution and thus far more power.

It's important to ensure a smooth motion and one movement, and not think of the individual elements. Having said that, try to eliminate dead spots by working hard on the bottom and top (6 and 12 o'clock) parts of the cycle. At first this drill feels very (very) alien, but stick with it: it doesn't take long to learn, and once mastered will give you great gains.

Cadence

Like running, cadence is important to cyclists. In running, a quicker cadence ensures a shorter stride, therefore more momentum forwards and less lost upwards or as the heel strikes the ground and possibly acts as a brake. In swimming, a slower cadence equals a longer more relaxed stroke to maximise the glide and power from each stroke. Most cyclists have a natural cadence of anywhere between 85–105 revolutions per minute (rpm), and change gear to match their cadence according to what they find most comfortable.

When we cycle our muscles propel the pedals and our cardiovascular system delivers oxygen to fuel these muscles and takes away waste products (any lactic acid as we jump into that energy system – see Chapter 2). Optimal cadence is all about keeping the two systems in balance. However, like everything, it's important to 'know yourself', as we're all different – just because in his recent Tour de France win Bradley Wiggins could climb hills at a cadence of 110rpm doesn't mean we all should. A high cadence reduces the watts per pedal stroke, making the effort more bearable for the muscles. It's thought this results from using less 'fast-twitch' muscle fibres (see panel below), usually thought to be recruited for speed and power, not endurance. If a low cadence is utilised too often too many fast-twitch fibres are employed and they produce more lactic acid (or so it's thought), which causes that uncomfortable burn in our legs that we know so well and means we have to slow down.

A higher cadence may recruit less fast-twitch fibres and therefore delay lactic acid accumulation, but it also wastes some energy: moving your legs fast with no resistance still gets the heart rate up, and obviously energy is being used. However, a cadence that's too high doesn't allow enough oxygen to fuel the cardiovascular system, while research shows that a lower cadence (under 60) utilises the least oxygen but won't get you the speeds you need without lactic build-up.

OK, so what's the solution? Fundamentally cycling at a high cadence is better as it doesn't overload the muscles, but it puts more strain on the cardiovascular system, so there's a far bigger requirement to be fit. However, as usual it's different for everyone, as each of us has an optimal point where a balance is reached between a high enough cadence that the muscles can handle it, but not so high as to overload the cardiovascular system. This goes to explain how Tour de France winners like Bradley Wiggins worked so well. He doesn't possess huge, powerful, muscular legs; he didn't need to – his cardiovascular system was second to none and therefore he could maintain a higher cadence, rarely overloading his muscles, and could just cycle away. To him, higher cadence, even with the energy loss associated, was the way forward.

⏱ The work required

The work required to move a bike down the road is measured in watts. Watts = torque x cadence, where torque = force x distance. 'Huh?' I hear everyone cry. In simple terms, how hard you press on the pedals multiplied by the number of times per minute you do it.

Let's look at it another way. Take a pair of identical twins. As they're identical they're the same height, weight and age. Now, imagine we give them identical bikes, identical aerodynamics, and they're riding next to each other at the same speed on a flat road. Since everything is the same they're therefore performing the same work, ie riding at the same wattage. However, twin A is using a cadence of 70rpm, while twin B rides at 110rpm. Twin A has to press hard on the pedals with each stroke, and less frequently than B, while B pushes lightly on the pedals but much more frequently. The lower cadence cycling of A requires him to push harder on the pedals, but to generate the higher force contraction his leg muscles must recruit more fast-twitch muscle fibres vs slow-twitch fibres. His brother B spins more freely, so recruits far less fast-twitch fibres, but has to breathe more heavily to supply his slow-twitch fibres with more oxygen, as they have to push the pedals more revolutions per minute.

So how does this help you? Well, first, you have to accept that we're all different (except identical twins!) and that our genetics and training backgrounds will affect whether we need a higher cadence or a lower cadence. In short, the golden rule is: if your legs burn

more than you feel out of breath, increase your cadence; if you feel more out of breath than your legs burn, lower your cadence.

Training your cadence
To make the most of your ability, and perhaps even to find it, the following can help:

1 **Train at different cadences**. Use a Wattbike, turbo trainer (with feedback) or exercise bike and keep the same wattage at the top and bottom ends of the cadence scale, say 75–80 and 105–110. These sessions can pay dividends to both low- and high-cadence cyclists.
2 **Remember specificity**. Perform sessions (most of them) the way you'll race. Otherwise, if you do too many 'easy', lazy rides you'll lower your cadence.
3 **Attempt high cadence**. If you decide you're a bit of a Bradley Wiggins rather than a Chris Hoy, then attempt high-cadence cycling. Bear in mind, though, that it takes time to develop the required cardiovascular fitness and for your legs to be able to produce good wattage at high cadence. Your effort will pay off, however, so stay at it. The following drill may help:
   – Cycle using an easy-ish gear and gradually increase cadence until you're bouncing a bit and feel like you can't stay in the saddle.
   – Gradually lower cadence to the point where you no longer bounce, but it's on the threshold. Maintain for 20–60 seconds depending on how long you've been doing this drill.
   – Lower cadence gradually, regain breath and repeat. It's important to maintain a smooth pedalling action throughout.
4 **Conditioning**. It's a bugbear of mine, but triathletes think they improve by cycling, swimming and running. They do, but only to a point. Look at the Brownlee brothers as a point of reference: they both perform strength training and power training by means of conditioning. Indeed, research has shown that weight training increases cycling efficiency for almost every rider at every cadence.

Work out if it's your legs or your lungs that are your limiting factor. If it's your legs, work to make your cadence higher. Once you've adapted it should make a real difference to your cycling.

⏱ Who benefits most

Those triathletes most likely to benefit from high cadence riding are those whose cardiovascular system is likely to outperform their muscular power: small, thin athletes, women and runners. Yes, if you come from a running background get your cadence up and you'll be a better cyclist. It'll also saves your legs for the run, as they won't be burnt out and full of lactic acid.

⏱ The Brownlee brothers

The UK has long had a successful history in triathlon, but the Brownlee brothers have really helped cement that place in the world rankings. Alistair and Jonny are constantly in the top three of pretty much every race they enter. In 2011 Alistair was Triathlon World Champion, with an astonishing season across the series. His brother didn't do badly either, coming second! They also won gold and bronze in the 2012 Olympics.

The Brownlee brothers mark the level of success of triathletes who grow up training for the sport as a whole instead of coming into it from one of its components.

Cycling position

Most of the effort you put in when cycling is against aerodynamic drag, so if you can minimise that it's going to make your life easier. The things is, you want to be comfortable and aerodynamic, but that's the issue: the more comfortable you are, the more drag you'll create; but the more aerodynamic you are, the less the drag and the faster you'll go, but the more uncomfortable you'll be. So compromise and efficiency are key, not just when cycling but in relation to the swim you've just done and the run you have coming up.

You need to make your front-on area as small as possible, as this is what will hit the air and slow you down. Simple, right – you just lean right forward so that only your shoulders face the oncoming air? Not quite. You may find that position uncomfortable and the run a little tricky. So here are some quick tips:

● Your shoulder angle should be 90° between torso and upper arm – any more and holding the upper body becomes a huge effort.

● Forearms should be parallel to the ground where possible, or at worst your hands should only be slightly higher than your elbows.

● Elbow angle should be 90° to begin with and then close the gap over time.

● The hip angle is very personal, so is down to each individual. Small is best for aerodynamics, but it's far harder to get power and performance.

● Dip the head to reduce overall frontal area.

Tweaking and changing your posture may make it feel better, but there's really only one way to check and that's to get out and ride. Best advice is to choose a set route of around one to two miles, with minimal traffic and wind tunnelling, ride it at a pace you can repeat and time it. Repeat twice more under the same conditions and take an average. Then change one thing to make yourself more aerodynamic (eg drop the handlebar height) and repeat three times over the same route at the same pace as before. An average speed drop could indicate a more aerodynamic position.

Riding skills

Changing gears

When training in the gym or on a turbo trainer, changing gears is just something you do; but remember, there's a reason for all those gears! Specificity is really important so train outdoors, even in the great British winter. Choose some routes with hills and practise your gear changes.

Just like when you're driving, getting the right gear is about planning ahead. You should be looking a good distance ahead while riding and planning your moves, be it race-wise or gear/turn wise. You should change your gears earlier than you actually need to, especially for hills. It's no good starting going upwards and then changing your gear – you lose momentum on hill climbs, and if you try to change while you're going uphill you'll fail to keep pedalling and pressure on the pedals is imperative for a smooth gear change. So start changing as you near the trough or flat before the start of the hill, use the momentum into the hill to finish the change and then you'll be on your way up in the correct gear.

Hill climbs

There are two ways to approach cadence for hill climbs: high for those more cardiovascularly competent, and low for those with a better lactic threshold. Having said that, hills are hard either way. Here are a few tips that may help:

- As described above, change gear early, not while going up the hill.
- If you're struggling, perform a set of revolutions sitting, then a set of revolutions out of the saddle. By breaking it down this can make the hill easier.
- Inside your head repeat 'Don't think, just do' (a friend of mine's favourite mantra).
- Switch into a harder gear for a couple of seconds, then when you go back down again the original gear feels much easier – a psychological scam!
- Don't relax at the top of the climb – you'll lose focus, momentum and any gains you've made. Recover, but work just as hard over the first 30 seconds after the ascent.

Downhill

Where you can, be fearless. Put the gears into the biggest ring on the front cassette and the smallest at the back. This will generate more power and allow you to actually pedal harder to go faster. Gaining speed downhill in this way, not just relying on gravity, will give you far more momentum into the next big hill climb.

Cornering

Like sighting in swimming, if you lose momentum you have to put a lot of effort into getting it back. Cornering is the same – you don't really want to brake unless it's really necessary. If you brake, so much energy is lost that could have been forward momentum that you have to put in far more effort to get back up to speed. It's all about confidence: new and inexperienced cyclists aren't used to the speed and consequently feel the need to brake for safety. The solution is to get out and cycle around the lanes and practise so that you get used to the speed and don't feel the need to brake. Again, it's necessary to look ahead, not down at your front wheel. Your bike will go where you look, so work out the best line for the corner then look at and follow it through the turn.

The correct way to corner

See the corner coming up and try to judge it. Stay in the seat, don't stand on the pedals. Drop down a gear, then stop pedalling and lean the bike into the corner to turn rather than use the handlebars. Speed is reduced, but not as much as if you braked as well. As soon as you're though the corner, pedal hard (in the lower gear, hence the change) to regain speed.

Coping with speed

You may find during a race, or even on a normal route that you know well, that you're feeling good and cycling hard and consequently you approach a corner a little too fast. That's fine, and a great training tool, but it can be a little hair-raising! The secret is to increase the cornering angle by leaning into the curve of the corner: follow these tips:

- Start at the outside of the turn (widest point).
- You want to negotiate the turn ASAP. Less time in the turn equals less time crashing.
- Put the pedal crank of the outside pedal down and the weight through it. This gives more grip to the bike.
- If you have to brake (try not to) then brake early, at the start of the turn.
- Brake on the rear wheel only and brake very lightly.
- Never use the front brake – it slides away and you'll crash!
- If a brake locks, release it immediately and concentrate on controlling the handlebars and keeping your weight equally distributed.
- Identify the apex (inside point) of the turn early and aim for it or just past it dependent on the sharpness of the corner: for corners under 90° aim for the apex (inside point) of the turn; for corners sharper than 90°, enter wide from the outside and aim just past the apex.
- As you exit the turn focus on where you're going – up the road.

Body position for cornering

- Head level with the horizon.
- Arms bent.
- Pressure on inside hand to allow turn.
- Grip handlebar lightly, not hard, either in drops position or hoods.
- Ensure access to brakes.
- Lean bike into turn and place pressure on outside pedal.
- Outside pedal down at all times.
- Backside touching the saddle, but not fully weighted.

Braking

If you do have to brake in a turn, slow before the turn using the brake, then release coming around the corner and accelerate out of it. As soon as you see the open end of the corner, cycle hard.

Braking in the turn loads weight on the sides of the tyres and often leads to crashes. Avoid it and you'll avoid a pile-up.

No hands riding

As a kid it was the ultimate cool, riding down the road with your hands placed on your thighs. As a triathlete it's not only a useful skill when you need both hands to refuel or de-layer on a training ride, it's also a useful training method for improving your steering.

When you steer round corners it should be done by leaning and by little saddle shifts that alter the line of the bike, with zero to very little handlebar steering. The ability to ride confidently without hands will make you a better rider with hands. However, start off easy: it's easy to fall off, especially in bad conditions. The following tips should help:

- Sit back in the saddle and move your backside to the rear of the saddle. This tends to give better control.
- Choose the right gear. It needs to be hard enough to push against but not so hard that it's difficult to gain momentum. The general rule is that high cadence is unstable.
- You need to ride at a speed between 12–16mph (roughly). This ensures enough pace to keep you and the bike upright. If you're scaring yourself you're probably going too fast!
- Take it slowly. If you've never ridden with no hands before, start by taking a loose grip; then a palm open grip; then raising the hands a few centimetres from the bar before sitting all the way up. Don't try doing anything fancy like eating or taking your jacket off until you're sure you're competent.

You can ride without hands to:
- **Corner**. By shifting your pelvis to one side of the saddle the bike will naturally turn in that direction. Practise in an open space such as an out-of-hours car park.
- **Eat**. Sit up and use your hands to open an energy gel, peel a banana or have a drink. Far less messy and more comfortable than having to hold things between your teeth.
- **Remove a layer of clothing**. Removing a rain jacket will always be difficult on the move, but it can be done without needing to stop by sitting up on the seat and ensuring the jacket steers clear of the rear wheel as it's removed.

Sliding

If the bike slides, due to surface conditions or braking, the following can help:

1 Release the brakes.
2 Don't turn until the wheels are turning and gripping.
3 Let the bike take you in the direction of the slide. This will eventually get weight over the tyres and enable them to grip again.

Specialist cycling training

The Wattbike

As Wattbike say in their advertising, 'The Wattbike monitors everything you need to know about your cycling and will help to track progress as your training develops. Whether you are looking to monitor your power output, cadence, heart rate or the effectiveness of your pedalling, there is a measurement parameter for you.'

It really is THE indoor cycling tool. Used extensively by British Cycling due to the amazing variety of feedback it can provide, it's certainly something you should try to train on if possible. If your local gym doesn't have one, ask the manager if they would be willing to get one or two in stock.

For the best cycling training on a Wattbike head to Wattbike. com and read resident sport scientist Eddie Fletcher's training guide, written and designed over two years of testing, monitoring and training athletes around the world.

Group training

Cycling with a club or a group of friends is a great way to progress, to complete sessions you otherwise might not finish and to gain confidence cycling in a group or behind other riders, as you need to in a race. My best advice is to start with people at your level and learn the basics:

● Keep a gap of a metre or so between you and the bike in front and ride in single file (to begin with). Close the gap as you gain confidence.
● Where possible choose a similar gear and similar cadence to the rider in front.
● Try not to freewheel at all.
● Be confident and only brake if absolutely necessary.

As you increase in confidence you can move on to cycling with people more used to group cycling. It's then worth cycling in two files so that you have someone in front, behind and beside you. This is quite daunting at first, but once you're confident with it you'll find it's a really great skill to have going into races.

○ Spit at the back

Groups often have their own rules, but a generic one they all use for obvious reasons is that if you wish to spit or clear your nose, you drop to the rear first. Get this wrong and group cycling won't be part of your training for long.

Key bike sessions

The programmes in Chapter 11 outline eight weeks of training for the various types of tri. However, alongside the sort of long, slow endurance-style bike sessions those shown below will also really help your cycling.

Tabata intervals

Izumi Tabata of the National Institute of Sports and fitness in Tokyo did lots of research to show that very high intensity interval training had a very positive effect of athletes' anaerobic and aerobic ability. He initially wanted to show that sessions lasting only four minutes could have a huge impact on fitness gains. Personally, I often complete three Tabata sessions back to back with a few minutes in between, but you can certainly perform just one as was his original intention. Tabata's idea was that this should be performed with a warm-up and cool-down, so the whole session would last about 25–35mins. For a significant increase in VO2 max it can be performed to Tabata's guidelines, five days a week for six weeks; alternatively just perform it several times once a week, as I often do.

The Tabata session revolves around maximum effort for 20 seconds, so you really have to work as hard as you can:

- Warm-up 10–15 minutes.
- Tabata session, 20 seconds as fast as possible, 10 seconds at lower speed.
- Repeat eight times.
- Cool-down 10–15 minutes.

Gibala intervals

Like Tabata, Martin Gibala wanted to show that short bouts of intense training were equivalent in fitness gains to long endurance sessions, perfect for those short of time and training for a triathlon. He compared athletes doing 2½ hours' intervals training over two weeks to athletes doing 'normal' 10½ hours' training over two weeks. Like Tabata, the sessions required maximum effort, but this time for 30 seconds. Fitness tests after two weeks showed little difference between Gibala intervals training and longer 'normal' training, therefore proving that short, hard sessions can continue fitness gains if longer sessions aren't possible. Should be performed six times over two weeks.

- Warm-up 10 minutes.
- Gibala session, 30 seconds as fast as possible, 4 minutes' recovery at lower speed.
- Repeat up to six times.
- Cool-down 10 minutes.

Microburst

This is said to be excellent for seeing fitness gains when 'normal' interval sessions have reached a plateau. Simply warm-up, then over a set period (10–20 minutes) sprint for 15 seconds, then slow for 15 seconds, then sprint, then slow, for the entire duration. Unlike Tabata and Gibala sprints these aren't maximal, but 'painful'; the 'slow' portions are just turning the legs. These sessions are very intense, so once a week only is necessary.

- Warm-up 10–15 minutes.
- Microblasts of 15 seconds sprinting, 15 seconds slow alternately.
- Repeat for 10–20 minutes.
- Cool-down 10–15 minutes.

Conclusion

Cycling is the part of a triathlon that most people assume they can do. We all learned to ride a bike when we were kids, but cycling is far more than a helmet and backpack on the route to work. Learn how to ride properly, learn how to set up your bike, practise cornering, changing gears and all the little things that seem insignificant. If they come easy, so will the rest of the race – except the hills, but then if you've sorted your cadence even they'll be less Marmite (to me anyway) and more peanut butter.

Top tips

Don't ride in headphones – the music may sound great, but you can't hear the traffic. Cycling with a mobile phone is even more dangerous, even on a hands-free. Stop, chat, and then get back to the training.

Have the following bits of kit with you at all times:

- **Safety pins** – Great for attaching a race number, even better if your clothes tear or your cleat buckle breaks. Either way, they're a good trouble-shooter.
- **Cable ties** – For attaching anything to your bike that breaks off, from onboard computers to lamps to water-bottle cages. They can even be used to join chain links together if the chain breaks.
- **Duct tape/electrical tape** – Great for attaching all sorts of things that aren't attached properly, from bar grip tape to loose bottle cages. Can also patch a tyre in an emergency.
- **Toe-clip straps** – Great if for any reason your cleats break, can be easily used to facilitate a proper cycling technique. They can also strap other bits of kit together, such as inner tube, pump, CO2 cartridge etc, or to strap them to a bike. In essence, can be used as any sort of strap if something breaks.
- **Thin disposable gloves** – Will keep your hands clean when changing a tyre or fixing the chain. Useful for wearing under racing gloves if the weather gets really bad, simply as insulation. Hopefully it won't be necessary, but if you ever come across an accident you can use them to help someone without having to touch their blood or wounds.
- **Bright clothing** – Vital if you're commuting or cycling in low light. British winters are bad all the time, so get a bright jacket.

Also, pack appropriately for the session. If you're going out all day, make sure you have money, a first aid kit, food, water, pump, energy gels and repair kit. Look at the weather and where you're going – you may need to pack warm or wet-weather clothing.

CHAPTER 07
RUNNING

Running is, or at least should be, the easiest of the three disciplines in terms of when and how to do it. Most of us at least believe we know how to run, even if once you've read this chapter you realise you have a lot to learn. As for when you run, it's definitely the easiest of the disciplines to arrange: other than a pair of trainers, some running clothes and a facility to shower afterwards there's not much else to be organised.

Not only is running easy, it should also be the least expensive, since you need nothing more than shorts, a vest or wicking T-shirt, socks and running trainers. Compare this to swimming's goggles, fins, trunks, swim hat and... OK, yes, there isn't actually a lot of difference, but you need to pay for pool usage or membership of a gym with a pool (unless you plan to always train in open water – in which case I hope you live in the Caribbean). Cycling, of course, is far more expensive than either.

However, just because running's cheap and easy doesn't mean it should constitute the bulk of your training – it should be shared equally with the other disciplines. In fact, if you're a proficient runner already it may well be less than equal (though as discussed previously, fitness gains for swimming can be better gained by running), as you'll need to concentrate on your weaker disciplines to bring them on.

Running kit

Trainers

Running shoes really do matter. Don't run in anything other than shoes specifically designed for running.

- If you choose to run in very supportive gel/air cushioned shoes, then heel strike to your heart's content.
- If you choose to run in very lightweight road shoes or specific barefoot-style shoes, you must readdress your running gait and run accordingly.
- Replace shoes every three to six months.
- Buy from a reputable running or tri shop and look at the varieties they stock.

1 Stability shoes – These are designed to offer increased support to the inside of the midsole specifically to stop the ankles turning inwards.

These are good all-rounders and suitable for beginners and seasoned runners alike, as they provide a good level of cushioning, grip, and are neither overly heavy nor too light.

2 Trail shoes – These are designed specifically for running off the beaten track. They don't generally have as much cushioning as other trainers, as the surfaces run

while wearing them should be more forgiving than a road.

3 Shock-absorbing shoes – These are best suited to seasoned or efficient runners whose feet, ankles, ligaments and bones are more used to

running compared to those of beginners. Despite their shock absorbance such shoes have the least added stability, as they're aimed at neutral runners who are unlikely to pronate.

4 Motion-control shoes – These are the most rigid of road-running trainers. They're specifically aimed at runners who collapse in at the ankles, known as

overpronators. They are often heavier because they contain a 'medial post' – basically a hard area under the arch to provide support.

5 Barefoot shoes – These are supposed to mimic running barefoot as closely as is possible. They generally have little or no stability, arch

support, motion control or shock absorbance. Most are literally a sole that protects the bottom of the foot and that's all. Some offer a very small amount of cushioning across the mid/forefoot (the ball of the foot area), as these shoes are designed for mid/forefoot runners only.

6 Performance shoes – Great for faster training and racing. They have more support than a racing shoe, more cushioning and more stability but are still light and easy to run in.

7 Racing shoes – Ultra-lightweight shoes known as 'flats', with no stability and minimal cushioning. Only suited to high-cadence light runners who don't

heel-strike. I wouldn't recommend them for every training session, especially for a marathon or ironman.

8 Spikes – Spikes are basic running shoes, almost like a midfoot shoe but with spikes for traction. Primarily used by cross-country runners and track runners (but a little

different in terms of shoe and length of spike). They're great to have if you're going to run cross-country races in the winter or train on the track in the off season.

9 Tri shoes – A few brands are jumping on the triathlon bandwagon to provide running shoes specifically designed for triathletes. They generally include elasticated laces or a lace lock, plus a lining that doesn't require socks but won't give you blisters.

Now that you have a good idea of the types of running shoes available, it's worth working out which is best and most

Swelling feet

If you're attending a week-long tri camp somewhere like Lanzarote (a lot are run there) then you'll be in the heat, and after an hour or so on a bike your feet will swell, so your trainers may need to be a little bigger.

suitable for you. You should take into account any injuries you've suffered, specifically collapsed arches, patella tendinitis, overpronation, Achilles tendinitis or shin splints. It's also worth considering where most of your runs will be done – the surface you'll be running on can make a huge difference to the shoes you'll require. Running on roads means more impact, so a more cushioned shoe will be needed, whereas running on a treadmill could mean less cushioning. Get your running gait tested to see whether you supinate or pronate, to determine whether you need motion-control shoes or stability shoes. If you're a forefoot runner you can use barefoot shoes.

Having read all this advice you may be thinking, 'That's all very well, but I'm not racing in a motion-control, stability (whatever) shoe – I'm racing in my super-lightweight, run like the wind trainers.' Fair enough. Race once a month, once every two weeks, in your 'super-trainers'. But train in shoes that will (along with your conditioning) prevent any injuries occurring or reoccurring. It'll also make you 'super-trainers' last longer.

The wet feet test

Normal print, normal arches: You're likely to have normal pronation, since you appear to land on your heel and the foot rolls only slightly inward.

Buy neutral shoes or perhaps a stability shoe to prevent rolling occurring.

Narrow print, high arches: Indicates underpronation, which means you run on the outside edge of the foot and get little or no shock absorption from it.

Buy flexible shoes that cushion, to promote movement.

Wide print, low arches: A wide print indicates overpronation, meaning your feet roll in too much, which can lead to injuries because you're pushing off with your big toe, not all your toes.

Buy stability shoes. Lace them up well and ensure the rigidity stops your foot from rolling.

Making your trainers last

Clean your trainers before you shower. Don't put them in a washing machine unless absolutely necessary as it will warp them or melt the glue. Use warm water and a little soap with a medium hard bristled brush. Remove the insoles to help the shoes air so that they don't smell. If they're wet, fill them with scrunched up newspaper, then replace the newspaper as it becomes sodden until the shoes are dry. Don't dry them in an airing cupboard or tumble dryer or on a radiator. Store them indoors, but not in real heat. If you store them outside they'll decay quicker than they should.

Don't use your trainers for anything else – EVER. And the best piece of advice I've ever received: buy two pairs – exactly the same, if possible, and use them equally. Both will last longer than either would on its own.

Laces

Triathletes often replace their laces with elastic or some form of draw cords, which allows them to pull their trainers on more quickly and not have to worry about doing up laces and wasting precious seconds in transition. Great, use this on race day when you actually have a transition, but when you're training use real laces done up properly. It'll save you injuries by allowing the trainers to work as they were designed to. It'll also (again) make them last longer.

Women-specific trainers

Not only are there differences between men and women in the structure of their feet, there are also major differences in sizing standards and running shoe designs. In general men have longer and wider feet, and the arch, first toe, lateral side of the foot, ball of the foot, ankle and overall foot shape are all significantly different. Running shoe manufacturers know this and have factored it in when designing their women-specific range. Most importantly, women tend to have a narrower heel and forefoot and a lower instep than men, so if a woman buys and runs in a man's shoe in her size, the likelihood is her heel will slip up and down, causing blisters from friction.

Elastic laces or lace locks

These allow running shoes to be put on more quickly. Elastic laces are set to a specific length, then pulled on with the use of talc or Vaseline in the shoes. Lace locks enable normal laces to be tightened without tying by pulling a lock up to the tongue.

CLOTHES

Always buy kit from a good sports brand, as you know the kit will be hard-wearing and fit for purpose.

Shorts

Buy proper running or sports shorts, not fashion brand cut-off tracksuit bottoms. They need to be decent, wicking, quick-drying running shorts. Buy gender-specific kit – the cuts are slightly better for the appropriate sex, so the fit will be better and the likelihood of rubs and chaffing far lower.

Leggings

Perfect for cold winter nights and even more when a small case of DOMS (delayed onset muscle soreness) is felt, as they provide compression. Most leggings are designed ergonomically so that they're more suited to men's or women's running gaits and help them stride correctly, therefore always buy the correct type.

Vests/singlets/T-shirts

Make sure they're made of a decent wicking material. For a long, slow, continuous run a T-shirt is fine, but if you're doing a fast pace or interval session a vest or singlet is better. Also wear what suits the weather and climate.

Sports bras

Research has found that breast movement when running was reduced by 38% with an ordinary bra but by 78% on average with a sports bra. It's important to get yourself correctly fitted for your sports bra and get re-fitted periodically thereafter, especially if you change size or weight. When you're in the changing room, jump up and down and sprint on the spot. Look in the mirror as you do so and check which reduces movement the most.

➔ Use and replace

Washing your sports bras as per instructions will prolong their life, but their shock-absorbing elastic 'suspension' will tire over time. Just like a pair of trainers they should therefore be replaced early to avoid injury and discomfort.

Layers
➔ Base layer

These are always made of wicking material and generally quite figure-hugging. The higher end versions are seamless to ensure there's no chance of chafing. Cold-weather variants are often very long so they can be tucked into shorts or leggings to prevent cold air entering waist-level gaps. Long sleeves are great when it's cold or if you're prone to sunburn and want to cover up.

➔ Warmth

Once you start running you'll heat up very quickly. For this reason you don't want to start off in too many layers. Best advice is to start off feeling a little cold – not unbearably so, but certainly chilly!

Most clothing manufacturers produce clever materials that provide warmth without having to be thick and baggy or needing multiple layers. My advice is to wear:

- A long-sleeved wicking T-shirt, long enough to tuck in to keep the core warm.
- A pair of full-length running leggings, keeping the legs and ankles warm.
- A windproof/showerproof soft or hard shell jacket of lightweight breathable material.
- Possibly a hat and gloves and a pair of breathable shorts over the leggings.

Jackets

Running jackets generally come in two variants: soft shell, which includes a warm fleece-like lining; and hard shell, which is thin and breathable but will protect from wind and rain.

Gilets

These provide warmth to the core, which is where it's most important, but allow cooling and breathability in the arms. Some full jackets are actually available with detachable sleeves, meaning they offer both.

Hats

You lose around 40% of your body heat through your head. Many sports brands offer running-specific hats that are made of the same wicking material as their shirts. Earmuff variants provide warmth to the ears but allow heat to escape from the top of the head during a run. There are also hats made of high-visibility material or with reflective strips – ideal on low-light road runs.

The dangers of hats

Wearing a hat over the ears can obstruct your hearing, so be careful when running on roads, especially in the countryside, since you may not hear the traffic coming.

Caps

Caps insulate the head somewhat, and in summer can provide shade and sun protection for your face and head. The running manufacturers again make these items from  high-tech materials to keep you cool and wick away sweat. Many triathletes even choose to race in a cap to prevent heatstroke.

Scarves

Snoods (basically a tubular neckscarf) can be pulled up over the mouth and ears when running in extremely cold temperatures, as they can protect the lungs from very cold air as well as keep the neck area warm.

Gloves

Just like hats, the top manufacturers produce gloves that keep the hands warm yet wick away the sweat. They may also be reflective and/or bright for additional visibility. With the major muscles of the body using all the blood, the extremities often have a restricted blood flow during exercise and so become cold.

Socks

Socks are a difficult issue for triathletes. Personally I think training in them is safer, as you shouldn't get blisters, and you want to minimise any aches, pains and ailments, so train in socks 90% of the time but maybe don't wear them for brick or race-pace sessions, nor races obviously.

Cotton should be avoided in preference for wicking materials, which most sports brand socks use. Many also offer cushioning in specific areas. Like trainers, when they look old they probably are, so should be thrown away or put in the 'conditioning session' pile, for which an old pair is fine.

Compression wear

The basic idea behind this gear is that the material – which generally contains spandex or Lycra in some form or other – separates and compresses the muscles, making them more efficient and warmer while providing support and preventing chaffing. By compressing the body the clothing constricts the blood vessels in the muscles, thus maintaining the heat in them. Not only does this aid warming up and prevent strains, it also helps recovery from DOMS.

How to run

I'm a great advocate of the maxim 'if it isn't broken, don't fix it'. What I mean by this is that although somebody may seem to run 'differently', if it works for them and they aren't looking to break any records or to compete, and it isn't causing them any injuries, I don't change it. I'll leave it and work with it. A great example of this is Michael Johnson. His running style was visually unorthodox and strange to watch; yet he was a double world record holder.

Foot strike

Despite forefoot (or midfoot) running having gained in popularity recently, the majority of runners (around 80%) are 'heel strikers'. This means that the first part of the foot to strike the ground is the heel. Following this, the foot rolls on to the toes to push off into the next stride. Core strength and stability is particularly important when heel striking, as it protects the back. Therefore heel strikers should ensure the abs are tight, which keeps the torso upright, the spine straight and the core engaged.

The other 20% of runners are 'forefoot strikers'. This means that the ball of their foot is the first part to strike the ground. Due to the heel being 'missed out' of the strike, these runners have a slight forward lean to their style and take short, quick steps. Their cadence is therefore slightly quicker than their heel-striking counterparts, which is actually a good thing.

Haile Gebrselassie is another great example of why there's no 'correct' way to run. Despite the fact that most of his peers are midfoot strikers, he's a heel striker, something that at his level coaches would have tried to change. It goes to show once again that we're all different and there's not necessarily a 'perfect' way to run.

Heel strike

With every step there is a sudden impact on the heel that travels up through the body. Some people believe it can lead to more injury, although this has never actually been proved.

Despite what I've just written, there are certain key pointers that can help, either by perfecting how you already run, or allowing a few small adjustments to be made. Both can could lead to a faster or longer run with less effort than before. In addition correcting a bad running technique might be exactly what's needed if an injury has occurred, or you're trying to recover from one.

Most people's running technique can be improved vastly by training, but 'training' doesn't just mean repeatedly running. Run training, like any sport practice, must be improved only by using the correct techniques, in order to make the practice perfect.

What makes the 'perfect' running style?

As someone who has re-taught or tweaked a number of people's running styles – whether to enable them to run a quicker 10km, to avoid injury, or to teach them to run midfoot – I've put together a list of pointers to help you improve your running. The problem is it's difficult to teach these; they're more something that becomes easy, economical and comfortable through practice, circumstance and implementation. So my best advice is to carry on with your normal training, but also try out these various suggestions for one minute in every three to five:

● Try to land with your foot directly beneath your hips, never out in front. If the foot lands in front, your forward momentum is 'stopped' slightly – in effect the leg acts as a brake. By landing underneath the body the leg allows momentum to continue, thus letting energy carry efficiently from the previous stride

into the next. Furthermore, impact and stress is reduced from entering the leg, thus saving the Achilles, knee, hip and back, which is why it's perfect for recovering injuries in those areas.

● Aim to keep the heel 'unweighted' throughout the stride cycle. This can feel very unnatural, yet it's the way the world's most efficient runners run. The heel hardly touches the ground, as almost all of the weight is put through the forefoot during the weight-bearing phase of each stride cycle. As explained above, this reduces the shock entering the leg and the body by providing both shock absorption and energy propulsion for the next stride via the natural flexibility of the foot.

● Aim to run with a cadence of at least 88–92 foot-strikes per minute. This should be the same no matter what speed you're running at. By simply running at this faster cadence there's a reduction in the need for vertical displacement, less fast-twitch muscle fibre is used, there's less impact stress and there's a greater energy return for the next stride – put simply, a better/ faster/easier run.

● Try to propel yourself forward using movement through your hips (hip extension) rather than through your knees (knee flexion or knee extension). This will make you more efficient, with more forward (horizontal) propulsion, by engaging larger muscles (the glutes and hamstring) to do it. This makes the whole running process more energy efficient.

Forefoot strike

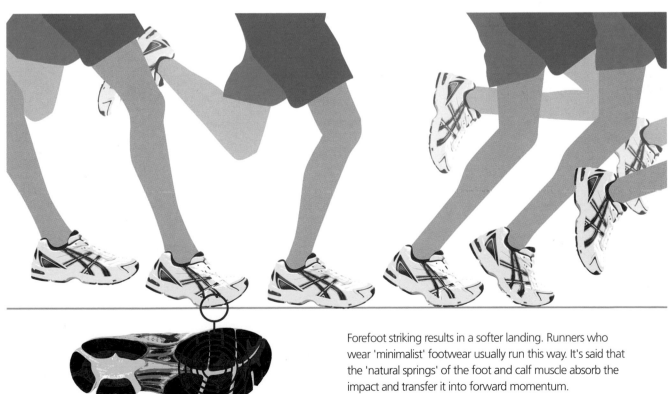

Forefoot striking results in a softer landing. Runners who wear 'minimalist' footwear usually run this way. It's said that the 'natural springs' of the foot and calf muscle absorb the impact and transfer it into forward momentum.

● Aim to accelerate the foot backward before it hits the ground. This too minimises any braking by the leg, and means propulsion begins as soon as the foot becomes weight-bearing.

● Try to keep the contact time between feet and ground to a bare minimum. This helps minimise energy wasted in vertical movements and makes the elastic recoil (natural suspension) in the foot more prominent.

Common mistakes

Rather than telling people what to do it's sometimes easier to say what not to do, and then what to do instead. The following is a list of common mistakes that people make when trying to run. They may help you to understand the correct way to run.

Cadence

Your leg speed should be fast (high cadence), perhaps faster than you might expect for a long 'slow' run (ie not a sprint). A high cadence will allow you to run faster no matter who you are and what type of triathlete you are (newbie or seasoned pro). Far too many runners make the mistake of thinking that 'bouncing' will make them less tired by giving them more air time. This may make you feel less tired, but it will certainly slow you down, because the air time actually wastes energy on upward propulsion instead of forward propulsion, which means that your run will take you longer. The opposite is actually advisable: cut the bounce down, which in turn reduces the time your feet are in contact with the ground and makes you run faster. In short, a high cadence is good and any form of bouncing is bad.

The feet leading the legs

The legs should be led by the knees rather than the feet. In a similar way to bouncing, people often feel that flicking the toes forward and lengthening the stride means they're travelling further with each step. This, too, is far from the truth. The foot landing in front of the knee is how we humans run naturally downhill, because it acts as a brake to slow us down. If the foot lands in front of the body on the flat, exactly the same thing happens – it acts as a brake, stopping forward momentum.

Knee lift

For any type of distance running as performed in a triathlon, knee lift should be low, as it's more efficient so will burn less energy. This will in turn lead to a delay in fatigue. If you're a swimmer-turned-triathlete and have done little running except on school sports days you may find you're more accustomed to sprinting, where the knee lift is far higher. So when you practise your running learn how to run economically over long distances: low knee lift, high cadence, no bouncing, and the foot landing under the body, not in front. The key is to get out and run while thinking about the techniques outlined in this chapter – this should lead to your body becoming economical as you train. 'The body becomes its function,' as I was taught in my Royal Marine days, and it does.

Breathing

Whether you're a seasoned triathlete or a first-time runner, when you run you get out of breath (see Chapter 2). This is because as we move faster our bodies require more oxygen, and with any exercise our muscles need more energy. The body meets these energy needs by supplying oxygen-rich blood to the muscles, which allows oxidative glycolysis (a method of making energy – see Chapter 2) to take place.

As we run we breathe – without conscious thought – in time with our cadence. The common way to breathe is in a 2:2 rhythm, ie two steps as you inhale, and two more as you exhale. If performing a very easy or recovery run our breathing may then become a 3:3 ratio. If running particularly hard during a race or interval session a 2:1 or 1:1 ratio may be reached, though this isn't true for everyone, and a 2:2 remains more common.

Most runners naturally breathe through both their nose and mouth, with neither being considered either correct or incorrect. Whatever way comes naturally without conscious thought should be maintained, since how the air enters is pretty irrelevant – it won't make you a better or worse runner, as long as the oxygen's getting in. The only thing I'd advise you work on if it doesn't occur naturally is which foot-strike you exhale on when running. It's believed that exhaling as the left foot strikes is most common and helps avoid a stitch, while exhaling on the right foot is thought to aid a stitch occurring, due to the diaphragm's position when exhaling and the effect of impact through the right side, where the liver is when exhaling on the right.

Staying relaxed

It's imperative to stay relaxed in every sport, and the three elements of a triathlon are no exception: swim when you're tense and you sink, cycle or run when you're tense and you waste energy. A relaxed running style will make you faster and, more importantly, ensure that you last longer; and as running is the final discipline in a triathlon, after swimming and cycling, going faster and lasting longer are vital, especially in half and full ironman events.

The most commonly seen mistakes are tenseness in the neck and jaw, especially when working hard, and clenched fists or rigid knife-like hands. Try to avoid these at all costs – a relaxed hand relaxes the forearms, and a relaxed jaw ensures breathing is relaxed and natural. Both will make your runs more enjoyable and easier!

> **⏱ Relaxed posture**
>
> **A natural relaxed posture is one of the most important things to remember as a runner. If you find it hard to relax, slow down, and perhaps even use headphones to listen to music that relaxes you.**

Body position

When running there are certain positions that the body must adopt. This isn't necessary for everyone, but for the majority of people it will make running easier. As I've said before, I'm a big fan of 'If it isn't broken, don't fix it'. However, when you finally reach the run in a triathlon you're already very tired, and it's then that bad technique will let you down. Coming from a running background I always coped better at this point, as my economic running style paid dividends, but I've seen great swimmers who now consider themselves good runners fall foul of the run, so work on your technique and don't take it for granted.

Arms

Often, but not always, what feels natural is best: therefore swinging the arms naturally like pendulums is the norm. For the majority of triathlon running there's no need to force the movement, though when sprinting for the line or performing intervals some power generation through the shoulders is necessary. Any arm swing should be at the side of the body and not across the chest, as swinging across the chest can restrict breathing and cause imbalance.

Hips

The hips should be straight on and shouldn't rotate or swing, as this will waste energy on an unwanted movement that then has to be counteracted, wasting yet more energy. Best case scenario the hips should stay in line with the shoulders, but for some runners, particularly women, this can be difficult. However, where possible try to keep any movement in a forward direction in the same plane as the run. Any sideways movement (swinging of the hips) will only slow you down.

Shoulders

Difficult as it may be, the shoulders must stay relaxed: rigid shoulders rotate the upper body in the opposite direction to the hips, which therefore slows the pace, wastes energy and can cause unsteadiness – all of which lead to a slower run.

Posture

A natural, relaxed (getting the idea?) posture is one of the most important things to remember. The key is to stay upright, and not to slouch. However, as the core gets tired this can be extremely challenging. To ensure it doesn't let you down during your runs train the core with specific conditioning exercises, which will help hugely with swimming as well (see Chapter 10 for exercises).

Cadence

Cadence is a measure of the number of full revolutions taken per minute (rpm) – in running that's the number of times both the right foot and the left foot strike to make a full revolution or stride.

Casual and non-professional runners generally overlook the importance of cadence, usually because other factors such as technique, stride length and breathing rate take precedence. However, it's a factor you need to be aware of if you want to see real improvements in your performance, especially following a leg injury or after hitting a plateau in training.

If you've ever watched an elite running race on TV, be it the last stage of a triathlon, the 10,000 metres or an Olympic marathon, the elite runners look as if they're finding everything easy, yet they're maintaining a pace for 26 miles that most of us couldn't keep for one! There are a number of reasons why it looks so easy and economical; yes, they're genetically gifted, highly conditioned and professional athletes, but a large part of their ability comes from their high running cadence.

A quicker cadence means the legs are moving quicker and therefore there's less impact on each leg with each step, which in turn leads to fewer impact injuries. You'd assume that a lower cadence means less forward momentum so less impact, but that isn't the case: a lower cadence actually means more air time, which causes a bigger impact with each landing, hence the higher rate of impact injuries. A lower cadence also means a longer stride, so the foot is landing in front of the body, not below it, leading to more shock through the leg and thus more impact.

A low cadence means the foot strikes the ground in front of the centre of gravity rather than directly under it. This acts as a brake and slows you down, and is known as 'over-striding'. A quicker cadence completely removes over-striding and leads to the foot-strike and push-off working together to conserve and generate momentum, meaning you run faster and it feels easier. This sounds counter-intuitive to most people, so just trust me.

Elite runners will keep the same cadence no matter what speed they run at. This is because a higher cadence allows more potential for speed when the pace is upped. Research shows that those with a higher cadence only increase their stride length when their running speed is increased. This means that the cadence they're using while running at a six-minute-mile pace is almost identical to the cadence used when running at a ten-minute-mile pace. It's only the stride length that's increased.

A large stride is essentially hopping from one foot to the other with very big steps, but we can only hop so far. What this means is that if your natural cadence is 80 and you want to run a 5k race at six-minute-mile pace you'll find it very difficult unless you change your cadence. So increase your cadence for your slower runs, get used to the different feel of it and work up from there.

On average top triathletes and long-distance runners have a cadence of around 88–95, which changes very little with speed.

Counting your cadence

To find your cadence, count how many times one foot (left or right) strikes the ground in 30 seconds or a minute. I usually get all my clients to do this on a treadmill, as it's easy to repeat, there's a clock in front of them, and weather and ground conditions can't affect their running.

If you choose to count for 30 seconds, then multiply this number by two, and if for one minute, then this is your cadence. Once complete, you can see how far you are from the 'magic' 90 strides per minute. If you're between 88 and 95, then great, you already have a good cadence (at that speed). If your cadence is lower – I've seen cadences of 74 for tall men, and 80 for girls over-striding, so you may be surprised what you actually are – you'll need to improve it by adopting some of the ideas set out below.

Improving cadence

If you've tested your cadence at different speeds and decided you need to increase it, the following tips may help. Of course, something that works for one person doesn't necessarily work for another – we're all different – so find the one that works for you and stick with it, and perhaps try another if things get stagnant.

- The first thing to address, and arguably the most important, is to ensure you're getting your body over your foot-strike. Get someone to watch you from the side and tell you if your foot is landing under you or in front of you. If it's in front, then you need to ensure you get forward over your foot. To do this you must get your hips forward so that it feels like you're falling into the next step. Practise running while ensuring that you keep your feet under your body. It may be necessary to do this with the feet individually, only worrying about one foot at a time at first and then with both feet at the same time.
- Run at a comfortable pace for a minute or two, then, staying at the same pace, try to put the feet down earlier than normal. A simple way to do this is to run directly behind another runner or very close to the front of a treadmill. This forces you to shorten your stride and hence quicken your cadence. Once a minute is up, go back to your normal stride. Do a couple of minutes at this, then repeat the shortened stride/quicker cadence.
- Reduce your up-and-down movement. This is imperative to speeding up your cadence and making your running more energy efficient. Run on a treadmill and watch your head movement in a mirror: if your head is bouncing up more than an inch or two each step then you need to work hard to stop this, as you're literally wasting forward momentum by going upwards.
- Run with your feet placed wider apart by imagining you have a box about 10cm wide and 10cm high between your legs. Because your feet can't strike in the middle you have to run by placing them to the side rather than front and centre, which – since it's impossible to over-stride doing this – shortens your stride and increases your cadence.

- Run with shorter and faster strides, which naturally forces you to increase your cadence. Beware of being unrealistic, though, and running well over 100rpm. Run naturally and relaxed, but shorten your stride.
- Use a metronome, either the old-fashioned type or a smartphone app version. Set this to 90 beats per minute and then make your foot strikes match it. Simple, easy, and after a long day something that doesn't need much thinking about.
- Music. Some songs have the correct beat and some fitness companies have actually created tunes that help you to increase your cadence. I haven't used them, but I've heard a couple of good reviews.

Once mastered, a cadence of 88–95 allows you to increase your run speeds far more than a low cadence, and thus allows you to push for faster times, avoid injury or re-injury, enjoy your run that little bit more or make the transition to midfoot running a bit easier. Whatever the case, you should become a better runner and find your overall tri time goes down.

Heel striking and forefoot running

As we've already seen, the majority of people (80%) run with the heel of the foot hitting the ground, but our ancestors were forefoot runners, and it's only recently (50 years or so) that the invention of cushioned running trainers has allowed us to run on our heels without causing huge shockwaves through the legs and body. Recently there's been much media attention on forefoot running, due to the popularity of barefoot running and, in the most part, Newton and Vibram FiveFinger running shoes.

In terms of triathlon running, the question is, of course, which is better, forefoot striking or heel striking? Should we recognise that our ancestors ran 'correctly' (for the human race) and return to our roots by forefoot running, or should we acknowledge that we've 'evolved', and accept that just as we now wear underpants and bras to stop our bits swinging around, we wear shoes to enable us to heel strike, and that this is how humans now run? I am, of course, being a little flippant; wearing underwear has not changed our biomechanics!

The main problem for me is the way we walk in school shoes, work shoes, work boots etc is by landing on the heel first. We walk this way, that's it, no question. We actually worry about toddlers who start by walking on their toes, but then the majority move into walking on their heels after just a few weeks or months. So, which is right? Have we evolved for the better, and what way should we run?

Manufacturers of barefoot running shoes and owners and advocators of barefoot running clubs claim that running shoe manufacturers have 'changed the way we naturally run' through running-shoe design, and the all-important heel cushioning. They see that without these gel-, air- and cell-cushioned shoes we wouldn't have adopted the heel-strike method. I can see their point, and the claim that if the shoe manufacturers admitted they were wrong it would cost them billions a year in sales is also a fair point. However, as I've already mentioned, what about our day-to-day shoes? When we walk in them we strike with our heels. Yes, there's less shock going through them when walking than when running, but it's still there.

I personally believe barefoot running has its place, and have no doubt that it was how we were designed to run. However, I also think we've evolved a little too far beyond it now and that it should be reserved for running in the park or on the beach every now and again as a form of cross-training or a bit of fun. Personally I don't think it's advisable on concrete roads and treadmills. The reason I say this is that to run successfully barefoot requires a fair amount of concentration, and if you slip out of that concentration you may well slip back into the natural running style you've used since you were a kid: heel striking. After a hard swim and long cycle the glutes and hamstrings will be tired, not to mention you'll be mentally fatigued too, and soon enough your stride stops being short and quick, striking on the ball of the foot, and becomes long, 'bouncy' and heel striking! Heel striking in a barefoot shoe (or indeed barefoot) will put a great amount of shock through the ankle, knee, hip and back, and is likely to cause injuries very quickly.

Having said all that, I'm a huge fan of forefoot running. I've personally changed my running style (although I always had a very short running gait and high cadence, so it wasn't much of a change) to see the effects for myself, so I can pass on accurate experience to my clients. I've successfully changed people from heel strikers to midfoot strikers to help them in a number of ways, from alleviating long-term hip pain and getting over ankle injuries to speeding up over 5–10km distances.

Personally, forefoot running has helped me avoid the return of a recurring patella tendinopathy injury, which I'd battled with for a good 18 months, so I'm definitely an advocate. However, I'd advise you run in trainers rather than barefoot until you're very competent.

Before you commence forefoot running

If you're planning or attempting to move from heel striking to forefoot striking the following may help you make the transition. If you think that you already midfoot strike, or at least do when you're concentrating during training, the following tips might help you in a race where the swim and bike sections have already taken their toll.

Finally, remember that all-round running superstar Haile Gebrselassie (the current marathon world record holder) is a

⏱ Midfoot style change

I've witnessed many amateur triathletes looking to better their running personal bests go out and buy midfoot running shoes without understanding that they must change their running style. Just because you wear a midfoot shoe doesn't mean you'll be a midfoot striker.

prominent heel striker. Heel striking hasn't and isn't hampering his performance, so as long as other coaching guidelines are stuck to (the weight of the foot contact is kept under the general centre of mass and landing is light and easy), then forefoot striking should have little to no effect when compared to VO2 max, aerobic capacity and correct mechanics.

How to forefoot run

Firstly, it's imperative to embrace and understand all the correct running mechanics laid out above. Then, take it slowly. Whatever you do, don't jump straight into long runs just because you can complete them as a heel striker. Pretend you're coming back from an injury and build up slowly. It's also important to strengthen the hamstrings and glutes, as they'll be used more due to the higher cadence and shorter stride of forefoot running. Pay attention to the specific conditioning drills and specific prehab to avoid injuries (see Chapter 10).

Shoes

Select the correct running shoes to help with your forefoot transition, although, having said that, you can learn to forefoot run in your normal trainers, you just have to make sure you land on the middle of your foot rather than the spongy heel. The problem with normal trainers is that their 'heel block' can make it difficult to miss this area in order to strike with the centre of the foot – hence the necessity (eventually) to buy specific midfoot running shoes such as Nike Frees (varying in their 'barefoot closeness' by the number associated with them, 5.0, 4.0 or 3.0), Newton's (probably the most popular amongst triathletes) and the various barefoot brands like Vibram FiveFingers, Merrell Barefoots and a few others.

The important thing to remember is that these shoes have little or no cushion at the heel and very little if any arch support. If a poor forefoot technique or a heel strike occurs in these shoes it will put a large amount of impact (six times your body weight) through your entire chain of movement, from the sole of your foot to your hip. Dependent on the mechanics of your gait and mileage per week, this could have disastrous consequences. I personally tried Nike Frees around 2005 without changing to forefoot running, unfortunately at around the same time that I was instructed and coached in Parkour/ Freerunning. As a result I suffered a collapsed arch and recurring patella tendinopathy. If these injuries were due to running heel-strike style in shoes that provided no heel cushioning or arch support then I learnt the hard way: learn from my mistakes rather than your own.

Don't rush

Just like coming back from an injury, slowly does it. You're essentially trying to abandon a well-rehearsed, economic and 'natural' technique in favour of one that's entirely new to you. This takes time. Whenever you stop concentrating, especially when you're fatigued, you're likely to slip back to heel striking. If

> ### ⏱ Midfoot style change
>
> **Before making the transition from heel striking to midfoot striking, it may be wise to ask yourself if you really need to. If you're pain and injury free and a successful and experienced heel-striker, why change? To date no independent long-term study has proven that forefoot running is more efficient, faster or more economical than heel-strike running.**

you're wearing shoes without heel cushioning when you do this, you're asking for an injury.

Successful transition will take a considerable amount of time. Realistically we're talking months rather than weeks. That said, everyone is different, so as long as you go at your pace and on your timescale there's no reason why you can't make a successful and injury-free transition. Furthermore, if you're currently running a lot and don't wish to cut your mileage down, then don't. Instead, supplement forefoot striking sessions with normal running. It's possible to do this by alternating sessions or by simply doing forefoot intervals in normal runs (one minute forefoot to five minutes normal running). Over the course of several months gradually increase the proportion of forefoot striking and reduce the proportion of heel striking, ideally by about 10% per week.

Preparation and rest

Prepare, prepare and prepare

Ensure that you actually do all your conditioning and prehab exercises each week, at least in the off season and pre-season if you're trying to change to midfoot striking. I actually get all my clients to perform these exercises pre-season, and find that weaknesses in technique can usually be solved by gym work. Too many triathletes, especially – but far from exclusively – females, only perform running sessions.

Normal exercisers are split into two groups, usually by sex (though many men fall into the female group). You have those that avoid CV training (running, swimming, cycling, rowing) and only do weight training, and those that avoid weight training and only perform their favourite CV training, which is most often running, with swimming and cycling close seconds. Triathletes often fall into the latter group, believing that the only way to improve is to smash themselves every day in the pool, on the bike or on the road. I've actually found that well over 50% of the triathletes I've trained have muscle imbalances and weaknesses that would be solved by one conditioning session a week in the gym and would make their swim, bike or run sessions far easier.

I appreciate that triathletes avoid the gym and conditioning for three general reasons:

1 Swimming/cycling/running is easier and more enjoyable than conditioning. Familiarity makes these sessions easier, so conditioning gets bypassed.
2 There's a fear that conditioning will lead to muscle growth, and that muscle growth will lead to a heavy, clumsy swimmer, a wind-catching lump on the bike and a heavy, slow body to drag round the roads, which in turn will lead to slower times and a less desirable physique. This isn't the case. Triathlon training across all three disciplines is greatly aided by conditioning. Stronger lats and shoulders lead to a more powerful swimmer and better swim times, stronger legs lead to faster bike times, and stronger hamstrings and glutes lead to more power and a sprint finish in the run – not to mention that a strong core makes all three disciplines individually faster and more economical. Conditioning is also key to avoiding injuries and recovering from little niggles.
3 There's a belief that only so much training can take place each week, especially in the light of overtraining (see Chapter 4), and I totally agree with this. So for many triathletes the thought of choosing a conditioning session over a run, bike or swim is ludicrous – it just isn't worth dropping a swim/bike/run to get a conditioning session in, is it? YES IT IS! Make the time, even if it's after an easy recovery or technique drill session. See the example training programmes on pages ???.

⏱ Volume

In Chapter 4 we discussed the principles of training and how to utilise it so that your body improves. However, an important factor not mentioned yet, and one that's relevant here, is volume. Whether specific to running or in relation to all three disciplines, and whether you're new to triathlon or someone trying to push on towards achieving half-ironman or ironman distances, something to remember is that the easiest way to pick up a running-related injury is to drastically increase the volume of running or training that you're doing.

The key is to start with very little and not every day, and build up from there. Obviously this is especially important for new triathletes, those returning from injury or after a long period of rest (such as the off season), and those making the jump from sprint or Olympic triathlons to half- and full ironman events. The general rule is to increase the volume of training by about 10% each week to achieve credible and manageable gains without the risk of injury.

Another group of triathletes who often encounter problems with volume are those trying to convert from heel striking to midfoot striking. This isn't easy (see below), and can take some time. My advice would be to start with distances as short as 200–500m and certainly no more than a kilometre. From there, increase the distance by no more than 10% per week. Although this is just a guide, it's certainly advisable.

Conditioning and prehab should be part of every triathlete's weekly schedule, especially pre- or off season. Conditioning before learning to midfoot run is equally important, if not more so.

Rest

In my first book 'overtraining' was my recurring point, so don't be surprised that rest, recovery and overtraining are my recurring themes again! For a triathlete, there's so much training to fit in that it's tempting to train all the time, and to feel guilty when resting. Well, don't. Instead make every session count, and then rest knowing you've worked hard and improvements are occurring.

When undertaking any sort of training programme, especially triathlon, overtraining is always a risk, and rest and recovery always a requirement. When training hard or after a long period of low-level or no training, DOMS (delayed onset muscle soreness) will occur. As volume increases and fitness is gained, this DOMS isn't as frequent, but whenever it does occur it's important to rest and recover. In relation to learning to midfoot run, DOMS will inevitably occur due to the change in biomechanics and slightly different muscles being utilised. Along with rest, mobility and stretching exercises, compression pants or a massage can be a great help. Just don't forget to rest!

Conclusion

People have, and always will have, different ideas on how to run, where to run and what sort of runs to do. Whether you're a treadmill enthusiast or hater, love the track or prefer country lanes, run training for triathlon should be fun. Join a running group and perform your long runs or intervals with friends. If you're considering upping your distances, take it slow and easy. The same if you're considering forefoot or barefoot running styles. Make sure you choose your kit and equipment wisely. If you want to keep abreast of things going on in the running world, check out some decent running magazines, such as *Men's Running* or *Women's Running*. Above all, remember that of the three disciplines, running is a natural thing to do. Don't be fooled by people who think they know what they're talking about: don't bounce, and don't try to reach the foot forward as far as possible. Follow the guidelines given and make time for rest, recovery and conditioning.

Big muscles?

Most women worry that heavy weights will give them 'big muscles'. However, I'd put money on the fact that most women lug big handbags around all day that weigh more than the weights the majority of their male friends use to try to get big muscles! Keep reps around 15–20 so that you work the muscles, but also work on muscular endurance. Having said that, always make the weights challenging. You won't get big muscles, and they won't slow you down: they'll help you, and all of a sudden you'll notice you're a better swimmer, cyclist and runner.

Most people think of triathlons as three disciplines: swimming, cycling and running. But there's actually a fourth discipline: transitions.
A transition is where we change from swimming to cycling (T1), and later from cycling to running (T2). Train the individual sports and forget about the transitions and you're in for a shock. Your aim is to pick up, not lose, time in these changeovers

Having your kit sorted – not just in clean, working order, but laid out as close as ready to go – and the ability to, for example, take a wetsuit off on the run, will make you a far more credible triathlete, and hopefully knock time off your personal best.

There's a running clock for a triathlon. It starts when the race starts and your time is when you finish the run. You have a tag on you throughout the race and this relays timings to a central computer as you exit the swim and enter T1, leave T1 and start the bike, finish the bike and enter T2, etc. You therefore get a breakdown not only of your swim, bike and run times, but of your T1 and T2 as well.

The transition area

In every race there's an area where only competitors and marshals can go: the transition area. This is where you keep all your kit for the various elements of the race and where you change your shoes and clothing. This area should be tidy and ordered so that you know where everything is. The best way to approach transitions is to practise. Set aside an hour a week to practise T1 and T2. Lay your kit out and practise everything, from removing your wetsuit (when wet) to getting on the bike, to getting off it and putting running shoes on. It's believed to save anywhere between 30 seconds and a minute if this is practised regularly.

Mind control

The top pros can get in and out of T2 in ten seconds or less. They do this by having everything prepped and learned. If it helps write a list of what you think you need to do and the order you need to do it. Practise it, amend the list, practise again. Once it's right learn the order. Repeat it as you swim if necessary, so that when you exit the water you know what you're doing.

The most important thing to do is remain calm. Even if your biggest rival is in transition as well, stay focused. As soon as you look at or worry about them you aren't concentrating on yourself, and you'll make a mistake. It's said we remember only about 30% of what we know when we're flustered or stressed, so the key is to stay calm and remember the order in which you practised things. Eventually T1 and T2 become second nature, and it's only when something's missing or out of place that things will go wrong, so I make no apologies for repeating the Marine mantra: 'Look after your kit and your kit will look after you'!

○ Bring it all

Bring everything. You don't have to use it, but at least if it's in the transition area you have it. If it's at home you're in trouble. Better to have it and not need it, than to need it and not have it. Having said that, less is sometimes more. Just like Marines with their big rucksacks that all their kit goes in, you have to carry it, so if it's unnecessary don't take it on the bike or run!

What to wear

Changing clothes takes time, end of story. Top triathletes will probably run/cycle in whatever was under their wetsuit or what they swam in, be it a swimming costume or a tri suit. However, you don't have to do that. If you want to change into cycling shorts and a cycle jersey, you can; if you want to change again into running shorts and a singlet, you can. As long as you

have your chest covered (both sexes, but the ruling is aimed at men!) and, if you choose to change, you're covered by a towel (nudity isn't allowed in transition), you're free to wear what you like.

The thing to bear in mind is time. Most pro triathletes don't wear socks for the run, but if you're not used to this it can be both uncomfortable and distracting, especially if you can feel blisters coming on. My advice is to try running in your trainers with tri laces (elasticated laces that you don't have to tie) and without socks a few times early in your training, and see if it works for you. If it does, brilliant. Try Vaseline on areas in your shoes that rub – these can be pre-Vaselined and left in transition. Again, it's all about 'knowing yourself' and prepping your kit.

Rehearsals

Walking through transition once it's set up is a great tip. Once you've arrived, found your spot and set up your kit (the most important parts) take a walk to where you'll enter transition; if there's a one-way system walk that way. Basically do what you'll do later, visualising and seeing where and how you'll do it. By rehearsing the transition in this way far less can go wrong, and any potential problems should become apparent now rather than during the race.

Split your kit

Most of the time T1 and T2 are in the same location. However, some events' logistics mean that the swim to bike transition is in one place and the bike to run somewhere else. This makes transition either easier or harder depending on your point of view. As long as you arrive in plenty of time before the race, read all the information correctly and prep your kit properly, it really shouldn't make any difference. However, remember if the transitions are separate that you need to split your food, separate out the right bits of kit, and maybe have two sunscreen bottles etc.

The T1 transition

Whether it's a pool swim, open water swim or sea swim, you'll have to get from the water to the area where your cycling kit is, having removed your wetsuit, goggles and swim hat.

There's usually some distance between the water and the transition. Whether it's through a changing room and a hall for a pool swim, or up a bank and into a car park for a lake swim, or across a beach and into a shower tent (to remove salt water which would lead to chaffing) and into a car park for a sea swim, you usually have time to remove your wetsuit, goggles and swim hat en route.

There's usually somewhere specific to put these bits of kit. They're expensive, so don't get caught up in the race and sling them off like you might see in the movies. A partner or friend can't enter transition but they could (possibly) pick up your swim kit as you pass them. If not, take it to transition and leave it there. This is probably the best advice anyway, as there'll come a day when you're on your own, so you'd best plan for a worst-case scenario and make that your practised method.

1 Exiting the water

Before we go into how to change from swimming to cycling mode, it's worth saying something about finishing the swim. Believe it or not this is a really important area to get right. Get it wrong and you'll be hurdle running out of the water and completely tiring yourself before you even get to the transition area. Equally, leave it too late and you'll give your wetsuit (and if you're unlucky your chin and nose) a nice sandpapered effect from the sand or stones on the bottom.

There comes a point where you can no longer 'swim' as the water's too shallow for a full arm stroke, but is too deep to run in without excessive energy expenditure. At this point the 'dolphin stroke' should be utilised.

Horizontal to vertical

A lot of people feel dizzy in T1. This is to do with being horizontal during the swim, then suddenly standing. A good way to avoid this is to kick hard with 200m or so to go. This will use more energy and make you more breathless, but if you're prone to nausea it's a good trade-off.

Dolphin stroke

Perfect at the beginning of a triathlon, or at the end. It's essentially what you see swimmers do after they dive in or perform a turn: they basically try to emulate a dolphin by allowing a wave of effort to travel along their body. It feels alien at first, but once mastered can be great at this point in a tri, or on each turn in a pool swim session.

The last little bit

After using the dolphin stroke to a point where it too is no longer feasible, you have to get to your feet and run. There's a right moment to do this, and a wrong moment. The best time is when the water is about kneecap height – any higher and it's too difficult to run and faster to swim. At just below kneecap depth, plant both hands on the floor (a bit like you're about to do a press-up), and pull the knees in between the arms (a bit like a squat thrust exercise). Plant the feet, drive forward on the strongest leg and begin running to the shore or (hopefully) exit ramp.

2 Removing your wetsuit

First of all pull your goggles up on to your forehead and leave your swimhat on. You don't want anything in your hands – you need them to remove your wetsuit.

Aim to remove your wetsuit before transition, but don't start taking it off until you're clear of the water and running. If you can get it off quickly and efficiently as you exit the water and move to the transition area it'll save you valuable seconds in transition. Avoid de-wetsuiting in congested areas.

Keep your momentum – ie keep moving, don't stop. Ensure you're completely out of the water before starting to remove your wetsuit – trying to remove it while running through the shallows can cause balance issues, and if you trip your arms may be too tangled up to save you!

Ten tips for smooth wetsuit removal are:

1 Use one hand to unfasten the Velcro at the back of the neck and the other hand to pull down the zip cord.
2 Take hold of the collar with one hand and pull it down over the opposite shoulder to give you more freedom of movement.
3 For now, leave the arm in the wetsuit.
4 Do the same as step 4 but for the opposite side, and this time continue down the arm and remove the wetsuit completely from that side.
5 Return to the original side.
6 Remove that arm from the wetsuit too, leaving you looking like a Californian surfer with just your legs in the wetsuit.
7 Grip the waistband of the suit and push it down the legs as hard and as far as possible by pushing it away, straightening the arms almost like an explosive bench press movement.
8 Once pushed below the knees, feed the suit down the legs until it becomes tight.
9 Use one foot to stand on the majority of the suit on the floor and then lift one leg as high as possible to free it from the wetsuit completely.
10 Do the same for the opposite side – stand on the suit and free the leg.

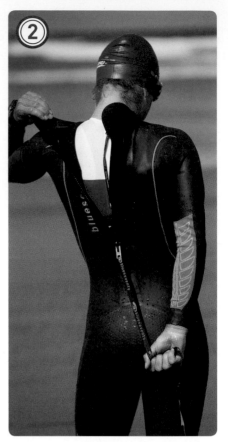

Visit the exit area

Top triathletes will visit the exit area prior to the race and go through in their mind where and how they'll negotiate the distance between the water and transition and how they'll remove their wetsuit. Follow their lead. 'Prior planning prevents poor performance,' as I learnt in the Marines.

Adapt and lubricate

A top tip from the pros is that if you have larger feet than most and your wetsuit often gets caught on your heels, either cut an inch or two off the leg length so that the suit has less grip at the bottom of the legs (this won't affect its performance at all) or apply lubricant (not Vaseline if you can help it, as it degrades the suit) to the suit's lower leg area prior to the race. This shouldn't come off in the water, though it may get a little sandy! Either way, precious seconds and extremely precious energy could be saved.

Once in transition, drop your wetsuit off in your box, Ortlieb bag etc, then take your goggles and swim hat off and put them in too.

You can actually run relatively long distances with the upper part of a wetsuit round your waist, but whether you do this or not depends on the distance the transition area is from the water. If there's more than a quarter of a mile (400m) it may be worth pulling the suit off your legs and throwing it over your shoulder. There are two reasons for this: you should be able to run faster without the suit on your legs, and it's easier to remove a wetsuit when it's wet. If it dries out it can be a little stubborn, hence removing it before a long trek to transition. Whatever decision you make, stick to it. Then remove your swim hat and goggles as you run, keep them in your hand and drop them in your allocated area in transition. If you remove them and then decide to remove your wetsuit you have the issue of dropping them in the sand, so keep them on until you've made your decision.

3 Cycle top and number

If wearing a cycle top, pull it on now, before anything else, and ensure your number is fastened with safety pins or elastic. If you're not wearing a cycle jersey, then attach your number if required. Some people like to wear their number under their wetsuit on their trisuit, but check if this is allowed. If so, attach it with elastic and it could save another five seconds.

You may not be required to wear a number on your top, but be prepared to if you are. Most tris now make you wear transfers on your legs and arms so that no matter what you're wearing on the bike or run they can see who you are.

If you do wear a running vest and have pinned a number to it, make sure you've not pinned the vest front and back together – many people do!

4 Cycle shorts

If you're wearing cycling shorts, pull them on now. Sometimes it can be worth towelling and talcing the legs slightly, as pulling Lycra over wet skin can be a nightmare!

5 Footwear

If you're cycling in trainers or want to wear socks with your cleats, put them on now. Top-level triathletes will have pre-attached their cleats to their bikes and pre-Vaselined them in areas that will rub or just to facilitate slipping them on swiftly. Very few bother with socks, but again it's down to personal preference. Try beforehand and see if you can manage it.

6 Helmet

Put your helmet on and fasten the clip – don't skip fastening it or as you run off it'll go rolling off in the opposite direction! It should take just seconds to put on your helmet if you've practised it.

Helmet practice

It sounds ridiculous, but how many times have you been asked to put on a helmet and spent a minute or so fiddling with the catch trying to fasten it? Exactly. So, practise. Practise putting your helmet on and taking it off as fast as possible. Make sure you can do it wet, out of breath and tired. If you're really dedicated, practise doing it in complete darkness (a military skill!). If you can, it'll be something you can do under the pressure of a T1 and T2. If you buy a new helmet or borrow one you'll need to start practising all over again.

7 Sunglasses

If you've attached them to your helmet they're with you already, but not on your face, which can hamper your peripheral vision when running to the T1 exit. My advice is find a way of threading the arms securely into your helmet in such a way that you can get to them without a struggle. You don't want it to be the brightest day of the year and have your glasses fly off your helmet and shatter into 20 pieces, or get stuck in your helmet so that you can't lower them. Again, it comes down to practice and preparation.

8 Get your bike

Run through transition to your bike. If it's with you in transition then just wheel it out and start running with it.

Where your bike is depends on how the tri is being run. A small event may require you keep your bike in your transition area, but this is less and less common these days. As more and more people enter tris and events get bigger and bigger, even if competitors are set off in 100 waves there are still a lot of people in transition at the same time, so bikes are generally kept in a separate location. Most large-scale tris have scaffolded racks in specific areas; your number will be on your rack spot and that's where you put your bike. If you've rehearsed getting to your bike you'll know what the route looks like. There are different ways to rack a bike, either by handlebars or by saddle, so practise de-racking it before the event and determine which way works best for you.

9 Mount your bike

If you don't get on your bike quite right as you leave T1 you may end up in a heap on the ground before you've even started! The best way to avoid this is to get your bike mount right. The easiest way (as with most techniques) is to break the process down into sections. We've already covered how to remove the wetsuit after the swim earlier in this chapter so you should now be ready to 'jump' on to the bike.

Your bike should be fully loaded with your energy requirements, puncture kit and everything else you'll require for whatever distance you're about to race. All that's left to do is to grab your helmet (with sunglasses attached), strap it on to your head, and grab your bike, run and mount.

Seat run

The easiest and quickest way to move with the bike is by holding its seat firmly in one hand. Hold the handlebars and you're likely to trip over the pedals. A decent pace will keep the front wheel going straight, and holding the seat will allow you to steer by just leaning the bike to one side.

Hand placement

Move the hands from the seat to the handlebars about three to four paces before you're about to jump on to the saddle. If you're holding the saddle with the right hand grab the handlebars with the left a split second before you let go of the seat and take hold of the bars with the right hand. It's personal preference whereabouts you hold the handlebars; the best advice is to practise this just as you would sighting or turning in the swim. Make it a technique you're good at so as to leave the opposition behind.

Mount

Again, this is something you need to practise, but once mastered it not only saves time but looks slick, and gives you a great start to the cycle element of any race. As you take the last few steps while running with the bike, holding the handlebars, take off with the outside leg and lift the inside leg as high as possible to the rear, thus swinging it over the bike and landing (under control) on the saddle. Be sure to look down for the seat as you're jumping; missing it can be uncomfortable, so aim to land towards the rear of your backside or perhaps on the inside of your leg to avoid landing on the 'wrong' area.

Adapt and lubricate

Note that there is a 'mount' line, usually a line painted on the road, and you can't mount until this point as it's too dangerous in transition with all the competitors running around. Use the skills opposite to run to this line then jump on as you cross it.

Pedal away

Once in the saddle your feet meet the already fastened cycle cleats on top of the pedals, and you start pedalling with your feet on top of the shoes until you reach a settled rhythm and an area clear of corners or other racers. Then slip your feet into the shoes. Don't risk doing this in a busy area as a crash at this point can be a race ender.

Then cycle for your race length until you get to T2.

Three top tips

● Make sure you've left a water bottle and energy bottle on your bike. You'll undoubtedly be thirsty after your swim and need to rehydrate and re-energise. This is easiest on the bike and better to do early than late.

● Don't be a 'grey' competitor. Transition is a difficult place – loads going on, lots of kit and everything looks like yours. In the military we wanted to be the 'grey man', not to stand out. In triathlon, be the opposite. Give yourself a fighting chance to find your kit and bike by making it personal. A horrendously bright towel across all your kit, a bright pink bike helmet, even – if the race organisers allow it – a flag or balloon tied above your kit and bike. It's called gamesmanship – anything that will help you win or have a good race.

● Stay calm. If you don't panic and just accept it'll take as long as it takes, you'll do far better. If you've prepared and rehearsed this will be easy.

The T2 transition

Just as there's a 'mount' line, there's a 'dismount' line. Many triathlons have marshals blowing whistles to remind you, as athletes are often 'in the zone' and would otherwise miss it. If you do miss it you could receive a time penalty, so again, rehearse beforehand – walk to the line, looking at the trees and the road so that you know where it is. A picture paints a thousand words, and you'll remember it as you see it.

1 Maintain speed

You want to keep forward momentum, so don't brake completely; keep your speed up for as long as possible.

2 Remove shoes

Undo your cleat Velcro and clips, take your feet out and place them on top of the shoes (still attached to the pedals). If you're cycling in trainers, loosen the laces unless you're also running in them.

3 Dismount

Do so before the required line and switch from holding the handlebars to holding the seat in your left or right hand (practise as for the mount to know which you want to do).

4 Run with bike

As practised for the mount, steer the bike from the back by holding the seat and run it to your spot on the rack in transition. Again, walk this route before the race to ensure you know where to go.

5 Rack the bike

Don't rush this. It's your most important piece of kit, so you don't want to damage it. Rack it properly and move on.

6 Remove helmet

You can't remove your helmet until the bike is racked (or at least in most competitions), and neither would you want to – you need free hands to rack the bike. Once it's away, unfasten your helmet and run to your kit.

7 Sunglasses

On the way to your kit pull your sunglasses up on to your head so you can see peripherally and make sure you can locate your kit and don't bump into anyone. Keep them there until you decide whether you want them on the run.

8 Footwear

If you haven't removed unwanted shoes yet, or you need to change shoes or put on socks etc, do that as soon as you've reached your spot and put your helmet down.

9 Remove cycle shorts and top

If you wore kit you're not running in, remove it now. Simply take hold of shorts at the waist and pull them straight down to the floor. Then step on and out of them like you did the wetsuit. Pull your top over your head.

10 Put on vest

If you're changing top, now's the time to put your running vest on. Your number should be pre-pinned to it.

11 Running trainers

Slide your feet into your (pre-Vaselined, if necessary) trainers, with elasticated laces if possible. This enables a quicker transition than having to tie laces.

12 Sunglasses and go!

Make a decision re your sunglasses, either to ditch them or wear them, and run out of T2 and into the run.

A quick guide to transitions kit

Choosing the right kit and equipment is important. (See Chapters 5, 6 and 7)

- If you're changing clothes, choose dry, wicking materials for the bike and the run. Not only do they go on to moist skin easier, they're far more comfortable to race in.
- Attach your number using four pins and check you haven't pinned the surfaces of your vest together!
- Lay your vest down with the waist opening upwards to facilitate grabbing and putting it on, and your shorts with waist opening upward ready to step into.
- Use elastic laces or lace locks to save time doing laces up.
- Have your sunglasses attached to your helmet, or in upside-down helmet ready to wear.

- Your helmet should be placed upside down with the front towards you, allowing you to pick it up and place it straight on your head, without having to work out which way round it is.
- Always fasten your helmet with the manufacturer's clip – don't try to make an elastic fastening, it's not permitted.
- Lastly, wear as little as you can – tri suit or swim suit for women and tri suit or swim trunk plus vest for men. Even in the worst conditions, you'll be exercising at an incredible level, so you won't (or will only rarely) feel the cold.

The Haynes seven secrets to transition success

Beyond the main points outlined above, here are seven prime recommendations that may lead to success:

1 Arrive early

Get to the race early, then you'll start calmly, as you'll have time to view the swim, the turning buoy, T1, T2 and the mount and dismount lines, rehearse, and...

2 Set up your kit

Despite your nerves, take the time and have the patience to lay out your kit in the order you'll need it. Think about details too. Look at the direction you'll be running into T2 from and place your trainers away from your incoming direction so that you can step straight into them. Equally, make sure they aren't in the way during T1 so that you won't trip over them.

3 Rehearse

This is so important: take the time to walk through the sequence and check all your kit is in exactly the right place, that you know where your bike is, and so on.

4 Vaseline

Use it for all sorts, from placing it in your cleats and trainers to stop rubs, to putting it on the bottom of wetsuit legs so they slide off more easily, and between the legs and on the nipples to stop chaffing. Buy a big tub and put it in a regular place so you always know where it is.

5 Multitask

Apparently women are better at it than men, but realistically it's all down to muscle memory and practice. So practise treading on your wetsuit legs to get them off while putting on your helmet (with sunglasses attached).

6 Find markers

If you can't mark your transition point and where your bike is physically, then when you do your walk-through stand exactly where you'll approach from and find a marker (sign, tree, house on the horizon) behind your number. Use this to navigate to your bike, then look for your number.

7 Plan for the unexpected

Most people have something go wrong in transition. If everything goes right it's a miracle, and something going wrong, especially with all those bits of kit, is far more likely, whether it's dropping your sunglasses, getting a leg caught in your wetsuit or trapping the back of your trainer under your heel. But if you go through everything that could go wrong and practise for it, then chances are you'll have experienced it before. Experience makes us less likely to panic.

Conclusion

So that's it, the fourth discipline. Simple, right? OK, maybe not, but if you take one thing – well, two maybe – away from this chapter it should be practise at home and rehearse (walk through) on the day. But remember, practice doesn't make perfect. It makes permanent. So make sure what you're practising is perfect, or on the day you'll find that what you've made permanent is a bad technique.

CHAPTER 09
WARM-UP & COOL-DOWN

Skipping the warm-up and cool-down before and after exercise are very common mistakes. We all do it when we're short of time, even seasoned triathletes. However, a mantra I learnt in the Royal Marines is 'If you haven't got time to warm up, then you haven't got time to train'. Take it from me, ignoring the warm-up is definitely the single most common way to get injured. A simple planned and constructive warm-up prior to exercise is worth its weight in gold.

Once it's learned it can be repeated every time, almost a pre-race/pre-training ritual. Equally as important is the cool-down, or, most important, the stretch routine at the end of a session. This again aids injury prevention and promotes recovery by giving the body time to return to normal.

The warm-up

Why warm up?

There are a number of specific benefits to taking the time to perform a 10- to 15-minute warm-up:

● **It prepares the body for the demands of exercise** – Warming up helps with performance, especially before a race. This is because as the cardiovascular system begins to work the blood vessels open more fully, allowing more blood to flow around the body and thus warming and supplying the major muscles and organs with an adequate supply. The increase of blood causes an increase in the rate of oxygen exchange from blood to muscle and tissue, which in turn allows the body to exercise to a higher aerobic level before the reduction of energy stores and rapid fatigue.

● **It warms the muscles, ligaments and tendons thoroughly** – A thorough warm-up ensures the muscle fibres, ligaments and tendons become more elastic, basically because they're taken through their full range of movements. This increases flexibility and thus reduces potential injury. Furthermore, there's an increase in the release of the joint lubricator, synovial fluid, which only occurs with increased activity and again reduces injury risk.

● **It increases the core temperature** – Exercise increases heat production, and this too enables the joints and muscles to become more flexible, helping to avoid injury. However, it also allows the body to start all the processes necessary in thermoregulation prior to the real session or race beginning, meaning the body will be more efficient when it actually starts.

● **It increases mental focus and prepares the mind for physical stress** – A warm-up allows the mind to start to focus on the session ahead. It allows all the problems of the day to be forgotten and the brain to concentrate on the upcoming exercise.

● **It rehearses neuromuscular channels and their function** – The warm-up rehearses the body for the specific movements necessary during the session, by sending messages from the brain that will also aid coordination. This is why a specific warm-up can be learnt and repeated. This prepares the body and mind like nothing else can.

● **It allows adaption to an extreme environment** – If the race or session is to be performed in radical heat or cold the warm-up will allow the body and CV system to gradually adapt to the climate. Forgetting the warm-up and heading straight into the exercise is more likely to lead to issues with the body's regulatory systems.

The phases of the warm-up

1 Passive warm-up
Increases the body temperature using external means such as clothing, direct heat and massage. However, it does little to motivate the body.

2 Psychological warm-up
Primarily used by professional sportspeople prior to races and personal best attempts. For the most part it requires bringing out a certain amount of physical aggression, which can be achieved by either visualising the high of achieving one's goal or by means of inspirational songs.

3 General warm-up, mobilisation and initial pulse raiser
The main bulk of the warm-up, which should be executed in a very controlled manner. Start slowly, ensuring all initial movements are neither dynamic nor ballistic; then gently increase the pace through joint mobilisation into the pulse raiser, to get the heart and breathing rates up and induce sweating.

4 Stretching, ideally dynamic
Dynamic stretching is simply stretching the muscles through active exercises in the range of normal movement.

5 Second pulse raiser
Like the first pulse raiser, but finishing at race/session pace or slightly quicker.

6 Activity specific
Not always necessary, but should be specific to the activity ahead – more shoulder rotations before the swim, practising the muscle memory regarding how to breathe etc.

Second pulse raiser

Following the dynamic stretch it's imperative to raise the pulse and develop the warm-up. The dynamic stretch allows more ballistic exercises to be performed such as sprints, strides, hops and jumps. Do them for five minutes or more to ensure the onset of sweating and that the neuromuscular pathways are firing.

Where possible perform suitable exercises for the event or session ahead: if you're doing a swim session, make the dynamic stretches more upper-body specific, but without neglecting the lower body. For a run, the upper body can be left out. Pre-race, most ironman competitors perform a very short warm-up, focussed on swimming – they don't want to waste energy. For sprint or Olympic triathlons, competitors often warm up for 45–60 minutes – riding the bike, ensuring everything's prepped, as they're such short races any problems will cost them. So again, 'know yourself'. Determine what works for you and stick to it. Ideally, your pulse rate at the end of a warm-up should be around the same as that expected during the coming session or race.

Dynamic stretching

➡ For a pre-tri dynamic stretch, simple examples are five slow squats to stretch the adductors and glutes (groin and backside), five lunges on each leg to stretch the quadriceps (front of the thigh) and five 'Russian walks' on each leg (scraping the bottom of the shoe down an imaginary wall from as high as possible) to stretch the hamstrings (back of upper leg), and five slow press-ups to stretch the shoulders and chest. Follow these with leg swings, pendulum swings, back kicks, arm circles, front crawl, backstroke, breaststroke, reverse breast stroke and back slaps (all on the shore, not in the water), which are all basically swinging the limbs through their natural range of movement.

The same dynamic stretches and warm-up routine can be performed on a treadmill.

1 Squats, run a few steps, then repeat.

2 Walking lunges, run a few steps, then repeat.

3 Leg swing.

4 Pendulum swing.

Psychological warm-up

Depending on the person and the session, it's sometimes necessary to prepare psychologically as well as physically. For obvious reasons this is more important when the warm-up precedes a competition or a particularly hard session.

The psychological warm-up can form part of the overall warm-up or can be something done while travelling to the event. For me, a piece of inspirational music is key to my psychological prep. Another method used by top athletes, especially to calm themselves and focus, is to visualise themselves performing or competing effectively and efficiently.

Dynamic stretching (continued)

5 Russian walk, run a few steps, then repeat.

6 Back kicks.

7 Arm circles.

8 Swim strokes.

The same dynamic stretches and warm-up routine can be performed on a treadmill.

The cool-down

Like the warm-up, the cool-down is often neglected. At some point I've heard nearly everyone I've trained say they'll skip the cool-down and 'stretch in the shower'. I've done the same myself! However, the cool-down shouldn't be skipped. Not only will it help avoid injury, it promotes recovery from the session and allows development of the muscles' flexibility, which will pay dividends in the long run.

A 5–30-minute cool-down helps return the body to its 'normal' state gradually, promoting recovery, providing time to consider the race or training that's just occurred and preparing the body for next time. A cool-down can be especially important if a subsequent session is going to be performed within 24 hours.

Cooling down also prevents blood pooling. This is where the muscles aid the heart and cardiovascular system moving blood around the body; as the muscles contract they help squeeze the veins and push blood back to the heart. If you just sit or stand still following a hard session the blood pools in the lower extremities, as the muscles are no longer contracting to help it return. The result is a lack of blood and therefore oxygen to the head, which can result in losing consciousness as the body renders itself horizontal to ensure that blood is recirculated.

Phases of the cool-down

The cool-down should focus on deliberate and controlled movements. There should be no need for any ballistic or dynamic movement – 'bouncing' when stretching is a dangerous practice and should be avoided. The phases of a cool-down should include:

Reduce

Continue to swim/cycle/jog or at least walk. Reducing rather than stopping exercise does the following:

➜ Ensures skeletal muscles remain active, which ensures blood is pumped around the body and doesn't pool in the legs, which causes fainting.
➜ Lowers the pulse rate slowly and steadily, which ensures blood is still pumped actively round the body, removing waste products from the muscles.
➜ Allows sweating to continue, which enables the body to control its temperature properly.
➜ Ensures the mind has something to concentrate on and stops the sick feeling that often accompanies hard exercise.
➜ Keeps the blood flowing to deliver nutrients to the muscles, which are essential for recovery.
➜ Continues to deliver oxygen to the muscles to ensure any lactic acid is cleared and the body is moved closer to normal levels.

Re-dress

It's easy to get cold very quickly after exercise, especially when training outside or in a cold gym. This means the warm muscles that are about to be stretched get cold and aren't as supple as you thought, and so injuries occur. By simply replacing some layers the temperature is maintained and the muscles kept warm in preparation for the stretch. For swimming this is difficult – still perform a cool-down, but if you feel your body temperature dropping go into the shower and do the cool-down in the warmth of the hot water.

Recover

Walk about, maintaining good posture and keeping your head up. Bending over or sitting down reduces the amount of oxygen the lungs can take in, while walking around and staying upright allows deep breaths to be taken. It's important to walk or even jog lightly to allow the pulse to lower slowly under control. Keep your mind focused on the session, don't allow it to wander. Think about the race or session, what went well and what could

> ### ⏱ Always do a cool-down
> Never skip the cool-down. Not only does it help avoid injury, it promotes recovery from the session and allows development of the muscles' flexibility. If you do skip it, you'll regret it when you start the next session and feel all your muscles aching!

be improved. A period of reflection after each event is highly rewarding, hence the numerous gadgets that allow feedback to be viewed on a computer.

Relax

Stop walking around but continue to take in deep breaths. Lie down on your back – this will aid in lowering the pulse further, as bloodpooling can't occur if the body is horizontal. Concentrate on relaxing – think of being somewhere else, on a beach, in bed, wherever relaxes you most. Soon the heart and breathing rates will return towards normal. This is an almost meditative state – in fact if you can't escape thoughts of work try meditating techniques such as concentrating on your breathing or slowly moving an imaginary ball of light from vertebra to vertebra until your reach your head.

Stretch

There are two types of stretches: maintenance and developmental. At first it's best to stick with maintenance stretches, which should be held for 8–10 seconds. These ensure the muscles stay flexible and help improve flexibility to some extent. In time it's worth moving on to developmental stretches, which should be held for 30 seconds on each stretch (done two or three times each).

Eat

It's important to eat something after exercise. As explained in Chapter 3, there's a small window of opportunity to replace the glycogen stores within your muscles. In fact, research suggests that those who ingest carbohydrates and protein within an hour of exercise will recover quicker and exhibit faster muscle repair than those who don't. A recovery supplement shake immediately on completion and a meal within an hour is the best option (see Chapter 3).

Treat

If any little niggles or muscle pulls have occurred, use an ice pack to start immediate recovery. Believe me; it will pay dividends! Using an ice pack on the area for ten minutes every hour or so can take days off recovery time. Obviously this depends on the severity of the injury, but either way an ice pack will certainly aid the healing process. (See Chapter 12 for correct icing technique.)

Stretching

The following stretches should be performed during the cool-down process. All can be performed as a maintenance stretch (8–10 seconds) or developmental stretch (30 seconds). For a maintenance stretch take a deep breath and then breathe out as you go into the stretch; count or time five seconds, take another deep breath, breathe out and increase the stretch as you do so. Hold for a further five seconds. At first these stretches will feel uncomfortable, but not painful. Be strong-willed and stick with them. However, stop if you feel any pain. Ideally perform each stretch two or three times.

Developmental stretches work in entirely the same way; they're just held for longer. Take a deep breath, put the stretch on as you breathe out and then hold for around 10 seconds; breathe in deeply again, breathe out and increase the stretch, hold it for 10, then repeat one more time and hold for 30 seconds. Again, try to repeat each 30-second stretch three times. However, once or twice is sufficient at first or if time is short.

Stretching routine

After a hard session it's always advisable to start from the bottom and work up. Besides, following the relax phase of the cool-down you should already be lying on the floor!

 ## Groin (adductor) stretch

Sit up with your legs bent as if you're going to cross them. Put the soles of your feet together and pull your heels in towards your groin. Take hold of your ankles and place your elbows on to the inside of your knees. While keeping the soles together, heels in, hands on ankles, use the elbows to push down through the knees, flattening the legs out and stretching the groin. You should feel a stretch on the inside of both legs.

 ## Single-leg hamstring stretch

Remain seated following the groin stretch. Keep the left foot tucked into the groin, but extend the right leg so it's straight and the left sole nestles into the inside of the right thigh. Reach forward as far as possible and take hold of part of your right leg (the bottom of the foot is the final aim, but at first the ankle or shin is fine). Try to bend from the lower back as you stretch, and don't round the upper back too much. Keep the leg straight. The back of the knee should be on the floor. Repeat for the left leg. You should feel the stretch on the upper back of the outstretched leg.

3 Quadriceps stretch

Roll on to your left side, ensuring your left leg is straight. Bend your right leg and take hold of your right foot and pull it up towards your backside. Try to keep your knees level with each other, and your shoulders, hips and knees in line. This will avoid structural injuries. To increase the stretch, pull the foot further into your backside and ease the hips in a forward direction. Repeat lying on the opposite side for the other leg. You should feel the stretch at the front of the bent leg.

4 Glutes (backside) stretch

Sit on the floor with your left leg outstretched and right leg bent up. Staying seated with your left leg outstretched, place your right foot over the left leg and allow it to nestle into the outside of the left thigh parallel to it. The right leg should now be up across the chest. Keeping the right foot on the floor, hug the right leg into the chest with the arms. Repeat with the opposite leg. You should feel the stretch in the buttock of the bent leg.

5 Double-leg hamstring stretch

Similar to the single-leg hamstring stretch, the double-leg involves sitting with both legs outstretched and then reaching as far down them as possible (taking hold of the shins, ankles or bottoms of the feet). Try to bend from the lower back, not the upper back. Stretch should be felt in the back of both legs.

> **! Relax**
> **When stretching, remember to remain relaxed and to breathe!**

6 Calf stretch

➡ Pushing with straight arms against a wall or partner, place one foot in front of the other about shoulder-width apart. The rear leg should be straight, front leg bent. Your body should be at an angle of about 45°. Force the heel of the rear leg into the floor. To increase the stretch, move the rear leg further away from the body without bending it. Repeat stretch for opposite leg. Stretch should be felt at back of rear lower leg.

7 Shoulder stretch

➡ Raise your arms up over your head and interlock your hands. Push your arms back to feel a stretch on the shoulders, then straighten them to bring your biceps to your ears.

8 Hip flexor stretch

➡ Kneel on the floor, then step forward with the right foot into a lunge-like position with the left knee rested on the floor. Place your hands on your hips and gently push the hips forward. Repeat stretch for opposite leg. Stretch should be felt at the top of the thigh, in the hip of the forward leg.

⑨ Abdominal stretch

➡️ Lie flat on your front and place hands under the shoulders as if you're going to do press-ups. Push down through the hands as if performing a press-up but don't allow the hips and legs to rise off the floor, ie rotate through the lower back. Try to straighten the arms as far as possible without allowing your hips off the floor. Stretch should be felt through the abdominals at the front of the lower torso.

⑩ Back stretch

➡️ Lie flat on your back, arms outstretched to your sides as if on an imaginary crucifix. Take one leg across the body (for example the right leg) and try to get the foot of that leg as far up towards the opposite hand as possible. To increase the stretch, allow the left hand to touch the right shoulder. Repeat on the opposite side. Stretch should be felt around the middle of the spine.

⑪ ITB stretch (best performed with a foam roller)

➡️ A form of iliotibial band stretch can be achieved by performing the quadriceps stretch described above and then raising the foot of the lower leg and hooking it over the knee of the upper leg. Repeat for the opposite leg. Stretch should be felt down the outside of the leg closest to the floor.

12 Chest stretch

→ Stand at the end of a wall or within a doorframe, facing towards it, and place the inside of your bent arm on the wall surface at shoulder height. Turn your body away from the positioned arm, pushing your shoulder and chest round in the same direction. Hold this position, then repeat with the opposite arm.

13 Lat stretch

→ Hold on to a bar or wall at waist height. Keeping the back straight, bend at the waist then let your head sag down, stretching the pecs and lats. Pull with one hand and push with the other to increase the lat stretch on one side. Release and repeat for the other side.

14 Triceps stretch

→ Raise an arm up and place it behind the head. Walk your fingers down your spine. Hold on to the elbow with the opposite hand and ease down the spine. Hold, release and repeat for the opposite side.

15 Deltoid stretch

→ Bring an arm across the chest and take hold of it with the opposite hand. Look away from the direction of the arm and pull it into the chest. Hold, then release and repeat for the opposite side.

These stretches are just a selection of the many you could use for the major muscle groups you'll use when training for triathlon.

PNF or contract-relax stretch

Proprioceptive Neuromuscular Facilitation (PNF) is a technique that 'cheats' the muscles and allows a stretch to be increased, sometimes drastically. The technique combines alternating contraction and relaxation of the muscle; this causes responses in the nerve that usually inhibits the contraction of the muscle being stretched. This results in a decrease in resistance and increased range of movement when stretching the muscle. Although PNF stretching usually requires a partner, this isn't always necessary. PNF stretching is supposedly far superior in improving flexibility. The technique utilises the fact that the Golgi tendon organs relax a muscle after a sustained contraction has been applied to it for longer than six seconds, thus an increased stretch can be seen.

The four stages in PNF stretching are: easy/maintenance stretch; six- to ten-second contraction; one- to three-second relaxation; and developmental stretch:

- Easy/maintenance stretch – During this stage the muscle stretches slightly but not to its maximum, ie the 'stretch' in the muscle just starts to be felt.
- Six- to ten-second contraction – During this stage the muscle is contracted as hard as possible, to build end of range strength, which is vital in developing flexibility. The breath may be held to increase the contraction and also assist in the contrast to the next stage.
- One- to three-second relaxation – Breathe out and relax the muscle for a few seconds.
- Developmental stretch – Increase the stretch as far as possible; this should be beyond the range achieved previously. Ideally the process should be repeated until no further increase in stretch can be seen.

Performing PNF

Start by stretching as normal at the limit of stretch for 10 seconds. Immediately following this, without getting up or moving, contract the muscle against a resistance (your own hand, a partner or a wall) for 10 seconds. Following the resistance, relax for a few seconds and then stretch again for 10–15 seconds. There should be a noticeable difference in flexibility. The first few times you perform such stretches it's advisable to do so in the company of others.

Points to note with PNF

You should judge how far you stretch by how it feels – never compare yourself to others performing the same stretch. Furthermore, PNF isn't recommended for use with lower back stretches.

⏱ Conclusion

Always warm up, always cool down. Find something that works for you and make it a routine. Sometimes you have to extend/shorten your warm-up depending on where you are and what you're going to do. Always stretch, as a flexible muscle is a healthy muscle.

CHAPTER 10
STRENGTH & CONDITIONING

To improve as a triathlete, it isn't enough to just swim, cycle and run. It's also necessary to strengthen certain muscles, not only to ensure they're strong enough to propel you at the speeds you want across all three events, but also to ensure you don't pick up injuries through weaknesses in certain muscles, joints, tendons and ligaments. Conditioning is something far too many triathletes, both novice and seasoned alike, neglect. However, a good tri conditioning programme will make you a better athlete.

Why condition?

Most triathletes, whether novice, amateur, experienced or pro, dislike weight training for fear of getting bigger. I totally appreciate that as a triathlete you generally don't want to build muscle mass. For sprint and Olympic triathlons it's perhaps not such a worry, but for ironman races extra bulk and weight isn't needed. However, this doesn't mean that longer distance triathletes shouldn't do conditioning – it just means doing more repetitions to increase muscular endurance. Conditioning the legs by doing just 15-plus repetitions increases the endurance of the muscles cells. This means that less cells/muscle fibres are needed for each stroke/revolution/stride, which in turn means less oxygen and less energy is needed – which means that over an entire race a triathlete is more efficient and can work harder for longer at a given speed.

When to condition

Conditioning sessions should be performed all year round, especially if they're prescribed specifically to rehab an injury or due to poor muscular activation and therefore poor technique is given areas. Having said that, more conditioning is likely to take place in the off and pre-season than during the season itself. Off/pre-season conditioning two to four days per week isn't unusual, reducing to one day a week during the season. If you're training for a specific triathlon you may want to perform one to three conditioning sessions a week at first, then drop this to one a week the closer to the event you get.

Bilateral training

The majority of triathletes who don't undertake regular conditioning are usually unbalanced in terms of their muscular strength, and such 'muscle imbalances' are injuries waiting to happen. They also make exercise more difficult than it needs to be. They're largely due to us being right- or left-handed and right- or left-footed, so that we naturally favour one side or the other. If there's a step, we usually step up on it with our favoured foot, thus strengthening it more than the unfavoured leg.

Another factor can be old or only partially recovered injuries, usually not rehabbed properly. This can have knock-on effects throughout the body and lead to compensation in the wrong areas. What this again leads to is favouring one side or one group of muscles. A great example is our hamstrings and glutes compared to our quads. Most of us spend far too long every day sat on our backsides, our glutes and hamstrings doing little more than supply a built-in cushion. When we stand up or sit down we primarily use our quads, so these get some low-level work, but our glutes and hamstrings get very little. This again leads to imbalances, where our quads are dominant in our cycling and running and our swimming is very much through the hip flexors. Unfortunately good runners use their glutes and hamstrings to support a short midfoot stride and high cadence, a good cyclist uses equal push and pull for a strong drive, and a good swimmer uses the glutes to kick efficiently. If you're imbalanced, you won't be doing any of these things correctly.

But enough scare tactics. The point here is that no matter who you are, which event you're doing or how good you think you are, conditioning is required for the muscles to function and fire at their best.

Equality is best

When starting a training programme you may notice that one side of your body is far stronger than the other, or that an exercise is far more difficult for one side than the other (this is especially true when returning from injury). However, it's important not to exercise one side more than the other – both must be increased at the rate of the weaker side, thus giving it a chance to catch up with the stronger side so that they're exercised equally.

Exercise descriptions

For all of these exercises, select a weight that's comfortable but testing. Generally speaking, the number of repetitions will determine what the muscles gain from the exercise. For strength gains perform 2–6 repetitions, for muscle growth perform 8–12 repetitions, and for muscular endurance gains perform 15-plus repetitions.

Personally I'd advise mixing between all three dependent on the time of the season (pre-, during or off) and your individual strengths, weaknesses and goals. For example, an ironman competitor might need just as much strength and power as a sprint triathlete during a hard hill climb, and an Olympic triathlete might need great endurance to keep going during the last 3km of their 10km run after a gruelling 1½ hours of cycling.

Rest between sets should be kept to a minimum when performing endurance sessions and a little longer for muscular growth and strength. For endurance sessions I'd recommend anything between 30 seconds and a minute; for growth and strength two- to five-minute rests are advisable, depending on

⏱ Training grows strength

Strength training combined with speed produces power, so although you might not feel like you want to train, I implore you to think about the power you need to push that bit harder to overtake in the swim, to get up a hill during the bike, or power past the last few opponents over the final kilometre of the run.

how heavy the weight and how hard the exercise is for you. When lifting at any rep range, quality of exercise is far more important, so resting a little more to ensure you can complete it properly is the way forward.

Whatever your goal, whatever you race, strength and conditioning training is a must, and you ignore it at your peril.

Rather than split the exercises into the three separate disciplines – as some would appear in two or three of them – the exercises are split into legs, core and upper body, with the areas they'll support stated.

Leg exercises

For two out of the three triathlon events the legs are the most important part of the body. For cycling and running, strong, healthy muscles with a good power-to-endurance ratio are imperative. Conditioning the legs with resistance exercises will produce a better runner/cyclist.

Squats Will improve: Swimming, cycling, running

Squats can be performed as a body weight only exercise, or with weight added. The technique for both is basically the same.

➡️ Stand with the feet parallel, pointing forward, shoulder-width apart. Ensure the arms are out of the way so they don't start pushing on the tops of the thighs if the exercise becomes difficult.

To perform the squat, bend at the knee until the upper leg is parallel with the ground, ie the knee is at a 90° angle. While squatting it's imperative to keep the back straight and upright, and not to bend forward. Furthermore it's important that as the knees bend they go forward over the big and second toes, and that the heels remain on the floor at all times. On the way up the back should remain tight and upright, the heels flat and the backside (glutes) squeezed. Once completely upright, repeat.

Progressions

➡️ Barbell weight back squat

The basic exercise is the same, but a barbell is placed across the back of the shoulders behind the neck, the hands gripping the bar either side of the head. Once you've mastered it the weight should nestle on the traps and won't cause discomfort, though a lot of people use padding at first or find they bruise slightly. It's even more important when using weight to ensure the back is kept upright, as if any forward leaning is allowed the balance can be lost. Again, ensure the heels remain on the ground.

Squats (continued)

➜ Front squat

Very similar to the back squat, but with the bar across the front of the shoulders. This adds to the instability of the exercise and therefore recruits far more of the core. It's important to keep the back straight and elbows high, and above all to avoid leaning forward. As with the back squat, keep your heels on the floor and control as described above.

➜ Dumbbell squat

Similar to the barbell squat but with weights in the hands. More emphasis is placed on the quads. Keep the head up and looking forward. Squat as normal so the knee is about 90° before returning to the start position.

➜ Jump squat

This exercise can be performed with just body weight and with a barbell across the back of the shoulders. A squat is performed as usual, either weighted or unweighted. From the bottom point, drive powerfully down through the heels to explode up into the air. As you land, cushion and drop down into a squat again and repeat.

Bulgarian split squat Will improve: Swimming, cycling, running

➡ Performed in a similar fashion to the lunge (see below), but with the rear foot raised on a step/bench. Stand with feet parallel and pointing forwards just under shoulder-width apart. The arms are crossed in front of the body. Place one foot, say the left, on a bench, step or block behind you. Toes should be an inch from the edge nearest the body but no more. With the right foot planted the right leg should be bent until the upper part of the leg is parallel with the ground and the rear knee is lowered to an inch off the floor (it shouldn't touch the floor). The right knee shouldn't go further forward than the right foot; if it does, then a longer step must be taken next time. It's important to keep the back straight and upright – don't lean forward. The right leg then powers the body upright by pushing off the floor through the heel. Do a set number of reps and then repeat for the left leg.

● Works the quads, hamstrings, glutes and core.

Progressions

➡ **Barbell and dumbbell variants as described for the preceding exercise.**

Lunges Will improve: Swimming, cycling, running

Like the squat, the lunge can be performed with or without weight. Again, it's basically the same in either case.

➡ Stand with feet parallel and pointing forwards just under shoulder-width apart. As with the squat it's important to keep the hands from supporting the legs, so the arms are crossed in front of the body. With one foot, say the right, take a large step forward, around shoulder-width and a half. Ensure both feet remain pointing forward as if on train tracks. With the right foot planted the right leg should be bent until its upper part is parallel with the ground and the left knee is just under an inch off the floor, not touching it. The right knee shouldn't go further forward than the right foot; if it does then a longer step must be taken next time. It's important to keep the back straight and upright; don't lean forward. The right leg then powers the body upright by pushing off the floor and the right foot is returned to its starting point next to the left. Repeat for the left leg.

● Works the quads, hamstrings and glutes.

Progressions

➜ **Barbell lunges**
With the barbell in the same position as for squats, the same exercise is performed, paying particular attention to staying upright and taking a long enough stride forward each time.

➜ **Dumbbell lunges**
As per normal lunges but with dumbbells of equal weight in each hand, allowed to hang naturally at the sides of the body. It's important to stop the dumbbells swinging wildly. This exercise has some effect on the grip (forearms) and shoulders.

Lunges (continued)

→ Walking lunges

These can be performed with or without a barbell or dumbbells. Start the exercise as normal, but instead of powering back to the start position off the right foot, the left foot steps forward to meet the right foot. The exercise is then performed on the left leg. In this manner a set amount of ground can be covered by 'walking lunges'.

→ Overhead barbell lunge

Holding a (light) barbell over the crown of your head, with hands gripping the bar as wide apart as is comfortable, perform lunges as normal, keeping the bar steady and in that position. This is great for core strength and shoulder stability, as well as leg strength.

Step-overs Will improve: Swimming, cycling, running

Using a bench or sturdy box, one foot (say left) is stepped up on to the box as in step-ups. The other foot (right) is then stepped over, without touching the box, and on to the ground on the other side. Step the left foot to join it. Turn around and repeat, but right foot first. Always ensure you step over in a controlled manner and don't just flop down as if you're tired. The step down is so controlled it's almost an eccentric lower.

● Works the quads, glutes and hamstrings.

Progressions

→ Barbell and dumbbell variants as described for the preceding exercises.

Step-ups   Will improve: Swimming, cycling, running

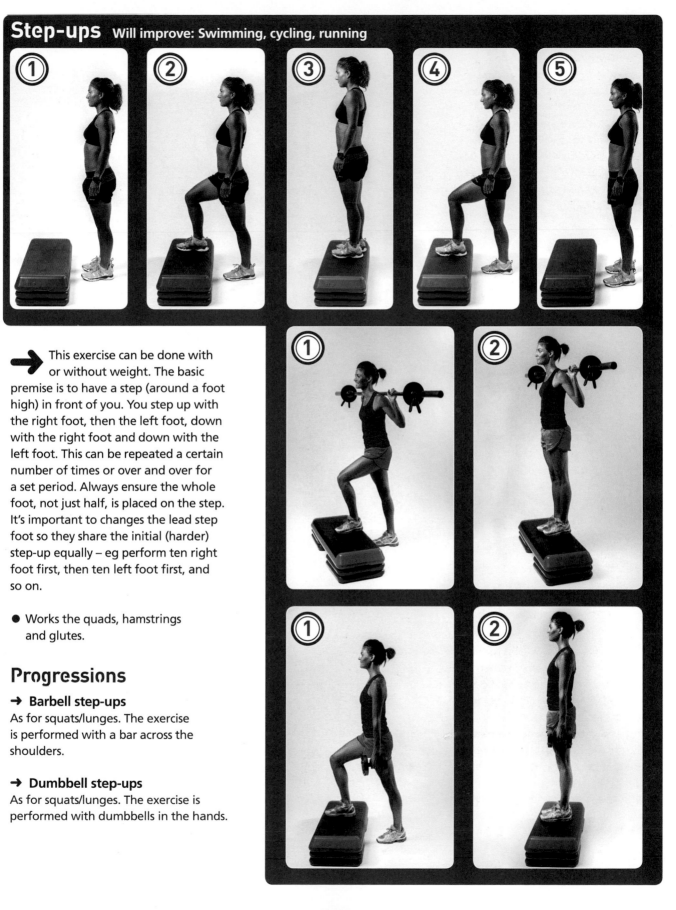

This exercise can be done with or without weight. The basic premise is to have a step (around a foot high) in front of you. You step up with the right foot, then the left foot, down with the right foot and down with the left foot. This can be repeated a certain number of times or over and over for a set period. Always ensure the whole foot, not just half, is placed on the step. It's important to changes the lead step foot so they share the initial (harder) step-up equally – eg perform ten right foot first, then ten left foot first, and so on.

● Works the quads, hamstrings and glutes.

Progressions

➔ **Barbell step-ups**
As for squats/lunges. The exercise is performed with a bar across the shoulders.

➔ **Dumbbell step-ups**
As for squats/lunges. The exercise is performed with dumbbells in the hands.

Side step-ups

➡ The same exercise, but standing side on. The lead foot must step on far enough to allow the other foot on as well. Remember to change sides. Any weighted variations could be used. The adductors (insides of the legs) are also worked during this exercise.

Leg press Will improve: Swimming, cycling, running

➡ A simple weights machine that mimics the squat action. Although it's effective it's not as good as the real squat exercise. Useful in a general muscular programme and especially good for building strength following an injury or long period of inactivity, as it requires less stabilising muscles than the squat.

Sit in the machine, ensure the knees are around 90°, select a sensible weight and press it through the heels. Control the weight and never just 'drop' it.

Leg extension Will improve: Cycling, running

➡ An isolation exercise for the quads using a specific machine. Especially good following injury or to correct a muscle imbalance. Sit in the machine. Ensure the cushioned supports are correctly placed for your body. The padding you push against should be in the ankle/lower shin area not the foot, as this would cause injuries to the ankle ligaments.

Leg curl   Will improve: Cycling, running

➡ An isolation exercise for the hamstrings using a specific machine. Especially good following injury or to correct a muscle imbalance, which many people have in their hamstrings when compared to their quads. Lie in the machine, ensuring the supports are correctly placed for your body. The padding you push against should be at the bottom of the calf. A common mistake is to lift too much weight, so be careful, the hamstrings are easily pulled. Ensure a thorough warm-up prior to this exercise.

Leg curl with partner   Will improve: Swimming, cycling, running

➡ A simple exercise that isolates the hamstring. The exerciser lies on the floor face down. The partner kneels over the exerciser's lower legs, putting weight though the exerciser's calf muscles thus pinning them to the ground. The exerciser then contracts the hamstrings to pivot through the knees to lift the whole body upright. Beware – some people find this exercise very tough.

Standing calf raise   Will improve: Cycling, running

➡ Either from the floor, or on the edge of a step, the calf raise involves going up on tiptoe from a position with the feet pointing forward just under shoulder-width apart. A momentary pause at the top should be followed by a slow return to the start point.

● Some balance is required for this exercise.

Progressions

➜ Barbell calf raise
As above but performed with a barbell on the shoulders as for the squat. Control must be maintained to ensure the weight doesn't cause the body to 'fall' forward. Therefore the core must be kept tight and the back upright.

➜ Dumbbell calf raise
As per squats/lunges, dumbbells can be held in both hands so that the grip/forearm is also worked. Balance is again key.

➜ Seated calf raise
While sat on the edge of a bench, a dumbbell is placed on the fleshy part of the end of the quad/knee of the leg to be exercised and the weight is 'lifted' by going on to tiptoe with the other foot. Pause at the top before slowly returning to the start point. Ensure both legs are exercised equally.

Deadlift Will improve: Swimming, cycling, running

➡️ Place a barbell (light to start with) on the ground in front of you with the bar touching your shins. Take hold of it in both hands a little wider than shoulder-width apart, ensuring your hands/arms are placed outside your legs. Many people prefer a 'split grip' (ie one hand overgrasp, one hand undergrasp), but it's personal preference. Ensure thumbs are around the bar. Arms should be straight, head up, chest up and out. It's important to look straight ahead with shoulders back to keep the back straight. Take a big breath and hold it to make the body/core/back solid and tight. Exhale as you complete the lift: the bar should be lifted in a slow controlled manner. Pulling is done by extending legs and hips and pushing the feet into the floor. Arms and back remain straight and the bar is kept close to the body. At the top there should be a slight pause before holding your breath again and returning the bar to the floor under control, pushing the hips back.

NB: Ensure the back is kept straight at all times! Always return the weight to a 'stop' on the floor before repeating. Do not bounce the weight.

A compound exercise that works the lower back, the glutes, adductors, hamstrings, quads, lats, traps and the grip strength.

Plyometric jumps Will improve: Swimming, cycling, running

➡️ Stand in front of a box or step with feet shoulder-width apart. The box should be knee to hip height depending on your ability and the time you've trained. Jump on to the box, landing on both feet at the same time. Cushion and try to land silently. It helps some people to touch the box with their fingertips on landing. Step down, reset and repeat.

Lower back exercises

Whether running, cycling or swimming, the lower back supports our upper body, flexes our hips and gives our legs that strong foundation. A weak lower back will lead to fatigue, bad posture, slower times and eventual injury.

Stiff-legged Romanian deadlift — Will improve: Swimming, cycling, running

Like the deadlift, place a barbell (light to start with) on the ground in front of you with the bar touching your shins. Take hold of it in both hands a little wider than shoulder-width apart, ensuring your hands/arms are placed outside your legs. The grip can be overgrasp or undergrasp. Arms should be straight, head up, and chest up and out. It's important to look straight ahead with shoulders back to keep your back straight.

The only real difference to the deadlift is that the legs are kept almost straight. They aren't locked, but only very slightly bent. The bar should be lifted up using the lower back muscles. There should be a slight pause at the top before returning the bar to the floor under control. The weight used is generally far lighter than in a normal deadlift.

● A compound exercise that works the lower back, glutes and hamstrings.

Dorsal raise   Will improve: Swimming, cycling, running

→ Lie face down on the floor with fingertips on temples and shoulders relaxed. Lift the chest off the floor while keeping the lower body on it. Hold briefly, then gently lower to the floor, breathing out.

● Works the muscles of the erector spinae of the lower back.

Progressions

→ Dorsal raise on fitball
As above but with hips/lower abs resting on a fitball and upper body curled over it. Toes should be in contact with the ground with feet more than shoulder-width apart for stability. Lift up and hold for a second before curling the upper body back around the ball.

→ Superman dorsals
Lie on your front with the legs straight and arms extended above the head. Lift one arm and the opposite leg a few inches off the floor and hold for a few seconds. Once complete, slowly lower back to the floor. Repeat for the opposite arm and leg.

Good morning Will improve: Swimming, cycling, running

➡ This involves placing a bar/barbell across the shoulders behind the neck. Stand with feet shoulder-width apart. Ensure legs are kept straight and back is straight and not rounded. While keeping the head facing forward, bend forward until the upper body is parallel to the ground. Hold for a split second, then return to the start position.

Progression

➡ **Holding dumbbells**
The same exercise but holding dumbbells instead of a barbell across the shoulders. Dumbbells have to be held, not rested. This is a harder exercise as the shoulders/arms must also work.

Streamline hold Will improve: Swimming

➡ Lie on a bench with your hips on the top edge. Have a training partner hold or sit on your lower legs. Perform a dorsal raise so that your body is in a straight line. Hold for a set period of time. Start with 20-second holds, then move up to 30, 40 and 60 seconds.

Core exercises

The core is similar to the lower back as it also supports the legs and upper body. A weak core will break under duress and injury will occur.

Pelvic lifts/bridging Will improve: Swimming, cycling, running

➡ Lie on your back with your knees bent and arms at your sides. Raise the pelvis up towards the ceiling so the shoulders, hips and knees are in line. Hold the position for a few seconds, ensuring the glutes are squeezed while holding. Release the position and lower back to the floor.

● Works the lower back, abdominals, glutes and hamstrings.

Progression

➡ Leg lift bridge
As above, but once in the upper position extend one leg from the knee until it's straight. Lower this leg and repeat with the other leg. There's a lot of control in this exercise. It's important to keep the hips steady and level – don't allow then to 'dip' or drop to one side. The core is exercised slightly more in this variation.

The plank   Will improve: Swimming, cycling, running

➡ One of the most underused and underrated core exercises around, but so simple and with so many variations that a whole workout can be designed around it. Despite its apparent simplicity it's actually relatively hard and commonly performed badly.

Lie face down, keeping the feet and legs together, and raise the upper body by leaning on the forearms and elbows. The head should be kept up and not allowed to hang. Shoulders, hips, knees and ankles should be in line at all times; the waist/lower back particularly shouldn't be allowed to sag or be raised into the air. Once the correct position has been achieved it should be maintained for a set period. Try 30 seconds to begin with, then increase a minute at a time. A five-minute plank is particularly impressive.

Progressions

➜ On hands
Instead of resting the weight on the elbows, the hands are used. Basically the fully extended press-up position is held.

➜ One arm
The normal plank exercise but with only one forearm, elbow or hand in contact with the ground. The other arm should be placed behind the back.

The plank (continued)

➜ On fitball
Performing the plank with the feet or arms on a fitball greatly increases its difficulty. The instability of the ball means the core has to work really hard to maintain the plank position.

➜ Leg lift
The normal plank is performed, but once the position is achieved the legs are raised alternately, completely straight, rotating from the hips. This works the glutes but also unbalances the plank and causes the core to work harder to readjust. This can be performed for a set time or a certain number of lifts.

➜ Arm lift
As above, but instead of raising the legs the arms are raised. The feet are kept together on the floor. Again, raising the arms unbalances you and makes the core work harder.

➜ Side plank
The body is turned to face one side or the other and the plank is performed on the forearm in contact with the ground, directly under the shoulder. It's important to keep shoulder, hip and knee in line and not allow the hips to sink to the floor.

173

Torso/abdominal exercises

The lower back and core go hand-in-hand with the abdominal muscles: the recurs abdominus, obliques and transverse abdominus. Training these will improve strength and power in all exercises and events, as well as making breathing easier when fatigued.

The sit-up   Will improve: Swimming, cycling, running

→ While lying on your back with legs bent, feet together, knees together and arms out stretched, sit up under control to a near vertical position. Ideally the feet should remain flat on the floor. Don't be tempted to put the hands behind the head and pull up through the arms – this will injure the neck. Once vertical, ensure open chest at the top position. Then lie back under control so that the head and shoulders are back in contact with the floor. Repeat the exercise ensuring your form is correct.

Regression

→ **The half-sit**

If you find the regular sit-up difficult, try putting your hands on top of your thighs and sliding them up to touch the tops of your knees. This should gently lift the torso off the floor and start exercising the correct muscles to improve regular sit-ups. However, don't allow the body to 'flop' back down to the ground – this will injure the back. Lower under control, eccentrically.

The sit-up (continued)

Progressions

→ Weight across chest

As for regular sit-up, but instead of placing fingers on the temples hold a weight placed on the chest under crossed arms. The abs have to work harder when sitting up.

→ Weight outstretched

As above but instead of holding the weight across the chest it's held in the air directly above the head. As the sit-up is performed the weight stays above the head, on the way up and the way down. It's important to keep it directly above the head and not allow it to come forward over the chest (which makes the exercise easier). This exercise has some effect on the shoulders depending on the weight held.

→ On fitball

As for normal sit-up, but instead of being done on the floor it's performed lying with the back on a fitball. Due to the instability of the ball the general core muscles and abs have to work harder to exercise and remain balanced.

Reverse crunch/knees to chest

➡ Lie on your back with hands flat to the floor, either by your side or just under your backside, to flatten the lower back. Keeping upper and mid back on the floor, bring the legs in towards the chest, sucking the abs in as you do so. The knees should be rocked towards the face, ensuring the hips/lower back are curled off the floor.

Toes to the sky

➡ Lie on your back with your legs straight up at 90° to your body. Place the hands next to the body or just under the buttocks to flatten the lower back. Push up from the abdominals with your legs pointing straight up. Aim to force the toes as high as possible. Control down (don't flop) and repeat.

Flutter kicks

➡ Lie on your back with your hands on the ground by your side or just under your buttocks to flatten the lower back. Raise your legs about 6in off the ground and perform 'flutter' kicks in the air as if you were lying on your back in water trying to propel yourself along (kick from the hip, not the knee). Keep the legs as straight as possible at all times and point the toes.

Heel push/hamstring contracted sit-up

The heels are used to pull against something put between them and the buttocks under the bent legs. A small rucksack, a 20kg disc weight or even a football could be used. By using the heels to pull in against the object, the hamstring muscles are contracted. This means that the hip flexors must relax. By relaxing these the exercise becomes very abdominal-specific and is thus surprisingly difficult at first.

Bar rotation

Sit on the end of a bench with an Olympic bar or broomstick across the shoulders. Rotate the waist as far round as possible while keeping the head facing forwards. This can be done relatively swiftly, which will increase momentum.

Jack-knife

Get into the press-up position but with hands on the floor and feet on a fitball. From here, bring the knees into the chest by contracting the abs and rolling the toes along the fitball. Return to the extended press-up position and then repeat.

Side bends

→ This is an oblique-specific exercise that involves standing up straight with feet shoulder-width apart, holding a dumbbell or other form of weight in one hand. Imagine the body is between two panes of glass so can't bend forward or backwards. Bend sideways to lower the hand holding the weight until it's in line with your knee, then lean all the way over to the other side to touch the opposite knee with your free hand. Repeat a certain number of times. Ensure you perform the same number on the other side.

Progressions

→ **Double weight side bends**
The same exercise as above, but with a dumbbell or equivalent in both hands.

→ **Saxon side bends**
Still imagining yourself between two panes of glass, a weight is held above the head with straight arms. A bit like a tree swaying in the wind the body pivots at the waist to the side, then back to the centre, then to the other side and centre. A small weight is best to start with, as this is quite a challenge.

Wood chops

➡ Usually performed holding a light weight, though it can be performed without. Holding the weight/arms out in front at about eye/chest level, bend the legs and rotate the torso to one side and lower the weight to the floor at the outside of the foot on that side. In an explosive movement, rotate the torso back and bring the weight back to the centre and beyond, up to the highest point of the opposite side, as if diagonally from the foot on the other side. Once the weight/arms are at the high point, repeat the exercise as quickly as possible, but still controlled. Ensure both sides are exercised equally.

● Works the core and legs.

Progressions

➡ **Cable wood chops**
Using a cable machine, select a relatively light weight. Take the cable handle in the hand closest to the machine and step out, taking up the tension. Allow your opposite arm to come across the body and take hold over the top of the other hand. Keeping your arms at arms' length, take them across the body to the far side without turning the hips at all: they should remain forward at all times. Hold for a split second, then return to start. Repeat for desired reps and change sides.

Upper body exercises

These exercises will generally only help with swimming strength, power and prehab. However, a strong set of arms and shoulders can be really helpful for generating power in running, so is certainly not worth ignoring if you feel your swimming is already of a good standard.

CHEST

Dumbbell/barbell chest press

➡ Lay on a bench or the floor with a barbell or dumbbells in the hands. From straight arms, lower on to your chest as you inhale, pause, then exhale as you push up again. Keep weights above chest at all times. Dumbbells are harder than a barbell as more control and stability is required from the shoulders.

Press-up

➡ Start face-down with hands flat on the floor shoulder-width apart, head up and forward, legs and feet together, and back straight. Lower chest to floor (or within 2–5cm of it). Push down through the hands to come up to start position, breathing out as you come up. Ensure elbows stay tucked into sides and arms are straight at top of the push. Pause, then repeat.

Pec flys

➡ Lay on your back on a bench or the floor holding a light set of dumbbells directly above your chest, with the elbows ever so slightly bent. Open the arms, allowing the weights to move down towards the ground. Keep in line with the shoulder, arms slightly bent, and don't over-extend. Pause at the bottom, then squeeze your pectorals and return the weights to the top. Exhale as you come back to the starting point.

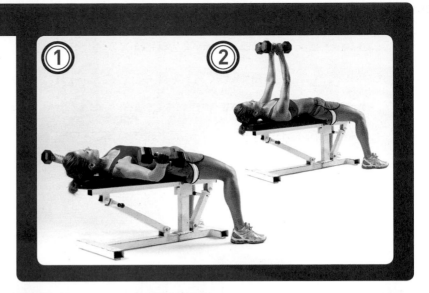

Pull-over

➡ Lay on a bench holding one dumbbell by the neck, above the head. Keeping the arms slightly bent and the back against the bench, allow the dumbbell to lower towards the ground over the head. Pause when in line with the body, then squeeze pectorals to bring dumbbell up above the head while exhaling. Pause and repeat.

Bar dips

➡ While supporting the weight of the body on two parallel bars or a wall, allow the legs to hang naturally below. Bend the arms so that the upper arm is parallel with the ground. Hold for a split second, then push down through the hands, exhale, and return to the top point with straight arms.

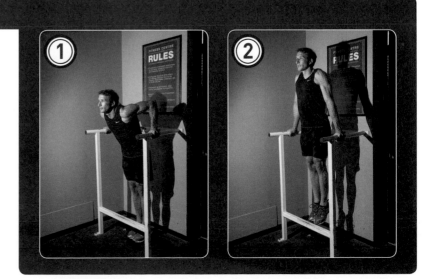

BACK

Pull-up

➡️ With both hands gripping a bar, palms facing away from you about shoulder-width apart, allow the body to hang naturally. Tensing the abs/core and holding the feet slightly in front of the body, pull up until your chin goes over the bar and your chest comes as close as possible to touching it. Exhale as you do so. Lower under control back into straight-arm hang. Pause and repeat.

Regression

➡️ **1 Chin-up (palms facing you)**
As for a normal pull-up but with palms facing towards you rather than away.

➡️ **Feet rested on floor**
Perform the same pull-up movement, but pull the chest to a bar while the heels are rested on the floor.

➡️ **2 Friend assist**
A friend holds your waist and helps, as minimally as possible, so that a pull-up can be achieved.

➡️ **Elastic support**
A piece of theraband (physios' elastic) or an elastic exercise band is attached to the bar to make the pull-up easier.

Lat pull-down

➡ Using a machine in the gym, grip the bar as for the pull-up above. Pull the bar down below the chin, pause, and return under control to the straight arm position. Then repeat. Keep the core tense throughout and don't swing the back.

Single-arm row

➡ While resting either one knee and a hand or just one hand on a bench, let a dumbbell hang naturally towards the floor in the other hand. Keeping the back straight and head up, pull the weight up towards the hip and lower ribs while exhaling. Hold this position for a split second, then lower under control and repeat.

Double-arm row with dumbbell/barbell

➡ As above, but with both arms at a time while lying prone on a bench.

SHOULDERS

Military press

➡ While standing straight, holding a barbell across the chest, tuck the pelvis under by holding the abs tight. As you exhale, push the weight upwards, allowing the head to come through the arms to ensure the weight goes above the shoulders and not in front of them. Pause, then lower under control. Keep the elbows high to control the weight. Repeat. Standing makes your core work far more, but you must ensure you don't lean back to use your stronger chest muscles.

Progressions

➡ **1 Dumbbells**
As above, but with two separate weights rather than one bar.

➡ **2 Standing lateral raise**
Same standing position as above, holding a dumbbell in each hand at your sides. While exhaling, raise the arms to a T position, hold for a split second, then lower. Don't swing the back. Keep the core tight and fixed.

➡ **3 Front raise**
A friend holds your waist and helps, as minimally as possible, so that a pull-up can be achieved.

➡ **4 Bent-over raise**
As with standing lateral raise, but bent over forward while standing, sitting on the edge of a bench or lying prone on a bench.

External rotation lying

 Lying on your side, with one arm bent from the elbow at 90 degrees, hold a dumbbell in that hand and raise as far as is comfortable. Hold for a split second then lower under control. Repeat.

Internal rotation standing

As above, but rotating in the opposite direction.

Prehab not rehab

Internal and external rotations are great exercises for all swimmers and triathletes, to protect the rotator cuff from injury. Remember, prehab rather than rehab.

TRICEPS

Close press-up

➡️ As for the press-up, but with the hands brought closer together. Elbows are kept into the sides.

Dumbbell extension

➡️ While lying flat on a bench, hold a dumbbell in each hand straight above the head. Inhale as you bend the elbows, still keeping your upper arms at right angles to the floor. The lower arms then move so they're parallel with the ground. Hold the position for a split second, then exhale and return to the start position.

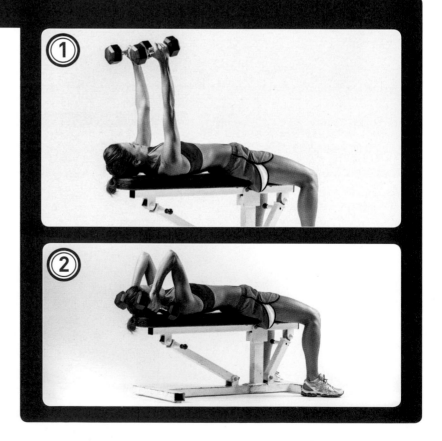

Bench dip

➡ With your arms and legs straight, place your palms on the end of a bench, box or wall. Lower so that your backside moves towards the floor and your upper arms bend to become parallel to the floor. Pause for a second, then exhale as you push up to the start point again.

Running backwards

Running backwards has gained momentum in recent years, not only as a rehab tool for certain injuries (jumper's knee) but also as a form of fitness and in particular as a form of conditioning for the leg muscles. Backwards running is classed as a 'retro movement', which means the reverse of any normal movement.

Running backwards initially feels very unnatural, but with practice a decent speed can be achieved. It's worth starting out with backward walking, and then move into very slow backward jogging. It's also worth doing only a short stint initially, say 3–5 minutes, then 8 or 10 minutes and before long 20 minutes, 30 minutes and beyond. Personally I'd advise running backwards only on treadmills until you achieve a degree of proficiency, then perhaps on grass. Running up and down hills backwards definitely adds difficulty, but is also relatively dangerous.

Downhill

Running backwards downhill is dangerous, full stop. Before doing it make sure you're very confident at running backwards on a treadmill or on grass. It's very easy to pick up speed when running backwards downhill, but don't be tempted to do so quicker than you're ready to. If you do fall, try to absorb any impact with your arms and your backside so that your head is less likely to hit the ground. Proficient backwards runners also advise learning to roll out using a backwards roll.

UK and London championships in backward running exist, so you could include these in your tri training programme.

I first encountered running backwards while in the Marines, when I suffered from quite a bad tear to my patella tendon. As I'd put up with the injury for around nine months it was going to take the same sort of time to heal. Part of my rehab, before I could run forwards again, was running backwards, the theory being that there's far less impact than running forwards, added to which backward running is almost an eccentric movement, which is what's necessary to help heal a tendinopathy (be it patella, Achilles or biceps).

Uphill

Compared to running backwards downhill, running uphill isn't very dangerous. It's not easy to run quickly when running backwards and doing so uphill makes it even more so, meaning it will always be at a lower speed. Again, if you do fall try to absorb any impact with your arms and your backside so that your head is less likely to hit the ground.

Physical benefits

Research suggests that running backwards helps balance out some of the stresses and strains that can occur during normal running. It's thought to work the tissues oppositely. In backwards running the heel is used to push off rather than the ball of the foot. Pushing off in this way works the tibialis anterior muscle (which gets little work in normal running) as well as the ball of the foot, which is good for prehabbing for barefoot running.

The main benefit of backwards running is that the muscles are used in the opposite way to how they are in forward running, ie an eccentric version of a concentric movement is performed instead of a concentric version of an eccentric movement (hence me being asked to run backwards when rehabbing my patella tendinitis, usually rehabbed using eccentric lowering). Whether for rehab or for general fitness training, both concentric and eccentric movements have advantages and hence backwards running could be included.

Other advantages include gains in balance, and enjoyment from doing something different and challenging. Lastly, due to the constant need to look behind more neck mobility is learned than in forward running. Although this can initially stress the neck muscles, in the long term it can lead to adaptations in them and a less rigid style when running forwards.

Prehab

The term prehab refers to an exercise programme performed to prevent injury, whereas rehab or rehabilitation is performed following injury to ensure full recovery and a swift return to fitness. In general a prehab programme will have one or both of two elements:

1 Sports-specific focused exercises and activities for all three of your triathlon event needs, to specifically avoid injuries that tend to plague triathletes.

2 Personal exercises to either prevent the return of an old injury, or prevent you from suffering an injury you're likely to be prone to (overpronation or rotator cuff, for example).

The philosophy of prehab is simply to prevent injuries, but its success depends on people performing the exercises. The major obstacle to this is that compared to swimming, biking or running, prehab can seem boring and uninspiring.

The sports therapy world suggests that everyone should include a prehab programme in their training, and the more advanced you becomes as a triathlete the more necessary it becomes. The thought process behind this is that as we undertake our daily training regime we can cause negative effects within our bodies, such as tight muscles and strength imbalances. Imbalances can occur naturally with any activity but can be reinforced with each workout, and it's such imbalances that are usually to blame for injuries.

Prehab programme

A good prehab programme should aim to aid total body balance and provide sports-specific exercises to strengthen the areas required in triathlon. Balances should include range of motion, strength, coordination and stabilisation. For tri competitors, much of the focus of these prehab exercises will be on coordination and stabilisation of the legs, knees, hips, shoulders, chest, back and core. Core instability is common for triathletes, yet the core is really, really important in all three disciplines, especially when you're fatigued. Such core instability is mainly due to a lack of education and understanding. Simply performing upper and lower body weights and tri session routines leaves the core without a direct focus or training routine, and can predispose us to injuries from a weak core.

When to prehab

Prehab can be done one of two ways: as part of a workout or as an independent session. If performed as part of a workout, simply perform a few prehab exercises as part of the warm-up or cool-down. Personally I prefer doing so in the warm-up, especially if the session is going to be hard, as afterwards fatigue may prevent good quality exercises. If doing prehab as a separate session, it's usually relatively low tempo, so can be used as rest days or as part of a long brick-style session to mimic the fatigue of a race (see Chapter 15).

You don't need to perform all the relevant prehab exercises every day. Far from it. Off-season, choose those that will strengthen the areas where you have weaknesses, though you may actually want to do a little of everything to support your active recovery. Start by following the exercises you choose two or three times a week; vary those that train certain muscles to keep the body guessing, and ensure overload (see Chapter 4) so that improvements are made. During the season you may only need to condition once a week, but ensure the exercises are those that will support your weak areas, as prehab to stop you getting injured or re-injured. Such exercises will certainly help you avoid injury, though some injuries are just bad luck.

⏱ Conclusion

Whether as prehab or for general conditioning, weight training is absolutely imperative if you want to be a decent competitor. If you look at professional triathletes you'll find they spend a significant time in the gym conditioning their bodies to be able to (1) cope with the training and racing they expect of it, and (2) to be faster, stronger and more enduring than if they only swam, biked and ran. Unfortunately conditioning is what most novice, amateur and even many pro triathletes neglect, their thought process being that the more actual swimming, cycling or running they do the better they'll be at those events. This is, sadly, wrong, and often results in plateaus, frustration and overtraining injuries, as their muscles aren't conditioned. Weight training and conditioning helps avoid injury, builds a strong healthy body, and tones the specific muscles needed to perform the functions asked of them. Simple.

CHAPTER 11
TRAINING PROGRAMMES

This chapter provides programmes for the various types of triathlon that you may be training for. Within these programmes there are sessions of varying difficulty or intensity. As per the heart rate training explained in Chapter 4, the heart rate percentages for the various sessions' difficulty levels are given at the beginning of each programme, to help you achieve the right training intensity for each session.

One for all and all for one

As I've already said, we're all different, and what works for you may not work for the next person. I'm therefore usually not a fan of a 'one size fits all' programme for any type of training/conditioning/preparation. However, this book wouldn't be complete without training programmes for the various length tris out there, so they're here to give you an idea or basis for your own training and training programmes.

I've included a cross-section of training types, from easy sessions to interval sessions, brick sessions and where necessary race length conditioning sessions. If they don't suit you, simply adapt them as necessary. Remember, if you are a runner coming into triathlon, chances are you need to weight the swimming and biking side of things more, as your running should just be kept up for technique and fitness.

Adaption and implementation

I have assumed that most people have a full time job and weekends off, so the programmes are designed around that lifestyle. If your training times need to be different, then adapt the programme to suit you and implement it as best you can. What do I mean by this? Well, for example, I've made Sunday the long training day and Monday the rest day for most of the programmes. This is perfect for the majority of us who work a five-day week, but people who work a four days on, two days off shift pattern or work at weekends will need to modify the programme to coincide with the appropriate days of their week.

1 Beginner's four-week programme

➔ Easy/enjoyable 50–60%.
➔ End/recovery zone 60–70%.

➔ Tempo/aerobic zone 70–80%.
➔ Anaerobic threshold zone 80–90%.

Week 1	Type	Intensity	Session
Monday	Run.	Easy.	1min run, 1 min walk x 8.
Tuesday	Swim.	Easy.	Alternate lengths – front crawl pull buoy, on back leg-kick, x 10.
Wednesday	Bike.	End.	30min.
Thursday	Rest.	Rest.	Rest.
Friday	Swim.	End.	4 lengths of every drill with 20sec rest after each 2 lengths.
Saturday	Bike.	End.	30mins.
	Conditioning.	Easy.	Upper body.
Sunday	Brick.	End.	25min bike straight into 1min run, 1min walk x 10.

Week 2	Type	Intensity	Session
Monday	Rest.	Rest.	Rest.
Tuesday	Run.	Easy.	1min run, 1min walk x 10.
Wednesday	Swim.	End.	Warm up with 1 length of every drill, alt 2 lengths pull buoy, 2 lengths kicking on back x10, 4 lengths front crawl to finish, 30sec between sets.
Thursday	Bike.	End.	40min.
	Conditioning.	Easy.	Whole body.
Friday	Rest.	Rest.	Rest.
Saturday	Swim.	End.	Warm up with 2 of every drill, then 2 lengths pull buoy, 1st easy, 2nd hard x 15, then 2 lengths front crawl, 2 lengths kick on back x 5, 30sec between sets.
Sunday	Brick.	End.	25min bike straight into 1min run, 1min walk x 10.

Week 3	Type	Intensity	Session
Monday	Rest.	Rest.	Rest.
Tuesday	Run.	Easy.	1min run, 1min walk x 12.
Wednesday	Swim.	End.	Warm up with 1 length of every drill, alt 4 lengths pull buoy, 4 lengths kicking on back x6, 4 x 4 lengths front crawl to finish, 60sec between sets.
Thursday	Bike.	End.	50min.
Friday	Rest.	Rest.	Rest.
Saturday	Swim.	End.	Warm up with 2 of every drill, then 4 lengths pull buoy, 1st 2 easy, 2nd 2 hard x 15, then 4 lengths front crawl, 2 lengths kick on back x 8, 60sec between sets.
	Conditioning.	Easy.	Upper body.
Sunday	Brick.	End.	40min bike straight into 90sec run, 30sec walk x 10.

Week 4	Type	Intensity	Session
Monday	Rest.	Rest.	Rest.
Tuesday	Run.	Easy.	90sec run, 30sec walk x 15.
	Conditioning.	Easy.	Legs.
Wednesday	Swim.	End.	Warm up with 2 lengths of every drill, 4 lengths front crawl x 20, 60sec between sets.
Thursday	Bike.	End.	60min.
Friday	Rest.	Rest.	Rest.
Saturday	Swim.	End.	Warm up with 4 lengths of every drill, 6 lengths front crawl x 10, 60sec between sets, 4 x 2 lengths kicking on back to finish.
Sunday	Brick.	End.	45min bike straight into 15min continuous run.

2 Eight-week sprint programme

→ **Easy/enjoyable 50–60%.**
→ **Recovery/end zone 60–70%.**

→ **Aerobic/tempo zone 70–80%.**
→ **Anaerobic threshold zone 80–90%.**

Week 1	Type	Intensity	Session
Monday	Run.	Easy.	15min.
Tuesday	Bike.	End.	6 miles.
Wednesday	Swim.	Drills.	2 lengths of each drill, 30sec rest between.
	Run.	Easy.	20min.
Thursday	Swim.	Easy.	400m as 2 x 200m blocks, 2min rest between.
	Bike.	Easy.	20min.
Friday	Run.	Intervals.	5min easy warm-up, Tabata 20sec flat out, 10sec rest x 8, 10min easy.
Saturday	Bike.	Easy.	6 miles.
Sunday	Run.	Easy.	20min.

Week 2	Type	Intensity	Session
Monday	Rest.	Rest.	Rest.
Tuesday	Swim.	Interval.	2 lengths of each drill as warm-up, 2 lengths fast, 20sec rest x 10, 4 lengths easy.
	Conditioning.	Easy.	Upper body.
Wednesday	Bike.	End.	7 miles.
Thursday	Swim.	Drills.	4 lengths of each drill, 40sec rest between.
	Run.	Easy.	20min.
Friday	Swim.	Easy.	400m.
Saturday	Bike.	Tempo.	7 miles.
Sunday	Run.	Easy.	20min.

Week 3	Type	Intensity	Session
Monday	Rest.	Rest.	Rest.
Tuesday	Swim.	Tempo.	100m at race pace x 5, 1min rest between.
	Run.	Easy.	25min.
Wednesday	Bike.	Tempo.	7 miles.
Thursday	Run.	Intervals.	4min warm-up easy, Tabata 20sec flat out, 10sec rest x 8, 2min easy, Tabata 20sec flat out, 10sec easy x 8, 6min easy.
	Conditioning.	Easy.	Legs/core.
Friday	Swim.	Drills.	4 lengths of each drill, 40sec rest.
Saturday	Bike.	End.	7 miles.
Sunday	Run.	Easy/tempo.	14min easy/6min tempo.

Week 4	Type	Intensity	Session
Monday	Rest.	Rest.	Rest.
Tuesday	Swim.	Tempo.	2 lengths of each drill warm-up, 200m tempo, 30sec recovery x 4.
	Conditioning.	Easy.	Upper body/core.
Wednesday	Bike.	Tempo.	8 miles.
Thursday	Run.	Easy.	25min.
Friday	Swim.	Drills.	4 lengths of each drill, 30sec rest.
Saturday	Bike.	End.	8 miles.
Sunday	Run.	Easy/tempo.	5min easy, 10min race pace, 5min easy.

Week 5	Type	Intensity	Session
Monday	Rest.	Rest.	Rest.
Tuesday	Swim.	Easy – open water (if possible).	20min continuous swimming.
Wednesday	Bike.	Tempo.	10 miles.
Thursday	Run.	Intervals.	1min fast, 1min slow jog x 10.
	Conditioning.	Easy.	Whole body.
Friday	Swim.	Easy/drills.	400m/2 lengths of each drill, 20sec rest.
Saturday	Bike.	Tempo.	8 miles.
Sunday	Run.	Easy.	25min.

Week 6	Type	Intensity	Session
Monday	Rest.	Rest.	Rest.
Tuesday	Swim.	Tempo.	600m.
Wednesday	Bike.	Tempo.	12 miles.
Thursday	Run.	Easy/tempo/ easy.	20min (5 easy, 10 tempo, 5 easy).
	Conditioning.	Easy.	Legs/core.
Friday	Swim.	Easy/drills.	500m/2 lengths of each drill, 20sec rest.
Saturday	Bike.	Tempo.	10 miles.
Sunday	Run.	Race pace.	3 miles.

Week 7	Type	Intensity	Session
Monday	Rest.	Rest.	Rest.
Tuesday	Swim.	Tempo – open water (if possible or being trained for).	20min.
	Conditioning.	Easy.	Upper body/core.
Wednesday	Bike.	Tempo.	10 miles.
Thursday	Run.	Easy/race pace.	5min easy, then race pace for 15min.
Friday	Swim.	Easy/drills.	600m/2 lengths of each drill, 30sec rest.
Saturday	Bike.	Tempo.	8 miles.
Sunday	Run.	Easy.	25min.

Week 8	Type	Intensity	Session
Monday	Rest.	Rest.	Rest.
Tuesday	Swim.	Race pace.	2 x half race distance (250m or 375m) with 5min rest and refuel between.
Wednesday	Run.	Intervals (on track where possible).	1 mile (1,600m), 8 x 400m interval, 60sec rest, 800m cool-down.
Thursday	Swim.	Easy.	800m.
	Conditioning.	Easy.	Whole body.
Friday	Rest.	Rest.	Rest.
Saturday	Bike.	Tempo.	12 miles.
Sunday	Run.	Race pace.	20min.

3 Eight-week Olympic programme

→ **Easy/enjoyable 50–60%.**
→ **Recovery/end zone 60–70%.**

→ **Aerobic/tempo zone 70–80%.**
→ **Anaerobic threshold zone 80–90%.**

Week 1	Type	Intensity	Session
Monday	Swim.	End.	1,600m (timed).
Tuesday	Bike.	End.	15 miles.
Wednesday	Run.	Easy.	30min.
	Swim.	Easy.	2 x 500m with 2–5min rest.
Thursday	Bike (as brick).	Tempo.	30min.
	Run (as brick).	Easy.	15min.
Friday	Swim.	Drills.	4 lengths of each drill. 30sec rest.
	Conditioning.	Easy.	Upper body and core.
Saturday	Bike.	Easy.	15 miles.
Sunday	Run.	Easy/tempo/easy.	10min/10min/10min.

Week 2	Type	Intensity	Session
Monday	Rest.	Rest.	Rest.
Tuesday	Swim.	Tempo.	1 mile.
Wednesday	Bike (as brick).	End.	15 miles.
	Run.	Easy.	15min.
Thursday	Swim.	Easy/drills.	Work on personal weak areas.
	Conditioning.	Easy.	Whole body.
Friday	Rest.	Rest.	Rest.
Saturday	Bike.	Easy.	20 miles.
Sunday	Run.	End.	40min.

Week 3	Type	Intensity	Session
Monday	Rest.	Rest.	Rest.
Tuesday	Swim.	Intervals.	2 lengths of each drill warm-up, then 400m intervals x 4 with 1min rest.
Wednesday	Bike.	Easy.	15 miles.
	Conditioning.	Easy.	Upper body/core.
Thursday	Run.	Easy.	30min.
	Swim.	Drills.	Pull buoy and kick on back, 100m each x 8.
Friday	Swim.	Easy.	1,000m.
Saturday	Bike.	End.	20 miles.
Sunday	Run.	Easy/tempo/easy.	15min/15min/15min.

Week 4	Type	Intensity	Session
Monday	Rest.	Rest.	Rest.
Tuesday	Swim.	Intervals/race pace.	750m x 2 with 5min to refuel and recover between.
Wednesday	Bike.	Easy.	20 miles.
Thursday	Run.	Easy.	30min.
	Conditioning.	Easy.	Whole body.
Friday	Swim.	Easy/drills.	500m then 500m of drills.
Saturday	Bike.	Easy/intervals/easy.	15min easy, 60min intervals, 15min easy. During the 60min intervals, once in every 15min perform a set of Tabata sprints, 20sec flat out, 10sec easy, x 8.
Sunday	Run.	Recovery.	45min.

Week 5	Type	Intensity	Session
Monday	Rest.	Rest.	Rest.
Tuesday	Swim.	Tempo (open water if possible).	25min concentrating on good open water/wetsuit technique.
Wednesday	Bike.	Easy.	15 miles.
	Run.	Easy.	20min.
Thursday	Swim.	Easy/drills.	1,000m then drills for personal weak areas.
Friday	Conditioning.	Easy.	Upper body/core.
Saturday	Various.	Tempo.	Race length session 2hr, 1hr conditioning, 40min bike, 20min run.
Sunday	Run.	Recovery.	50min.

Week 6	Type	Intensity	Session
Monday	Rest.	Rest.	Rest.
Tuesday	Swim.	Intervals.	2 lengths fast, 20sec rest x 10.
Wednesday	Bike.	Easy/race pace/easy.	20 miles – 5 easy; then 10 miles of 1 mile race pace, 1 easy, x 5; then 5 easy.
Thursday	Run.	Easy.	40min.
	Conditioning.	Easy.	Legs/core.
Friday	Swim.	Easy.	1 mile (1,600m).
Saturday	Bike.	Easy.	6 miles out, rest/refuel, 6 miles back.
Sunday	Cycle (as brick).	Tempo.	20 miles.
	Run (as brick).	Easy.	30min.

Week 7	Type	Intensity	Session
Monday	Rest.	Rest.	Rest.
Tuesday	Swim.	Intervals.	400m x 4 as fast as possible, 1min rest between sets.
Wednesday	Bike.	Recovery.	20 miles.
Thursday	Run.	Easy/race pace/ easy.	10min easy/400m intervals at race pace x 8 with 2min easy between intervals/10min easy.
Friday	Swim.	Easy.	Drills for 1,600m.
	Conditioning.	Easy.	Upper body/core.
Saturday	Bike.	Intervals.	20min warm-up easy, then 2min hard, 1min recovery x 10, 20 min cool-down easy.
Sunday	Run.	Tempo.	40min.

Week 8	Type	Intensity	Session
Monday	Rest.	Rest.	Rest.
Tuesday	Swim.	Tempo.	1,600m (timed).
Wednesday	Run.	Tempo.	40min.
Thursday	Swim.	Easy/drills.	800m easy/800m drills.
	Run.	Intervals.	5min warm-up, 1min flat out, 1min recovery x 10, 5min easy, 5min race pace, 5min easy.
Friday	Conditioning.	Easy.	Upper body/core.
Saturday	Bike.	Tempo.	25 miles.
Sunday	Run.	Recovery.	60min.

4 Eight-week half-ironman programme

→ **Easy/enjoyable 50–60%.**
→ **Recovery/end zone 60–70%.**

→ **Aerobic/tempo zone 70–80%.**
→ **Anaerobic threshold zone 80–90%.**

Week 1	Type	Intensity	Session
Monday	Swim.	End.	1,600m (timed).
Tuesday	Bike.	End.	25 miles.
Wednesday	Run.	Easy.	40min.
Thursday	Swim.	Easy.	1,600m.
	Bike.	Tempo.	60min.
Friday	Swim.	Drills.	4 lengths of each drill, 30sec rest between. Normal stroke easy at end to make up to 40min.
Saturday	Bike.	Easy.	35 miles.
Sunday	Run.	Easy.	1hr.

Week 2	Type	Intensity	Session
Monday	Rest.	Rest.	Rest.
Tuesday	Swim.	End.	1,800m.
Wednesday	Bike.	End.	30 miles.
Thursday	Run.	Easy.	45min.
	Swim.	Easy/drills/easy.	800m/2 lengths each drill/800m.
Friday	Swim.	Easy.	2,000m.
Saturday	Bike.	Tempo.	40 miles.
Sunday	Run.	End.	1hr.

Week 3	Type	Intensity	Session
Monday	Rest.	Rest.	Rest.
Tuesday	Swim.	Intervals.	200m fast with hard pull x 10, 30sec rest between, 2 lengths each drill to finish.
Wednesday	Bike.	End.	30 miles.
Thursday	Run.	Easy/tempo/easy.	45min total, middle 15–25min tempo if feel good.
	Swim.	Easy/drills/easy.	800m/2 lengths each drill/800m.
Friday	Swim.	Easy.	2,000m.
Saturday	Bike.	Tempo.	40 miles.
Sunday	Various.	End.	Race length session 4hr+, made up of 1.5hr bike, 2hr conditioning, 1hr run.

Week 4	Type	Intensity	Session
Monday	Rest.	Rest.	Rest.
Tuesday	Swim.	Tempo.	1,000m at hard fast pace, 5min recovery and repeat. Must be within 10% of first time for second.
Wednesday	Bike.	End.	35 miles.
Thursday	Run.	Easy.	45min.
	Swim.	Drills.	Work on personal weaknesses.
Friday	Swim.	Easy.	1,800m.
Saturday	Bike.	Intervals.	30min warm-up, 5min hard, 3min easy, repeat 10 times, 10–20min cool-down.
Sunday	Run.	End.	1hr.

Week 5	Type	Intensity	Session
Monday	Rest.	Rest.	Rest.
Tuesday	Swim.	Easy (open water if possible).	1hr.
Wednesday	Bike.	End.	40 miles.
Thursday	Run.	Tempo.	45min.
Friday	Swim.	Drills/easy/drills.	Work on personal weaknesses, then 1,800m concentrating on keeping stroke perfect in those areas just drilled; then repeat drills.
Saturday	Bike.	Easy.	30 miles.
Sunday	Run.	End.	70min.

Week 6	Type	Intensity	Session
Monday	Rest.	Rest.	Rest.
Tuesday	Swim.	Intervals.	100m, 20sec rest x 10.
	Conditioning.	Easy.	Upper body/core.
Wednesday	Bike.	10 miles/intervals/15 miles.	1 mile hard, 5min easy, repeat 10 times.
Thursday	Run.	Easy.	45min.
	Swim.	Easy/drills/easy.	800m/2 lengths each drill/800m.
Friday	Swim.	Easy.	2,000m.
Saturday	Conditioning.	Easy.	Upper body/core.
Sunday	Bike/run (as brick).	Bike tempo/run easy.	40 miles. 1hr.

Week 7	Type	Intensity	Session
Monday	Rest.	Rest.	Rest.
Tuesday	Swim.	Intervals.	200m fast with hard pull x 10, 30sec rest between.
	Conditioning.	Easy.	Legs/core.
Wednesday	Bike.	Easy.	40 miles.
Thursday	Run.	Intervals.	10min warm-up, 800m as fast as possible, same time easy, repeat x 8.
Friday	Swim.	Easy.	2,000m and drills concentrating on personal weak areas.
Saturday	Bike.	Tempo.	40 miles.
Sunday	Various.	Endurance.	Race length session 4hr or more: 40min swim, 2hr bike, 1hr conditioning, 1hr run.

Week 8	Type	Intensity	Session
Monday	Rest.	Rest.	Rest.
Tuesday	Swim.	Drills.	Concentrate on weak areas, 2,000m
Wednesday	Run.	Intervals.	10min warm-up, 800m as fast as possible, same time easy, repeat x 10.
Thursday	Swim.	Easy/tempo/easy.	500m/1000m/500m.
Friday	Run.	Easy.	40min.
Saturday	Bike.	Tempo.	50 miles.
Sunday	Run.	End.	90min.

5 Eight-week ironman programme

➜ **Easy/enjoyable 50–60%.**
➜ **Recovery/end zone 60–70%.**

➜ **Aerobic/tempo zone 70–80%.**
➜ **Anaerobic threshold zone 80–90%.**

Week 1	Type	Intensity	Session
Monday	Swim.	End.	2,500m (timed).
Tuesday	Bike.	End.	40 miles.
Wednesday	Run.	Easy.	45min.
	Swim.	Easy.	2 x 500m with 2–5min rest.
Thursday	Swim.	Easy.	2,000m.
	Bike.	Easy.	90min.
Friday	Swim.	Easy/drills.	1,500m/4 lengths of each drill.
Saturday	Bike.	Easy.	60 miles.
Sunday	Run.	Easy.	60min.

Week 2	Type	Intensity	Session
Monday	Rest.	Rest.	Rest.
Tuesday	Swim.	Easy.	1,600m, 5min rest and refuel, 1,600m.
Wednesday	Bike.	End.	50 miles.
	Run.	Easy.	15min.
Thursday	Swim.	Drills.	Work on personal weak areas.
	Run.	Easy.	60min.
Friday	Swim.	Intervals.	Warm-up, 800m, 1min recovery x 4, cool-down.
Saturday	Bike.	Easy.	75 miles.
Sunday	Run.	End.	75min.
	Swim.	Drills.	Mix of drills for 20min, 2.5min rest/refuel, 20min mix of drills, 2.5min rest/refuel, 15min personal weakness drills.

Week 3	Type	Intensity	Session
Monday	Rest.	Rest.	Rest.
Tuesday	Swim.	Intervals.	100m slow, 100m drills, 10 x 100m with 30sec rest between.
Wednesday	Bike.	Easy.	60 miles.
Thursday	Run.	Easy/tempo/easy.	30min/15min/15min.
	Swim.	Drills.	45min of personal weakness drills.
Friday	Swim.	Easy.	2,200m.
Saturday	Bike.	End.	75 miles.
Sunday	Various.	Easy.	Race length session 5hr or more: 2hr bike, 2hr conditioning, 1.5hr run.

Week 4	Type	Intensity	Session
Monday	Rest.	Rest.	Rest.
Tuesday	Swim.	Intervals/race pace.	600m x 4 with 5min to refuel and recover between.
Wednesday	Bike.	Easy.	60 miles.
Thursday	Run.	Easy.	60min.
	Conditioning.	Easy.	Legs, core and arms exercises.
Friday	Swim.	Easy/drills.	1,000m, 2min rest to refuel, 1,000m.
Saturday	Swim/bike (as bricks).	Drills/end.	45min/75 miles.
Sunday	Run.	Recovery.	90min.

Week 5	Type	Intensity	Session
Monday	Rest.	Rest.	Rest.
Tuesday	Swim.	Tempo (open water if possible).	60min.
Wednesday	Bike.	Easy.	60 miles.
Thursday	Run.	Easy.	45min.
	Conditioning.	Easy.	Upper body/core/legs.
Friday	Swim.	Easy.	2,500m then drills.
Saturday	Bike.	Tempo.	100 miles.
Sunday	Various.	Recovery.	Race-length session 5hr or more: 1hr swim, 2hr bike, 1.5hr conditioning, 1hr run.

Week 6	Type	Intensity	Session
Monday	Rest.	Rest.	Rest.
Tuesday	Swim.	Intervals.	100m slow, 100m drills, 10 x 100m with 30sec rest between.
Wednesday	Bike.	Easy/race pace/ easy.	50 miles: do 5 easy, then do 10 miles, then do intervals of 2 miles race pace and 1 mile easy, x 6, then complete the 50 miles easy.
Thursday	Run.	Easy.	60min.
Friday	Swim.	Intervals.	Warm-up, 100m fast, 50m slow x 16.
Saturday	Bike.	Easy.	25 miles.
Sunday	Bike (as brick).	Tempo.	75 miles.
	Run (as brick).	Easy.	70min.

Week 7	Type	Intensity	Session
Monday	Rest.	Rest.	Rest.
Tuesday	Swim.	Intervals.	900m, 1min rest, 800m, 1min rest, 700m, 600, 500, 400, 300, 200, 100.
Wednesday	Bike.	Recovery.	60 miles.
Thursday	Run.	Easy/race pace/ easy.	40min easy, 15min race pace, 10min easy.
Friday	Swim.	Tempo.	1,900m fast, 5min rest and refuel, 1,900m within 10% time.
Saturday	Bike.	Tempo.	40 miles.
Sunday	Run.	Recovery.	18 miles.

Week 8	Type	Intensity	Session
Monday	Rest.	Rest.	Rest.
Tuesday	Swim.	Tempo.	2,000m, 5min rest and recovery, 2,000m.
Wednesday	Run.	Intervals.	10min warm-up, 800m fast, recovery equal to time taken, repeat 10 times, 10min cool-down.
Thursday	Swim.	Easy/drill.	2,400m easy/1,000m drills.
Friday	Run.	Easy.	45min.
Saturday	Bike.	Tempo.	60 miles.
Sunday	Run.	Recovery.	20 miles.

Training diary

Recording your training and races is something all serious triathletes should do, whether novice or experienced. The reasons are many, but, as an example, let's say you complete a normal 1,500m swim or 10km run and find it particularly difficult, or you're doing a standard session and feel aches in the joints or in certain muscles. If you've recorded your training sessions over the last two weeks, a quick glance would show you if you've been training too hard, had a few really intense sessions already that week, or even that nothing you've done has been any different, in which case you may be coming down with a cold and it's time to whack in some vitamin C and Echinacea.

Conversely, let's say you absolutely smash your personal best for an Olympic triathlon. Short of having great conditions and a good field that push you, reference to your training and nutrition for the weeks leading up to it would enable you to prepare just as well for future races. I keep harping on about 'knowing yourself'. Well, what better way to know yourself than by documenting what's going on and then studying the results?

We've spoken about goal setting and milestones in Chapter 1, and logging your training goes hand in hand with this, enabling you to aim for those goals, analyse if you've hit them or not and keep track of everything else along the way. Although your goals will remain the same, it's often necessary to remain flexible regarding how you get there – how you hit your milestones and when you hit them.

Sunday evening is a great time to look at the week's training logs and see if you need to tweak your training for the next week – up the number of intervals, put another conditioning session in etc. Although you won't change things drastically or often (if at all), it's great to have the information available if you need to.

Sometimes you won't feel like filling in a training log after getting in at 8:00pm from a soggy bike ride in April, but make yourself. Maintain that dedication and effort at all times. The more detailed you can be, the more useful these logs will prove, whether you hit a plateau, pick up an injury or achieve a personal best.

The log need be no more complicated than the example I've included here:

Training Log

Date:

Type	Swim	Bike	Run	Brick/other
Distance				
Time				
Intensity/heart rate				
Notes				

Strength and conditioning

Exercise	Reps	Sets	Rest	Notes

Intervals

Swim/bike/run	Distance	Time/splits	Heart rate	Notes

Notes (time of day, temperature, conditions, training partners etc)

CHAPTER 12

INJURIES & REHAB

Injuries are the nightmare of all sportspeople. It not only means being unable to exercise, it may also mean losing the fitness and strength you've attained so far. The purpose of this chapter is to describe the injuries that most commonly plague triathletes and provide guidance on how to diagnose them, how to treat yourself if you get injured (though a trip to your A&E or GP should always be your first port of call!), how to spot the early signs, and ideally how to prehab in order to avoid injury altogether.

Losing all you've worked for

If you become injured or just have no time to train, the effects of 'detraining' can seem devastating. Whether you take your fitness levels seriously or not, you'll have worked hard to attain them, and will feel that any time off will result in losing everything. But believe it or not, detraining isn't all bad. First of all, think of it as another motivation to continue training wherever and whenever possible. Put a positive, not a negative, spin on it.

In addition, research suggests that losses in performance and efficiency occur only after training has ceased for around two weeks, so taking a few days off for a cold, the flu or a niggly hamstring isn't going to do you any harm. For most of us the contrary is true – it'll do us some real good to have a rest. However, if a few months pass due to serious injury, illness or any other reason, then the majority of real fitness gains and physical improvements made will be lost – in fact studies show that VO2 max levels can decrease by as much as 25% over 20 days if injury or illness means you're almost sedentary.

Regaining past glories

If illness or injury does prevail, and fitness levels are lost, it isn't the end of the world. For example, a nasty injury to my right hand meant I couldn't use my arm for the best part of six months or run for the best part of three (the scars had to heal without getting sweaty). Obviously I was distraught, as prior to the injury

Repair and refocus

When you get injured, it's important to accept it. Know when you're beaten and find a new way round the obstacle, but never, ever give up. Just rest, recover, repair and refocus.

Rest and recovery

A common theme across all my books is that overtraining leads to injuries. Rest and recovery will turn you into a well-rounded, continually improving triathlete who most of the time is able to avoid injury.

my fitness levels were pretty much at their peak. However, studies suggest that once a certain level of fitness is gained, even if it's lost again it's easier to regain than it was to gain the first time. I've now surpassed my previous fitness and found more ways to train and improve, as I had to adapt and 'think outside the box'. Furthermore I enjoyed striving to regain my old fitness level, as it gave me another motivational goal. As a result of all this I can now empathise when people I train get injured, and find I'm far better at rehabbing them due to my complete understanding of both the frustrations and the importance of the process.

Common triathlete injuries

Achilles tendinitis

What is it?
Inflammation of the Achilles tendon, the strongest tendon in your body, which connects the large calf muscles to the heel bone and provides the power in the push off phase of the running gait cycle. It presents as an ache just above your heel that increases as you run or walk. Studies suggest that it makes up 11% of all running injuries.

→ Causes
In general it's due to your calf muscles being too tight or your ankles being slightly inflexible. Increasing your mileage too quickly (ie overtraining) and the back of your trainer rubbing on the Achilles tendon area can also be factors.

→ Treatment
Replace old inflexible trainers with new more cushioned ones. Increase the flexibility of your calf muscles by stretching and reduce or stop training until it's pain-free. Reducing hill training, sprints and interval training is also a good idea as these involve more heel impact. Lastly, ice the area after any training to help reduce the pain.

→ Prevention
Stretch, and if new to training or suddenly upping the mileage take it slowly.

Shin splints (periostitis)

What is it?
Shin splints refers to any shin pain picked up by a sportsperson, but originally and still most commonly to medial tibial stress syndrome. This is basically inflammation and the resulting pain of the inner part of the shin, which feels almost like a bruise.

→ Causes
Usually too much impact from training, particularly on hard surfaces. If biomechanical weaknesses such as overpronating or weak muscles below the knee are also present these can be the major cause (which brings us back to conditioning again).

→ Treatment
Ice and possibly massage of the area to reduce inflammation and relieve pain. Cut down on training – stretch and train the muscles of the lower leg before building training back up. It's a good idea to run on softer surfaces where possible. Don't be tempted to run through pain. Warming up the area passively and actively prior to training can help alleviate the problem.

→ Prevention
Conditioning, prehab and not training too much per week too quickly. Keep up strength and conditioning training of the lower legs including flexibility. Vary training and running on grass and treadmills. Trail and cross country runs are also a good idea.

Runner's knee

What is it?
Runner's knee – chrondromalacia or patellofemoral pain syndrome (PFPS) – is characterised by pain at the front of the kneecap. The pain usually increases going downstairs after long periods of sitting.

→ Causes
There are multiple causes, but commonly overpronation, too much downhill running, tight hamstrings, weak quad muscles and (yes) overtraining.

→ Treatment
Reduce and remove inflammation through 'PRICE(A)' (protect, rest, ice, compress, elevate, anti-inflammatory medication, ie ibuprofen). To protect or rest, cut down or stop running and avoid activities that cause pain. Build up imbalances of the quads and gluteus medius – stabilising exercises do this very well.

→ Prevention
Get your running gait analysed, as overpronators are more prone. Replace your running shoes regularly. Try to focus on swimming and cycling to avoid the problem, and when running avoid hard surfaces and steep downhills. Maintain your flexibility by stretching and keep on top of prehab/conditioning so leg muscles are strong.

Jumper's knee

What is it?
Jumper's knee or patella tendinitis is characterised by pain at the front of the knee underneath the kneecap. The pain is usually increased with prolonged use, such as standing, walking or, in my personal experience, driving.

→ Causes
Like runner's knee there are multiple causes, such as direct impact or jumping sports such as basketball and gymnastics. Tight and overworked quadriceps (common for most office workers) can also be a major cause.

→ Treatment

Reduce activity and remove inflammation with PRIA (protection, rest, ice, anti-inflammatories). Cut down or stop running training in favour of seated cycling (out of the saddle riding puts the same pressure on the patella tendon) or swimming, to allow the tendon to heal and calm down. Build up imbalances of the quads and gluteus medius – stabilising exercises are perfect for this.

→ Prevention

Replace your running shoes with cushioned versions, learn to midfoot run and avoid running on hard surfaces all the time. Avoid steep downhills, especially on hard surfaces, and where possible, avoid sports that involve jumping and landing on hard surfaces. As always avoid overtraining.

Lower back pain

What is it?

A dull aching in the lower back, centrally or to one side. Often leads to restricted movement and can lead to cessation of running.

→ Causes

Most common cause is a previous pain in that area that's worsened by activity or training, whether swimming, cycling or running. Poor technique in one or all three disciplines and bad footwear can also be to blame, as well as bad posture from sitting at a desk all day. Also increasingly common these days is running with a backpack (carrying the day's work requirements, change of clothes, lunch etc) but not running correctly with the weight. Tight hamstrings or weak abdominals can also play a huge part.

→ Treatment

Anti-inflammatories will drastically reduce the pain and inflammation but won't cure the problem. Improving posture and addressing core weakness is of utmost importance (see Chapter 10 for core strengthening exercises). In particular, strengthening the transverse abdominals, glutes and erector spinae can help with back pain. Flexibility can also be an issue, so if you tend to neglect stretching after training, start performing a good stretch routine involving the lower back, hamstrings and hip flexors immediately. Ice and heat on the area can help relieve pain and tightness, as can a good sports massage.

→ Prevention

Avoid training that hurts – only do exercises that are pain free, be that swimming, cycling or running. Try different training environments, grass or treadmill, and perhaps different cycling positions or bikes. Ensure you have your running gait assessed by a professional and then wear the appropriate cushioned trainers to run. Improving your core strength and abdominals is an absolute must, and if you must run wearing a backpack make sure it's a bag fit for purpose.

⏱ Keep a strong core

A poor core is terrible for a triathlete. If your core is weak your swim stroke will be poor and will make you use far more energy than necessary. More worrying than that, running is core intensive but is the last of the tri events, so your core will be fairly fatigued by the time you run, and your pelvis position changes because your core can't fix it; and your lower back will start to ache. If that sounds familiar start training your core every other day.

Iliotibial band syndrome

What is it?

ITBS is a dull ache felt on the outside of the knee. The iliotibial band is a thick, fibrous band of fascia that runs down the outside of the thigh and inserts just below the knee. The pain can be severe enough to make running too difficult to continue, especially as tenderness may also be felt in the gluteal area in more severe cases. Like Achilles tendinitis this is a very common runners' injury. Triathletes who hit their road runs hard (especially if increasing the mileage too quickly) often suffer from this as much as runners.

→ Causes

If the IT band becomes tight it can rub against the outside of the knee, causing pain and inflammation. This pain is unfortunately aggravated by running, particularly downhill. In severe cases pain is felt even when bending the knee. Overtraining or training without sufficient rest is a common cause.

→ Treatment

PRICE (see page 218) and stretching your ITB using a roller is by far the most successful way of alleviating this injury. However, running on even ground, general stretching and increased flexibility and strengthening of the leg, hip and muscles in the backside can help. Conditioning is key!

→ Prevention

Stretch at the end of EVERY session. Try not to run downhill on hard surfaces too often and ensure you wear cushioned and correct-fitting shoes. A good conditioning routine to ensure leg muscles are strong is also imperative, as well as utilising a midfoot strike if you've suffered previously. Ensure your training programme includes conditioning and prehab and not just run, bike, swim.

Bruised toenails

What are they?
Repeated bashing of the toes while training, especially in badly fitting cycling cleats or running shoes, causes blood to pool underneath the toenails, turning them black.

→ Causes
I lost five toenails from this on one military course. I think on that occasion it was down to my boots being half a size too tight. Usually it's due to the impact of the toe against the end of the shoe or by blood being pressed into the toe from the shoe being too tight. Too much running, especially downhill can also be a cause.

→ Treatment
The toenail will eventually fall off of its own accord and a new one will have part grown up underneath. Don't pull the toenail off prematurely – it's still protecting the soft skin underneath and removing it will cause pain and long-term damage, including ingrown toenails. If the nail is catching on socks or in bed, tape it down or visit your local surgery and they can remove it.

→ Prevention
Try a new set of cycle, running or work shoes, perhaps a different brand, or at least a half-size bigger. Less running downhill, especially on hard surfaces.

Blisters

What is it?
Blisters can occur anywhere on the body, but among triathletes they're generally found on the feet and toes from running and cycling without socks. The human body protects itself from friction by forming a bubble of fluid over the affected area.

→ Causes
Many things can cause blisters, from ill-fitting trainers to ruffled socks and dampness.

→ Treatment
There are two schools of thought. Either leave the blisters to disappear or burst by themselves, by wearing shoes that don't rub the same area or by protecting them with plasters or blister-specific medical kit; or, if wearing other shoes isn't realistic, burst the blister with a sterile needle by making two holes – one to let the fluid out, the other to let the air in. Clean the area immediately by soaking up the fluid and dressing the wound. However, don't remove dead skin, as this protects the tender layer of new skin beneath; it will die and fall off when the new skin has grown. Removing it before this will cause far more discomfort than the blister itself and delay the healing process.

→ Prevention
Keep the feet dry and clean and get perfectly fitting cleats and shoes. After a while the skin hardens in the problem areas anyway. If 'hot spots' are known where friction is beginning, use tape or Vaseline on the foot and put Vaseline inside your shoes and cleats in those areas.

♥ Personal experience...
During my time in the Marines we dealt with blisters in many different ways. For some, taping problematic areas was the key. This meant layering the areas that usually blister with zinc oxide or Leuka tape, which then took the friction instead of the foot. I've done this myself and it works very well. As a triathlete, it's possible to swim with tape, but not common. For training it's fine, but for a race Vaseline preparation is more likely the way forward.

Plantar fasciitis

What is it?
The plantar fascia is a broad, thick band of tissue that runs from under the heel to the front of the foot. Plantar fasciitis is a pain felt under the heel and usually on the inside, at the origin of the attachment. Pain is usually worse first thing in the morning, as the fascia tightens up overnight. After a few minutes it eases as the foot gets warmed up. However, pain can worsen through the day as the area gets overused.

→ Causes
The most common cause is thought to be very tight calf muscles, which leads to overpronation of the foot. This causes overstretching of the plantar fascia, leading to inflammation and thickening of the tendon, which in turn leads to a loss of flexibility and strength. Wearing footwear that doesn't provide much arch support has been associated with the increasing incidence of plantar fasciitis. Triathletes' long runs in bare feet from the swim to transition 1 can cause or aggravate the injury, especially if on concrete.

→ Treatment
Correct footwear at all times (not just when training) is imperative, especially when running. A decent pair of shoes with good arch support and cushioning are a must. Beyond that, rest as much as possible and desist from unnecessary activities that hurt. Taking stress off the area by applying strips of tape across the plantar fascia can help, but should be learnt from a physio or sports therapist. Ice and anti-inflammatories can also help.

➜ Prevention

Correct shoes are most important, as unsupportive footwear causes the problem. Studies show that overweight individuals are more at risk of developing the condition due to the excess weight impacting on the foot, so a weight loss programme may be of benefit. Lastly, stretching techniques such as rolling the bottom of the foot on a golf ball are important as both treatment and prevention if the area is tight. Midfoot running from swim to transition should also take pressure off the area.

Swimmer's shoulder

What is it?

Injury to the rotator cuff caused by repetitive swimming, especially front crawl, forcing the shoulder to undergo repetitive overhead motion. This repeated movement sometimes results in the development of an inflammatory response and, ultimately, pain.

➜ Cause

An increase in volume and/or intensity overload can be a cause, but mainly it's down to poor technique.

➜ Treatment

PRICE, reduction in training volume or mileage, the use of non-steroidal anti-inflammatory drugs (NSAID), rehab, and correcting poor technique to prevent future injury.

➜ Prevention

Ensure the technique used for your stroke is correct. Get professional coaching if you're concerned. It's well worth filming your swim stroke and reviewing what you actually do.

Saddle sores

What is it?

Saddle soreness results from a number of ailments, including chaffing, rubbing, boils, inflammation of the thighs and buttocks, and even skin ulceration. Pretty much any chaffing causes lesions in the skin.

➜ Cause

Simply spending a lot of time doing hard physical exercise on an unnaturally small seat in a fixed position. Although often considered a beginners' ailment, it can affect anyone, especially if they've changed their clothing, saddle or bike or have got bigger or smaller themselves.

➜ Treatment

The most important factor is hygiene: wash your kit immediately after each use. Never use more than once, and shower on

completion of exercise immediately. Use anti-bacterial creams and keep the area(s) dry and clean until healed.

➜ Prevention

Good kit is always best. If it needs replacing, replace it. If you're suffering from soreness try a new saddle or new shorts etc. Seek the advice of an expert and invest in a decent saddle, making sure it fits you personally. Equally important is the saddle's position: it shouldn't move from side to side with every single pedal stroke, as this will cause rubs. Clothing and shorts are just as important – they're your skin's protection from friction. You get what you pay for, so invest in a good pair of shorts or tri suit. Lastly, Vaseline and tape saved me in the Marines: both work well on triathlons too!

Road rash

What is it?

The skin abrasions or grazes caused by crashing on your bike or stumbling while running.

➜ Cause

Basically caused by friction of soft skin hitting a hard surface, leading to layers of skin being rubbed off. Most aren't serious and rarely break more than a couple of layers of skin. However, a high-speed bike crash or falling while sprinting can lead to deeper cuts.

➜ Treatment

Clean dirt and grime out of the wound, as it will cause infection. Soap and water is fine. While cleaning, check the wound and remove any debris. Check for deeper cuts that need further medical attention. If a cut bleeds for more than 15 minutes or has edges that pull apart it will need stitches. Cover any cuts with a semi-permeable dressing that will protect the wound and keep it moist, to aid the healing process. Change the dressing every few days until the wound heals.

➜ Prevention

Very difficult to prevent, as crashes and accidents just happen. Wearing protective clothing (such as below-knee tri suits, jogging bottoms or long-sleeved tops) can help protect the skin massively, but may hamper your race and training.

Athlete's foot

What is it?

Athlete's foot is a fungal infection of the skin on your feet. True athlete's foot is where the skin splits and cracks between and underneath the toes. Serious and untreated cases are extremely painful, as the wounds can be deep and expose raw skin.

➜ Causes

Athlete's foot is generally transferred from people already infected, in particular from the floor in damp changing rooms, by sharing socks or trainers, and by using other people's towels.

➜ Treatment

Keep the feet aired and dry, and use anti-fungal creams, athlete's foot powder and over-the-counter sprays to treat the infection.

➜ Prevention

Don't share towels, shoes, socks etc with others. Wear flip-flops in changing rooms and around swimming pools. Keep your feet as dry as possible and always dry them thoroughly after washing. Use of talcum powder, particularly anti-fungal types, can help. Also, ensure trainers have completely dried out after use before wearing them again.

Stress fractures

What are they?

Stress fractures are small cracks in or fragmentations of the bones. Among triathletes they're most common in the metatarsal bones and shins, due to doing long runs when the muscles are highly pre-fatigued. Symptoms are chronic pain that gets worse when running, tenderness to the touch and swelling.

➜ Causes

When muscles, tendons and ligaments become too fatigued from training and stop providing adequate shock absorption the bones of the feet end up taking the brunt instead. Worn-out trainers that lack cushioning can also be a major contributor – as can running in shoes not designed for running, or running barefoot with bad technique, especially after a long swim and cycle when the leg muscles are fatigued. However, sometimes stress fractures just occur due to overuse, especially if distances or times are increased too quickly.

➜ Treatment

PRICE(A) must be rigidly followed for anywhere between four weeks and four months depending on the severity of the fracture. All running and perhaps even cycling (hard sessions anyway) must cease until completely healed, or the injury will be back to square one.

➜ Prevention

Wear shoes with cushioning and replace them often. If attempting barefoot running, ensure you understand the technique and increase very gradually, starting on soft ground. The same goes for progressing any running – increase distances gradually and carefully, and where possible have a day's rest between each run session to stop stress fractures taking place.

Bursitis

What is it?

Bursitis is the swelling of a bursa in any joint. The bursae are sacs of synovial fluid that lubricate the movement of tissue and bone against bone and cartilage. Pain and stiffness is felt in the joint itself and is usually worse in the morning or after long periods in one position, such as when driving. Shoulders, hips, knees and ankles are most common for triathletes.

➜ Causes

Usually associated with overuse and impacts, ie long periods of repetitive movements of a joint.

➜ Treatment

Yet again PRICE(A) is the answer. Rest allows recovery and ice helps remove the problem over time. Don't train on the affected joint, as injury reoccurs if not fully healed.

➜ Prevention

As this injury is related to overuse/impact, well-cushioned shoes are imperative. Where possible train on softer surfaces, like grass or a treadmill. Trying not to increase session length too fast is essential for the overuse factor. Good technique can also avoid the problem.

Hyperkeratosis

What is it?
Hyperkeratosis is the thickening of the skin on the feet, in particular on the heels and balls. Calluses (layers of skin) build up on top of each other to protect the area that's constantly under stress to avoid blistering. Problems arise when these hard areas become painful.

→ Causes
There are multiple reasons for the skin to form calluses, from simply cycling or running for long periods to ill-fitting shoes that cause rubbing. Overly large trainers or trainers done up too loosely, thus leading to excessive rubbing, are a major cause.

→ Treatment
Removal of some of the callused skin with a pumice stone can help, as can moisturising the area.

→ Prevention
Ensure shoes fit well and are replaced often. Treat and repair your feet – if you ignore them they'll get infected and cause you pain. A god foot admin routine of exfoliating and moisturising and removing hard skin can be the answer.

♥ Personal experience...

In the Marines, Recruits were expected to administer their own feet during down time to enable them to keep soldiering. If blisters, trench foot, calluses or any other foot problem means they become 'out of action' this is seen as a failure on the Recruit's part. Looking after your feet as a runner should be part of a standard routine.

Sciatica

What is it?
A numbness or electric-shock type pain felt in the glutes, lower back or in some cases the back of the entire leg, caused by some form of compression or irritation of sciatic nerve.

→ Causes
There can be multiple causes, such as an uneven running posture, which is in turn often caused by particularly tight glutes, hamstrings, calves or iliotibial bands. In more severe cases, damaged vertebrae can be to blame. Just sitting on your bike in an unnatural position can cause it.

→ Treatment
Since sitting in one position for long periods can aggravate it, stretching and mobility – particularly of the spine – are important. If the problem persists seek medical advice, and in the meantime, combat pain with painkillers and anti-inflammatories.

→ Prevention
Compression wear, mobility and stretching.

Chafing

What is it?
Chafing occurs where areas of the skin become irritated (usually by friction) and can be rubbed raw. Most often occurs between the legs, on the feet, backs and sides of the arms and nipples (among men).

→ Cause
Your skin rubbing against itself or your clothing. It's especially common when clothing becomes soaked in sweat.

→ Treatment
Applying Vaseline to known problem areas, and wearing the correct kit for your sport (wetsuit, trisuit etc). Ensure that it fits well. It's also important to use antiseptic cream on any raw patches to prevent infection.

→ Prevention
Use plentiful amounts of Vaseline on problem areas before starting. Purchase and wear triathlon-specific, well-fitting clothing and replace where necessary. Furthermore, wash it after every use! Lastly, stay hydrated, as this can help reduce chaffing as well.

Cramp

What is it?
Cramps are spasms that cause muscles to contract but then won't release. When severe the affected limb can't be used normally. Severe cramps can last for a considerable time.

→ Causes
Cramps result from an imbalance of the minerals/ions that generate the electric impulse that allows a muscle to contract. A number of factors can lead to this: fatigue, dehydration, salt deficiency, overtraining and performing a session too difficult for present fitness levels.

→ Treatment
In most cases it's a case of rehydrating and eating to rebalance mineral and electrolyte levels. However, gentle

stretching and massage of the affected muscle can help. If someone I'm training in the pool constantly gets cramps I make them have an electrolyte drink (like Electro Tabs from Maxifuel) prior to the session and keep two water bottles at the end of the pool ready for use, one with electrolytes and the other with water.

→ Prevention
Ensure you eat and drink prior to your sessions and don't exercise too long without topping up, especially in extreme heat. A thorough warm-up and stretch can help prevent cramp.

DOMS

What is it?
Stands for delayed onset muscle soreness – the soreness that occurs in muscles between 12 and 72 hours after exercise.

→ Causes
The aches result from microscopic tears in the muscles. They're usually worse the day after, as this seems to be when the proteins of the muscle are broken down and repair occurs. DOMS are always worse if you're returning to exercise after a sedentary period, trying something new, or extending a distance or time considerably.

→ Treatment
If symptoms are bad PRICE can help. Other than that, rest the painful muscles and massage gently if necessary. Anti-inflammatories can be taken, but shouldn't need to be.

→ Prevention
Warming up, cooling down and stretching can help reduce the onset. Compression gear (see Chapter 10) and building up slowly after sedentary periods can help.

Heat exhaustion

What is it?
The body overheats and symptoms such as nausea, dizziness, disorientation and headaches take hold. If left untreated it can lead to potentially severe, even life-threatening heatstroke.

→ Causes
Generally results from lack of fluid and increased sweating, which leads to severe dehydration and causes the body temperature to climb rapidly.

→ Treatment
Immediately you feel you're suffering stop exercising, and if you're in a hot place or the sun get out of it as quickly as possible. Sit down and drink water slowly without gulping – if you gulp you're more likely to be sick. Energy drinks can also be used at this point to replace electrolytes, but make sure water is taken on as well.

→ Prevention
Eat and drink sensibly before your session or race, and if you're susceptible to heat train early or late in the day when it's cooler. If you have to race in the heat take it slowly at first and acclimatise. The correct kit and equipment is imperative, so make sure you're dressed appropriately for the conditions and have some way to hydrate throughout your training or race and afterwards.

Sprains

What are they?
The over-stretching or, worse, tearing, of the ligaments that connect bones. Common sprains for triathletes are ankles and wrists, either from falling on run, bike or transitions, or fatigued leg muscles on the run that lead to an inversion or eversion of the ankle, which feels like a sharp pain and then feels like an ache. The joint generally swells considerably and quickly following injury.

❤️ Personal experience...

When training Marine Recruits on one occasion, a young Recruit sprained his ankle while we were training outside. On speaking to him, the injury seemed relatively serious. It was winter and there were puddles in potholes in the ground, so I made him take his boot and sock off and submerge his foot and ankle in the cold water. When he received medical attention the feedback was that the injury might have been far worse but for the immediate application of cold. So remember, acting quickly and starting PRICE(A) as fast as possible can pay dividends.

→ Causes
Any twist, eversion or inversion of the ankle, wrist or joints that damage the connective tissue, often caused by uneven ground or weary muscles, tendon, joints and proprioreceptive sensors.

→ Treatment
Commence PRICE(A) as soon as possible. It's often necessary to keep activity to a minimum and where possible stop using the joint completely for two weeks, at which point the majority of swelling should have gone down.

➜ Prevention

Wrist injuries are unavoidable if accidents happen. However, if you have a tendency to ankle sprains perform proprioreceptive exercises during prehab/conditioning sessions to strengthen them (see Chapter 10). Avoid runs over uneven ground and ensure your running shoes have good support and stability. A thorough warm-up is also a good avoidance measure. However, most ankle sprains are just unfortunate accidents.

Stitches

What are they?

A sharp stabbing pain just under the rib cage, usually on the right-hand side. It's said to be a straining of the ligaments that connect the diaphragm to the other internal organs.

➜ Causes

Results from the diaphragm and organs receiving impacts during running. If you breathe out as the left foot strikes the ground you shouldn't suffer, but if your routine gets interrupted and you breathe out as the right foot lands, then the ligaments connected to the liver get stretched by the movement of the diaphragm (allowing you to exhale) and a stitch occurs. Eating too soon before a run can also cause the problem, as a full stomach affects the whole process.

➜ Treatment

Try to run through the pain and regulate breathing by slowing down. If this fails to cure it, stop and walk and control breathing that way. Breathe in deeply and stretch the affected side of the body by leaning away from it. Stretching usually alleviates the pain.

➜ Prevention

Ensure you exhale as the left foot strikes. Breathe deeply and evenly when running. If you get breathless and get stitches regularly then run slower until fitness improves. Don't eat within two hours of your session and drink plenty, as dehydration can cause the cramping pains associated with a stitch.

GI distress

What is it?

Runner's diarrhoea – the need and often the inability to prevent yourself from needing to go to the toilet when exercising extremely hard.

➜ Cause

It's thought that gastrointestinal (GI) distress stems from reduced blood flow to the GI tract, stress or anxiety and impact while training. Other suspects are poor posture on the bike and poor pre-race or race-day nutrition. Dehydration can also play a big part. Exercise reduces blood flow to the digestive system, causing bloating and diarrhoea as a result.

➜ Treatment

Go to the toilet! If symptoms persist an anti-diarrhoea medication can help.

➜ Prevention

Look at the foods ingested over the few days before a race or hard session. Reduce fibre intake by avoiding large quantities of salads and vegetables in the 24–48 hours prior to a race. Best advice is to try some different foods during training, work out what's best for you and stick to it; don't try anything new pre or on race day. Hydrate, as it aids blood flow to the muscles to digest food.

Mental crash

What is it?

A complete lack of morale and self-belief that comes out of nowhere.

➜ Cause

Morale slumps are common in long events and are the result of low blood sugar and fatigue. Mental strength is essential for triathlons, but low blood sugar or general fatigue leads to your hormones telling your body that it's tired, resulting in this slump.

➜ Treatment

Be prepared. You won't feel 'up' throughout a long race or session, but knowing in advance that you'll face a slump and survive it helps. 'Knowing yourself' yet again plays a part, as does specificity of training so that you don't experience such a crash for the first time on race day. Distract yourself by repeating a phrase in your head or counting your steps or revolutions etc.

➜ Prevention

Nutrition is vital. Constantly refuel, as blood sugar (around 60g of carbs per hour) is essential to maintaining mental as well as physical focus. Be honest with yourself. Don't set out to break your personal best if you've trained only half as much or been injured. You'll disappoint yourself and your morale will suffer.

Swimmer's ear

What is it?

Swimmer's ear, or otitis external, is inflammation of the outer ear and canal. Symptoms include pain, redness and discharge from the ear. Itching is particularly bad, as scratching the infected area can lead to broken skin and therefore infection. The ear canal may swell so much that it closes, affecting your hearing.

➜ Causes
Unclean water is the main culprit, with open water swims being mainly to blame. The trapping of water in the ear canal after swimming or showering is another common cause.

➜ Treatment
Keep it completely dry until symptoms have disappeared, so no swimming even with cap or earplugs. Flying can also be harmful so should be avoided where possible.

➜ Prevention
Wear earplugs when swimming. These must be a good fit and not scratch or break the skin. The most effective versions can be rolled into a ball to fit. Clean and dry the ear carefully, but don't insert anything into the ear canal as this may worsen the condition by disrupting the layer of wax inside your ear that protects against harmful bacteria. Eardrops can help.

Post-ironman blues

What is it?
After finishing any big event, like an ironman, disappointment and even depression can set in. This is often termed 'post-ironman blues'.

➜ Cause
All of a sudden there's no goal to look forward to, and after all the months of hard training there's suddenly too much free time and an emotional slump. Chemically speaking massive amounts of adrenaline and the stress and anxiety hormone cortisol are released into the body; also exercise produced endorphins, meaning that a lapse in your exercise regime can create a withdrawal effect.

➜ Treatment
Relax, take a week or two off, eat the wrong things and use the extra time to reconnect with your family, friends and hobbies. Start active recovery, as your body will be addicted to endorphins. Swimming is a great way to recover and maintain activity levels. Sharing your thoughts and feelings with other athletes and your friends and family will help you move past the race.

➜ Prevention
Remember that an ironman is only one race and one day of your life. However, depression is common and may be just the tip of an iceberg, so if the feelings continue go and see your GP.

Muscle strain

What is it?
Any small or large tear within a muscle. Tears range from minor micro tears (or pulls) to full-on ruptures. Micro tears are characterised by a dull ache that gets continually worse as it's used and gets steadily bigger. A full rupture is a sharp, stabbing pain, sometimes accompanied by an audible noise.

➜ Causes
The most common cause is over-exertion of a tight, cold, un-warmed muscle. For triathletes, most common causes are sudden acceleration or anything that puts undue and unnatural stress on a particular muscle.

➜ Treatment
If you suspect a pull or tear stop immediately – continuing will make it far worse. Yet again PRICE(A) is the only real remedy, along with resting until the pain subsides. Length of rest can be anywhere between two and eight weeks dependent on severity. On return to activity, be very careful. Do thorough warm-ups, including dynamic stretching, and a shorter/easier session than normal to start with.

➜ Prevention
Correct technique, correct kit and equipment, and most importantly a thorough warm-up and post-workout stretch routine.

❤ Personal experience...
I was undergoing an interval training session of three sets of eight intervals, with a minute between each set. I'd performed the first two sets (16 intervals), and was on the first rep of my last set when I felt a twinge in my hamstring. I finished the rep, took my rest, then started the second. I felt it again. I stopped, and then spent about three days icing, resting, NSAID (taking non-steroidal anti-inflammatory drugs) and massaging. I returned to gentle exercise, and was squatting with weight less than a week later. The moral? Stop early, rehab correctly, return quickly.

Stomach distension

What is it?
A bloated, sick feeling after exiting the water, which isn't any fun while trying to do the bike leg of a race.

➜ Cause
Commonly believed to be due to swallowing too much water during swimming, but more likely to be due to taking in too much air, as breathing through the mouth, down the oesophagus and into the lungs causes excess air to enter the stomach. The rapid, laboured and snatched breathing during a swim creates this build-up of air, leading to distension of the stomach and nausea.

→ Treatment
Let the vibrations of the road through your bike help your body rid itself of any excess gas naturally. Excessive drinking or eating while on the bike can make you feel sick.

→ Prevention
Getting your breathing technique right will help you, as will practising in open water to avoid panic and over-breathing. When you're not breathing in during a swim you should be breathing out. This helps rid the stomach of air and allows a more natural 'in' breath, with enough air to feed your muscles. When breathing out, be sure to do so through the mouth as well as the nose, otherwise you're likely to be sucking in more air than you're exhaling.

Tarsal tunnel syndrome

What is it?
The tarsal tunnel is the area along the inside of your ankle that houses several nerves, ligaments and tendons. When any of these (usually the tibial nerve) become inflamed, pressure builds up inside the tarsal tunnel, resulting in pain in your toes and a tingling sensation in your heel. In acute cases it can lead to pain all over the affected foot and a build-up of fluid in the tarsal tunnel.

→ Causes
Common in regular runners. The main reason cause flat-footedness, as the flattened arch puts increased pressure on the nerves and muscles in the tarsal tunnel.

→ Treatment
NSAIDs help reduce swelling in the nerves, ligaments and tendons, thus allowing them to move more freely through the tarsal tunnels. Getting a running gait analysis could also be a good option. Some cases of tarsal tunnel syndrome require surgery. The operation involves cutting the laciniate ligament to increase the amount of room in the tarsal tunnel.

→ Prevention
Wider-fitting shoes and trainers with arch support will help combat the effects of flat-footedness and should reduce the chance of developing the injury. The use of orthotics to address flat-footedness is also worth considering, as it will correct the arch of the foot to increase mobility.

Torn rotator cuff

What is it?
The rotator cuff is a group of four muscles that together act as tendons to keep the top of your arm in your shoulder socket. If the muscles are torn the pain can be excruciating, and swimming has to cease. There are two forms of tear – acute and degenerative – and swimmers mainly suffer from the latter. Symptoms are feeling pain at night when resting on that shoulder, pain when lifting and moving, and a cracking sound when rotating your arm.

→ Cause
The injury is often brought on by repetitive stress, and swimming front crawl is one of the major causes.

→ Treatment
Seek medical advice if you suspect a tear and use NSAIDs to reduce pain and swelling. In extremely painful cases you may have to be prescribed a steroid injection. As soon as you feel pain it's important you stop swimming and avoid movements that cause discomfort, but don't stop movement in the affected arm entirely as this could potentially lead to frozen shoulder (adhesive capsulitis). Rehab exercises like external rotation are imperative, and will then become part of your prehab. In acute cases surgery may be required: surgery to repair a torn rotator cuff has an almost 100% success rate, so isn't a major cause for concern.

→ Prevention
The injury may be due to poor technique, so invest in some coaching and do prehab on the shoulders by performing strength and conditioning sessions.

Insomnia

What is it?
Put simply, not sleeping.

→ Causes
A myriad of factors contribute to sleepless nights, including stress, diet, temperature and hormones. Sleep is crucial to your training. If you're unable to sleep properly your mental and physical ability will be impaired and you won't train or race well. This adds to the stress, hormones and lack of routine that caused your sleeplessness in the first place.

→ Treatment
Regularity and routine, from your time of going to bed seven days a week to your diet and work routines. Worrying about not sleeping only makes it worse. The real key is to keep your stress levels under control. Consequently time relaxing with your friends and family can help.

→ Prevention
Nutrition and timing of nutrition is very important, from eating your evening meal as early as possible to avoiding caffeine and alcohol. Have a routine that works for you, from a warm bath and some reading to listening to music. Avoid anything that prevents you from relaxing, especially work.

Ice treatment and injury

Injuries are split into two groups: acute and chronic. An acute injury is one that's happened recently and from a known cause; a twisted ankle is a perfect example. A chronic injury is one that's been around for some time and persists; patella tendinitis is a good example. An untreated or unrested acute injury can become a chronic injury.

With any injury (acute or chronic) it's worth seeking medical advice to ensure serious damage hasn't been caused. If your injury is to the head, neck or back you should seek medical attention immediately. In general triathlete injuries are leg or core/lower back related, but it isn't uncommon to hear of injuries to the shoulders and – if we consider asthma or allergies to be injuries – to the cardiovascular system. Whatever the injury, in general you should seek professional advice, as if it's nothing to worry about you have at worst wasted your time, while if it's a real injury you might prevent yourself causing complications by continuing to exercise the damaged areas.

♥ Personal experience...

Following a fall I thought I'd simply sprained my wrist, so I left it for a month before seeking medical advice. Following X-rays, an MRI and finally an arthroscopy I was diagnosed with a complete rupture to some major ligaments of the wrist, which if left much longer might have seen me lose the use of my thumb. I required surgery to repair the damage and was left with a reduced range of movement for some time.

Last warning: always seek medical advice if you're ever in any doubt about an injury. However, if you're positive medical advice isn't needed, or have sought advice and the injury is minor rather than major, you may find the following guidelines to be of use.

Injury treatment

The acute phase of an injury is said to be the first 48 hours from the instant it occurs, and this is the period in which to use ice. The types of injury you can treat yourself are sprains to ligaments (eg going over on your ankle), strains to muscles (eg a pulled hamstring) or impacts causing bruising (usually from a fall or contact sport). If left untreated all of these injuries will be dealt with by the body's natural biological pathways, but icing can drastically speed up the process. Such injuries lead to classic inflammatory responses, ie heat, pain, redness and swelling, all of which are to protect them from further injury and are characteristic of this acute phase, along with discolouration and loss of function.

PRICE(A)

'PRICE', now often accompanied by an 'A' at the end, is a simple mnemonic used to help you remember how to treat an injury, standing for protect, rest, ice, compress, elevate, plus anti-inflammatory medication when required:

→ Protection

It's important to protect the injury to aid recovery and prevent further injury. No painful activities should be undertaken where possible, but obviously your everyday lifestyle and work commitments have to take priority. Where possible immobilise the injury entirely and never be tempted to just press on, as there's a huge risk of making the injury worse.

→ Rest

Rest is arguably the most important part of injury management in the first 48 hours, and makes a direct contribution to the healing process. Again, where possible anything causing pain or discomfort must be avoided. Having said that, as soon as activities can be done pain-free it's important to begin active recovery.

→ Ice

Ice is THE tool for injury treatment. It reduces swelling and heat by narrowing the diameter of the blood vessels; the cold also numbs the area, which reduces pain. Once ice is removed the injured area reheats and blood rushes in, bringing with it all the nutrients to aid healing.

⏱ Hearts are special

If you have an injury to the chest or left shoulder it's worth asking for medical advice prior to icing, due to the area's proximity to the heart.

→ Compression

Compression helps to control swelling by providing counter-pressure to the injured area. Pressure can be applied in a number of ways, from a Tubigrip-style bandage to a regular crepe bandage or a 'compression bandage'. However, it's imperative to check the circulation of the compressed area by pinching the body below the injury to ensure that blood is seen to return. If pain is felt above or below the injury the compression is probably too tight and should be removed or at least loosened.

→ Elevation

The injured area (a leg, most likely) should be elevated above heart level, eg by putting the feet up. This allows the drainage of blood and inflammatory fluids from the injury site, thereby reducing swelling. While elevated it's important to perform active recovery exercises within the pain-free range, ie static exercises and joint mobility (like rotating the ankle left and right after an ankle inversion). This encourages the muscles to aid the drainage of the swollen area as they 'pump' while they contract.

Anti-inflammatories

Ibuprofen, Nurofen and chemists' own-brand anti-inflammatory medications will help alleviate the five characteristics of the inflammatory process:

- Pain (due to chemicals released by damaged cells).
- Swelling (due to an influx of fluid into the damaged region).
- Redness (due to vasodilatation – the widening of blood vessels and bleeding in the joint or structure).
- Heat (due to an increase in blood flow to the area).
- Loss of function (due to increased swelling and pain).

When taking these drugs always read the label, stick to the dosage, and take with a full stomach.

Another acronym, 'PRIA', has also come into common use for dealing with smaller, less significant injuries, standing for protect, rest, ice and anti-inflammatories.

Icing

Although a simple bag of frozen vegetables can be used, it may be worth purchasing an ice pack system from a sports shop. Most are under £10 and consist of a gelatine ice pack for the freezer (which can also be microwaved to act as a heat pack), a cover to put it in (to protect the skin from hot or cold burns) and an elastic Velcro strap for attaching to the injured site.

⏱ Keep your ice pack ready

Keep your ice pack in the freezer ready to go, as you never know when you'll be injured and you won't want to have to wait for it to freeze, as speed is vital to quick recovery.

➜ How to ice

Ice should be applied until the injured site is numb, which usually takes around 10–20 minutes. Where possible this should be done every two hours while awake. It's important to protect the skin from ice burns by wrapping the ice or icing implement in a damp towel or cloth (or the cover an ice pack is provided with). Additionally it's important, when icing a joint (knee, elbow, ankle, wrist etc), that the ice is removed briefly every five minutes or so to allow movement of the joint in the pain-free range. Due to the cold's numbing effects this pain-free range may be greater once iced.

⏱ Prehab after recovery

Prehab is the most important thing once you've recovered from an injury. This essentially involves performing the same exercises that you used to get strong, but doing them all the time to prevent re-injury. The easiest way to get injured is to just swim, bike, run. Condition and you're far more likely to stay injury-free.

Conclusion

As careful as you are, as much conditioning and prehab as you might perform, as good as you are at avoiding overtraining, you'll eventually pick up an injury. It's inevitable and almost unavoidable. However, by being aware of the common injuries, what causes them and how to avoid them you can lessen your chances of getting and limit the onset of common and returning injuries. Just ensure that when you do become injured you rest up, use PRICE and/or PRIA and take your time coming back – see it as another challenge, not a setback.

CHAPTER 13
WOMEN AND TRIATHLONS

In recent years, especially amongst young professional women, triathlon has become hugely popular. Running has always been the most popular sport for women and is now one of the fastest growing hobbies for women of all ages. Swimming is hot on its heels as it's a non-impact sport, and great for easing back into exercise after a long absence (pre/post natal etc). Throw a bike into the mix – a popular piece of gym equipment with women – and it's no surprise that more women are edging towards their first triathlon.

As I've said before, we are, genetically speaking, all different. Therefore we need to be realistic about whether we've chosen the right sport and whether we've set ourselves realistic goals. In some countries children are assessed on which sport they're most suited to. For example, is a child who is likely to be stocky and heavy better suited to triathlon, rugby or mixed martial arts? I'm not trying to put people off – look at the Marines – they're an example of people of all shapes and sizes who, so long as they have the mental robustness, can fulfil any role. Amateur sport is the same – if you love your sport, compete and enjoy it. So why am I talking about genetics? It's to make the point that we're all different and suited (supposedly) to some things more than others.

Extensive research has shown that female athletes are twice as likely to suffer from lateral knee injuries and kneecap damage, that female runners are three times more likely to suffer injury to their glutes and, astonishingly, around ten times more likely to report lower back injuries, than men.

OK, but so what? It's best to be aware of an issue so you can try to avoid it. Look at it this way: if we look purely at size, proportions and movement, men and women are very different. In fact we all have little differences, and no two humans are exactly the same. It's believed to be these differences in body shape and structure of the legs and feet, leading to sometimes very different swimming, cycling and running patterns, that are the main cause of higher injury rates amongst female athletes.

Biomechanical differences

All women have a wider pelvis than their male counterparts and shorter upper legs. These characteristics mean that a typical woman's running gait has hips and thighs turned inwards and legs taking on a kind of 'X' shape. This bending sideways at the knee causes strains and impact on the hips, knee joints and lower back, which can lead to injuries.

⏱ Team entry triathlons

Many competitions now allow 'team' entries, ie three people complete one triathlon. This allows three people to do individual events without having to worry about the other two stages, and is a great way to 'get the bug' to do a full event individually.

Resistance training

Conditioning your muscles by resistance training (which can be seen as prehab) will help protect you from female-specific injuries. Rest and recovery is also important, especially if you feel a muscle niggle or pick up an injury.

This is where triathlon is actually a great sport for women to take up if they love running and/or swimming. If you constantly pound pavements, tracks and treadmills these biomechanical differences will have more time to take effect (as you'll be running more often) than if you have to fit in cycling and swimming sessions as well, since the volume of running you do will decrease to accommodate the other events. In addition, many women – and swimmers in general – train breaststroke, and unfortunately the action of the breaststroke kick also puts pressure on the knees and back, so training triathlon and changing your stroke to the front crawl is far better.

One of the major problems with running is that the same muscles get trained repeatedly, whereas by swimming and cycling too, other patterns and muscles also get trained, or at least trained in a different way, which helps protect you against the issues that can result from repetitive exercise.

Can kit help?

Manufacturers of clothing and shoes have tried to combat women's 'X'-shaped running gait with specific trainers and leggings that can alter the angle of the feet and the way the muscles act on the joints. This technology can apparently help stop the 'X' shape and thus protect the joints and prevent the associated injuries. Whether this is true or not, if you've suffered from this type of injury and are looking to run again, any preventative measure is worth trying. Even if it just helps with your confidence – placebo or not, if it works, it works. To reiterate, though, conditioning, rest, recovery and variation would be my first advice.

On top of the biomechanical differences, there are obvious differences to the equipment needed by women, and not just different swim costumes, bike sizes and sports bras. There are actually woman-specific versions of nearly every item of equipment required by triathletes, from Lycra leggings and wetsuits to heart-rate monitors and trainers. These take into account a woman's physique, body shape and other differences to ensure that she's comfortable while training or racing. These bits of kit are all covered in Chapters 5–7.

Tips for women

Tying back your hair

Whether wet from sweat or swimming, damp strands of hair stuck to your face and the back of your neck can be off-putting. When performing a triathlon you can do without anything that might distract you.

My girlfriend described to me a time when she forgot her hairband when training intervals on a treadmill at the gym. She still tried to perform the session, but the constant need to wipe her hair from her face distracted her so much that she felt unfit while running her normal speed, and was forced to get off the treadmill to find some other way of tying her hair back.

Make-up

Some people feel the need to look just the same when training as they normally do; this is especially true in a gym where work colleagues or clients may be seen. But it's much better for your skin to remove all your make-up, it will aid your skin by allowing it to sweat out impurities, breathe properly and prevent the pores clogging, which would lead to spots. Even if you do keep it on, the intensity or duration of your training is likely to make it run anyway. Make sure you drink plenty, exfoliate after the run and wash your face properly before reapplying any make-up. It's far better to train hard, shower and then look great afterwards.

And if you're new to tri training and think that unless you're in the pool or the rain you probably won't get wet, then all I can say is that if you're not sweating, then you're not working at the right intensity to achieve your desired goal.

That time of the month

In the past women of all ages were advised to stop exercising for a few specific days a month. This may be good advice if pain is particularly high but it just isn't practical in today's busy world. Professional athletes and sports players can't afford to sit out an event because it's their time of the month. I appreciate I'm a man and writing about women from a man's point of view, but I was also a Marine and worked with both sexes in the forces where

A time to be aware

Research suggests that women in their premenstrual phase are more likely to suffer from injuries. It's thought that the imbalance of hormones can affect the motor neurones and leave you less reactive than usual; added to which blood sugar levels tend to be lower, meaning energy levels will be lower too, all of which can cause an injury to occur.

there's no excuse for not getting on with the day's work, short of collapsing. Nevertheless, I appreciate that the pain associated with the menstrual cycle can be debilitating – which brings me back yet again to my favourite mantra: 'Know yourself'. If you know you suffer badly, then take a break.

Powering through

At that time of the month a little bit of depression is quite common, due not just to discomfort but also hormonal changes. Consequently motivation can be a problem. It seems that the solution to this is to simply power through. By doing this, the post-exercise buzz leads to a real feeling of achievement and helps with your general well-being. Conversely, there's no harm in having a rest – there's no point hurting yourself, especially if you may cause yourself injury.

Triathlon for pain relief – really?

Female triathletes have apparently reported that training through the premenstrual syndrome actually helps alleviate pain. Whether it's the physical act of training, where the pain becomes focused on the effort exerted, or because of the endorphins that are released during exercise, pain apparently subsides to some degree. So if you're feeling low, a swim/bike/run could help boost your spirits.

Reduce bloating

The bloating associated with premenstrual syndrome, which is caused by sodium retention, can be vastly reduced and alleviated by sweating from hard exercise. Drinking plenty of water is a must.

Sanitary towels

I've again taken advice on this, and apparently different women report different things in terms of the effects of exercise on blood flow. Try out a few different tampons and pads and see which work for you. If you have friends who do tri training, or you've joined a swim/bike/run club, ask for other opinions. Key advice, though, would be to put fresh in before you run, cycle or swim, and change it on completion. This can prevent embarrassment if your session does encourage more flow than usual. Lastly, avoid light coloured clothing, just in case. Black tights are probably a good item to cycle or run in during periods, and open water swims in a wetsuit may be more appealing than a swimming pool. Again, the bottom line is to know yourself. If you aren't happy swimming in a pool at that time of the month, then increase your training, conditioning and run and bike sessions until you can return as usual and throw in a few extra pool sessions.

Differences to men

Added to the biomechanical differences in the legs, hips, knees and feet as mentioned above, there are physiological differences that are important to factor in, especially when starting triathlon or training with men. In general women's cardiovascular systems are proportionally smaller than men's. This means they have to work harder for similar gains. In addition, women have less oxygen-carrying haemoglobin than men, which again means the heart (which is already smaller) must beat more times to get the haemoglobin to deliver oxygen around the body. However, don't be disheartened. Despite these differences women generally show greater improvements than men during training. So what's the key? Stick with your training, work hard and compete with yourself, not the men.

⏱ Triathlon suits women

There's an old theory that women are better at endurance sports than men because they have more body fat to burn. Over shorter distances men tend to use their strength to push ahead, whereas women are generally content to find a comfort zone and stay there – an approach ideally suited to triathlons over long distances, such as an ironman. So if competition with your partner is your aim, why not sign up for a sprint first, and then convince him to race you over an ironman?

Hormones

Women's hormones fluctuate through the month and can have various consequences on the body, from increased temperature to lethargy. But what effect does training have on hormone production? Research suggests that if you train regularly you produce a less potent form of oestrogen than if you were sedentary. This form of oestrogen isn't problematic in any way and is said to reduce the risk of developing breast and uterine cancer by 50% and the form of diabetes that most commonly plagues women by 66%.

Female athlete triad syndrome

This term refers to the condition of athletic women who train extremely hard and suffer from one of three interlinked disorders: amenorrhoea, osteoporosis and anorexia.

Amenorrhoea

The downside to hard, frequent tri training is that you might develop amenorrhoea (lack of a monthly period), which means that little or no oestrogen is circulating in your body, due in part to the overproduction of exercise-released endorphins and catecholamines. You may first think, 'great, no period', but oestrogen is essential for maintaining healthy bones, and hence a lack of oestrogen will lead to serious health risks. By taking oestrogen and a calcium supplement amenorrhoeic women can stop – but not reverse – the damage to their bones. Consult a doctor if your periods do become infrequent or absent.

Osteoporosis

This almost seems a paradox, as varied exercise like tri training is known to help promote healthy bones and increase bone density. However, amenorrhoea is caused by low levels of oestrogen, and oestrogen is necessary for strong bones. This means females suffering from a lack of menstrual cycle are at risk from stress fractures and osteoporosis. This is true not only for women suffering from amenorrhoea, but also post-menopausal women.

Again, the answer is to cut back and consult medical advice. However, the problem can also be treated by insuring calcium and vitamin supplementation, and the contraceptive pill, which raises oestrogen levels and re-orders menstruation cycles.

Anorexia

Whether you're a gym-goer, runner, triathlete or just an exercise addict, many women (and even more men, especially those involved in endurance sports) develop anorexia. This results from an assumption that the lighter and smaller the body, the faster the athlete. However, this notion is sadly misguided. Obviously, large bodybuilders' muscles aren't required, but muscles are still needed for swimming, cycling and running to take place efficiently and properly. Furthermore, without adequate fuel, performance is greatly hindered and the body will metabolise itself if put under stress. This muscle breakdown and lack of energy leads to a fatigued athlete with less muscular support than necessary, and injuries inevitably occur. The other side effects of anorexia should also be watched for, and again, medical attention should be sought if this becomes a problem.

Women's dietary needs

Chapter 3 outlines diet in general, what to eat, when to eat and what to avoid, and applies to women as well as men except for two specific minerals: calcium and iron. Calcium is needed for bone health, particularly if oestrogen levels are low. Iron is needed – especially for menstruating women – to enable the blood to carry oxygen more readily. Women require more iron than men each day, as much as 18mg when menstruating. A high proportion of women are in fact iron deficient. This is especially true for vegetarians, who can develop anaemia relatively easily if training for long periods or over long distances each week. This is because distance athletes use a huge amount of iron. Sources of calcium include dairy products, dark leafy vegetables, broccoli and canned oily fish, like sardines and salmon. Foods rich in iron include liver, fortified dry cereals, beef and spinach.

Pregnancy

The best advice is that if you already train all three elements of a triathlon then you can continue at the start of your pregnancy. If you don't, then taking up any form of exercise while pregnant is probably not the best idea – your body won't be used to it so will start to make the adaptations that any human does when they start training. However, your body is also adapting to the foetus inside, and it isn't advisable to have both adaptations occurring at the same time. Consult a doctor and do what you feel is comfortable.

Drawbacks of training during pregnancy

● Overheating – Any form of exercise makes us hotter; it also raises our metabolism after we train. However, both of these raise our temperature. If your body temperature gets too high it can harm the foetus.

● Dehydration – This can reduce blood flow around the body and specifically to the uterus, which can in turn cause contractions to start. If you do choose to train, make sure you drink more water than you did when running before you became pregnant.

● Injury – Hormones released during pregnancy make the joints loose to help with childbirth. This can lead to injuries occurring far more readily.

Advantages of training during pregnancy

● Healthier mother and baby – Women who were regular exercisers before becoming pregnant are more likely to have a larger baby. This isn't necessarily something to wince at, as larger babies tend to be stronger and cope better with physical adversity.

● Blood pressure – As long as it's comfortable and not painful in any way, training during pregnancy can keep your blood pressure down, which is more healthy for you and the baby.

● Weight loss – Weight loss after pregnancy will be easier if you continue to train through the early stages, as you'll have kept the metabolism high. However, this is again only good if comfortable, otherwise restup, for both your health and the baby's.

A few guidelines

Pregnant women are far more robust than people give them credit for. Just look at any of the world's tribeswomen, for example: they're known to walk long distances, work hard and carry heavy weights well into their third trimester. This is something that occurs naturally and isn't going to change any time soon. We in the Western world have developed a culture of protection and segregation towards pregnancy. I'm not knocking this – we should still give up our seats on the bus to pregnant women and be aware that pregnant women may lose their

breath or feel sick doing mundane tasks. However, we should also remember that as long as a pregnant woman is healthy she is strong enough to carry on exercising, as long as a few guidelines are kept. It's important to use common sense and if something doesn't feel right, stop and check with your doctor.

● If you were active before becoming pregnant then stay active but cut back. If you were doing full or half-ironman events once a month this may be a little too much! Always err on the sensible side. If you weren't active before pregnancy, you must ease in gently. Of the three events, swimming will be the best until you've given birth.

● Strange cravings during pregnancy are said to be the body's way of saying it requires a vitamin or mineral, so take a multi-vitamin and multi-mineral supplement and ensure you're getting enough red meat and calcium.

- If you're going to keep running as well as swimming and cycling, choose a softer surface to run on to avoid too much impact to the foetus. This may also help to avoid too many stretch marks.
- Despite the extra cost, don't scrimp if you need larger leggings or a sports bra – many companies produce maternity sports bras. Just buy one set and wash them to death for six months. It'll be worth it. The same is true for shoes – wear a more cushioned pair during pregnancy to save your joints.
- When cycling, the recumbent bikes at the gym can be really useful. The position is perfect for pregnancy and allows a (semi) comfortable position that's completely non-impact.

Pregnancy itself

The three trimesters are all very different and each has things that you can and can't do. The key is to listen to your body – whether you're tired, hungry or have aches and pains, just make sure you act accordingly.

First trimester

It's fine to train, but ensure you keep it aerobic and not anaerobic, ie long, slow, steady sessions are fine, but don't make them too intense. Interval training will quickly take you into anaerobic glycolysis, which is too intense and can be harmful to the foetus.

Second trimester

At this point all your life's needs are being split between you and your foetus. For this reason you'll start to feel breathless when active. This isn't due to your fitness levels; it's due to your diaphragm being unable to move as freely because of the little person sitting on it. Continue to exercise if you feel able. Realistically the runs and road bike sessions will probably have to go, but gym recumbent bike sessions and swims can stay, although again, within the aerobic threshold.

At the end of the second and beginning of the third trimester a woman's body starts producing a hormone called relaxin. Its main role is to relax the pelvis to allow it to enlarge during birth; the problem is it acts on the other joints too, and leads to them becoming hypermobile. Advice at this stage would be not to do any high-impact training and to stick to 'closed chain' exercises (ie exercises where the feet stay on the floor), hence swimming and cycling are the way forward. Conditioning can continue, as long as the exercises are also 'closed chain'.

Any exercises that involve the feet leaving and hitting the floor ('open chain' exercises) aren't recommended for ankles, knees and hips weakened by relaxin. Weighted exercises shouldn't be done for the same reason. Body weight exercises are fine if they're 'closed chain', but avoid exercises that open the joints and pelvis, like sumo squats. However, always listen to your body and err on the side of caution.

Third trimester

By this stage the breathlessness of the second trimester has eased off, as the 'bump' has dropped, but due to the size of the bump you can't exercise easily anyway. Strangely though, energy levels usually increase, so staying active is still important. Due to the presence of relaxin, however, lower-impact exercises must be chosen to avoid injury. Walking, swimming, recumbent cycling and aquarunning (you'll be even more buoyant than usual) are all excellent. Exercise should be easy and enjoyable, so don't exercise to the point of breathlessness, which can divert oxygen away from the baby.

Post-pregnancy

For some women relaxin can stay in the body for up to six months after birth, and for others, up to six months after breastfeeding finishes. Unfortunately this means that hypermobility continues and exercise must be progressive, done with low weight, and care must be taken when doing exercises that involve opening the legs, which can be detrimental to the pelvis. It's a good idea to do core strengthening exercises to reverse the action of relaxin and pregnancy; a strong core will stop most injuries, and is imperative for all triathlon events anyway.

> ### Express milk
> Research has suggested that babies dislike the taste of post-exercise breast milk as it's high in lactic acid, which gives it a more sour flavour. Therefore collect milk beforehand or breastfeed before your session, and drink a little more than you usually would.

Final word

The most important thing to remember is to come back into training progressively. You also need to remember the effect the new addition to your family is having. It's likely that baby feeding through the night, added worry and the realisation that life will never be quite the same again will be taking its toll. At this point, assess the importance of training to all your lives. Above all, remember to eat well, ensure you remain well hydrated and use your common sense: listen to your body, know yourself and get enough rest.

> ### Check with your doctor
> If you have any form of operation and have stitches, check with your doctor that it's safe to train before you do.

Conclusion

Men and women are different. We need slightly different kit, we can suffer slightly different injuries, and we're capable of slightly different achievements. So know yourself – take a look at your training schedule in relation to your life. Ensure you're fit, healthy and doing everything you can to be the best you can – whether by wearing a good sports bra, resting at 'that' time of the month, changing your training while pregnant or seeking medical advice as your periods have stopped. Safety and a happy lifestyle must be paramount.

CHAPTER 14
CASE STUDY: MEL BRAND

Melissa Brand is a Maxifuel, Timex, Compress Sport, Zero D-sponsored triathlete who competed in the 2012 World Triathlon Championships. Oh, and she also has a full-time job in the centre of London and has to fit all her training (up to half-ironman events) around her working lifestyle.

I've included Mel in this book not just to get some great tips from a pro/semi-pro triathlete, but also because she is a true inspiration to anyone wishing to get into triathlon who doesn't feel they have the time. If Mel can hold down a full-time central-London job and train twice a day, six days a week, sometimes for five hours on Sunday alone, then surely you can fit in the training for the local sprint race?

Yes, Mel is dedicated, but we already know it takes motivation and dedication. She is organised, focused, and plans her year, months, weeks and races to ensure she can make everything work around her life. She is also a firm believer in strength and conditioning, and the use of food first, and supplements only in support.

Training

As I've said previously, the training programmes in this book are guidelines. Everyone is different, so if you're a strong swimmer you'll spend less time in the pool and more time on the road and bike. If I described Mel's training programme in detail many people would follow it word for word and expect to become a world qualifier, but it doesn't work that way. So instead, let's look at certain elements of Mel's training and how they might help you plan your own.

Mel usually trains twice a day six days a week, though this varies between the race season and the off season, depending on races, tapering and – of course – injury and illness. This doesn't mean Mel smashes herself for 12 sessions a week; she has key sessions that push her stamina or endurance while other sessions keep the heart rate lower to allow for recovery.

⏱ Cycle to and from work

Mel cycles to and from work and the gym, utilising her commute time as a session. Her other sessions are made up of pool and open water swims, runs inside and outside, and cycling on Wattbikes. She's also a firm believer in utilising local 5km, 10km and half-marathon races – along with swim trials, cycle trials and cyclocross events – to test her 'race head' and performance.

During the race season she also includes strength and conditioning. This doesn't mean hitting the weights to increase power and size; much of her conditioning is focused around prehab, to stop problems from recurring. She had to really focus on her glutes and hamstrings last season to take her to the next level, so keeping on top of her conditioning ensures she doesn't lose that strength. This conditioning is focused on the movements and covers all body weight. It's low tempo, often for long periods of time, and used as a pre-fatigue exercise before a bike or run session. It's worth mentioning that although she conditions during the season, it's more important to do this during the off season in order to provide a base foundation for the season ahead.

Most of Mel's training revolves around a seven-day cycle, including a rest day. This changes if she's racing – especially for a big race that she wants to taper for, or a race that involves overseas travel. The only change to this cycle is a nine- or ten-day block if a race is on the cards, so that specific training and rest can be planned for.

In an off-season week Mel's seven-day cycle may well be repeated four to six times over, but she still sees the training as a seven-day cycle.

As has already been mentioned, Mel is a big believer in race practice. She enters races, puts them into her training programme, but doesn't taper for them. She isn't bothered by her placement, she just uses them to her advantage, racing against other athletes in half-marathons, cycling and swimming time trial races to get an idea of how she feels when racing in these disciplines. She says that whatever type of tri you're racing, experience is paramount. Use half-marathons if you're a half-ironman competitor, or 5km or 10km races for sprint and Olympic triathlon competitions respectively, to know what it's like to 'feel this much pain for an hour, two hours etc. If you've never felt it, it's an unknown. You need to feel it to know how to push through it.'

Doing race-length sessions also enables her to test her nutritional planning. She finds race-pace sessions that are also race length test her nutrition pre and during, enabling her to make tweaks by taking more or less with her. Mel has discovered that nutrition doesn't matter as much in the shorter tris, as the body pretty much has the ability to get round. But for half and full ironman events she states that it's imperative to get a good hold on your nutrition needs.

Develop a proper understanding of the amount of calories, therefore the amount of energy gels and drinks, you'll need on a specific race. Mel recalls people carrying dozens of energy gels during Olympic and sprint triathlons, when their energy expenditure is far less than the gels being ingested, so be realistic. Try and test your nutrition in advance so that you don't waste your money and don't make yourself sick!

As discussed in Chapter 4, specificity is key to any sort of fitness training, and triathlon is no different. Mel has found this to be true for her own training, and thus has some sessions that aim to mimic the amount of time for which she'll be competing. Mel is concentrating on half-ironman events at the moment and this is her pre-season training:

- Two hours strength and conditioning. Low level, body weight, but continuous.
- One-hour bike ride, endurance, and time to refuel while cycling.
- Two-hour run, relatively high tempo, meant to mimic the tiredness in the legs after a swim and cycle prior to a long run.

For the half-ironman she'll be aiming for five hours, so this session needs to be as long. The first two parts aren't stressful – they are designed to fatigue the legs like a half-ironman – but the run is meant to be more taxing.

The great thing about this session is that it shows how someone at the top of their game not only values strength and conditioning, but utilises it to mimic fatigue prior to other areas of training – a great example of time management and clever training planning.

It can be argued that this is far less important for sprint and Olympic events, as they aren't long enough for the body to require refuelling or suffer a loss of performance from lack of fuel (provided pre-race food and nutrition has been ingested), but it's still useful. Specificity is, arguably, along with strength and conditioning, one of the most widely accepted and important strategies adopted by professional sportspeople over the last decade.

One thing to consider is that if you're going to use race-length sessions you should allow for similar rest after that session, as you would after a race.

Specificity

Specificity is key to an athlete's performance on many levels, but for me the most important are confidence and knowledge. Before I entered Royal Marine Training I knew the Royal Marines Fitness Test would be used. I wanted to not only pass it, but to be so used to it that it wasn't difficult. I therefore made the test my normal Sunday routine, but always after a 5km run as quickly as possible. I also used specificity while watching football – I'd choose a match on TV, go to the gym and run for the first 45 minutes on a treadmill, stretch and refuel at half-time, then run for another 45 minutes. That way I knew I could run for 90 minutes without any problem.

Rest

As you'll have noticed, rest and recovery has been a constant theme throughout his book. Without it, you can't improve, won't perform at your best and will probably become injured. Mel's take is the same: train hard then rest to allow the body to adapt. She also has no fear of taking a week's complete rest at any point if she's ill or burnt out. Although her training is set and planned in the cycles mentioned above, she's always willing to change it if her body tells her to.

Strengthen a weakness

At one point, Mel's coach 'banned' her from cycling and running until she'd sorted her hamstring and glute strength. Like most triathletes, she was trying to get better by hammering the event's disciplines instead of looking at her personal weak areas. She's now very conscious of the importance of doing core work and prehab: body-weight squats, step-ups and concentrating on the hamstrings and glutes while conditioning. Her running and cycling improved following her coach-enforced 'ban', showing the importance of conditioning at all levels.

After the last race of the season she has a week of complete rest. This doesn't mean doing nothing, but she doesn't do any training. She utilises this 'complete recovery' period to let her body repair, recuperate and relax without undergoing the rigours of triathlon or fitness training. Her diet is also relaxed.

After her rest week Mel's periodisation starts with four weeks' active recovery. This is basically a 'do what you want in terms of fitness' month. It's meant to be enjoyable and just keep the body ticking over, but without any structure or routine. At this point Mel could swim, cycle and run, but she doesn't have to, and there's literally no structure if she does. Equally, she might practise none of these elements, or even do no training at all. Mel says that this period is important for mental, more than physical recovery.

Off season

The off season training programme starts relatively easily, but always concentrates on any weaknesses, either noticed during the season or resulting from old injuries. In a sense this prehab and rehab is the cornerstone of Mel's strength and conditioning. It's therefore functional, with no weights used until she's functionally fit, with a real focus on learning pathways and feeling the body – which muscle works in which movement; which doesn't, and so on. Body weight exercises such as half-lunges, hamstring bridges and squats are key.

Pre-season training

As we'd expect, pre-season Mel continues to work at the individual disciplines, with strength and conditioning, tapering off and key sessions each week working her hard, allowing for recovery sessions. A surprising element, however, is the use of cross-country running races of around 30 minutes and cyclocross races of around an hour through the winter. They're great high-intensity workouts and require concentration, so they keep the mind active in a way a treadmill wouldn't.

Cyclocross is technical, so helps with her cycling ability, as you have to be able to use the bike properly. She firmly believes that these races stop her getting sluggish and makes winter training (which can be gruelling) fun.

 Cyclocross bike

A cyclocross bike is another piece of expensive kit. It can be used in bad weather – snow, ice etc – and since you race with cyclists rather than triathletes it really pushes you and keeps you working hard in rain and cold, and, above all, at a high intensity.

Tapering and choosing races

Mel, like most pro-level triathletes, has a series of races through the season, but has to pick and choose which to race as there are so many. Mel's technique is to grade the races 'A', 'B' and 'C'. She picks a handful of races across the season, decides which are very important, and those 'A' races will be the ones she rests and tapers for. If she didn't do this she wouldn't train, as she would always be tapering for races – some of which aren't that important so she'd rather see them as a really good training session.

General guidelines regarding how many races a triathlete should enter in a season are:

● Sprint – Two a month, as these shouldn't last longer than an hour, so the body can cope with more. If one race is particularly important then just do that one.

● Olympic – One a month.

● Half-ironman – Four half-irons in a season on average, but racing any good sprint or Olympic triathlon is training, so one or two a month.

Nutrition

In terms of diet, Mel is not overly controlling. She has no prescribed diet and doesn't use a dietician. Her diet is a normal one, full of variety, containing carbs, fats and proteins. She does make a conscious effort to eat more protein than less active people. This is to support her high-tempo, high-volume training and ensure she has the necessary building blocks to repair post-session.

She believes in variety across the spectrum when it comes to food, but she does concentrate on lean meats for her proteins and natural carbohydrates such as potato, sweet potato and rice (wholemeal, of course). For breakfast Mel has a no-sugar, no-sodium muesli with yoghurt or soya milk. 'For my level of training I need to eat well, but I don't rule out any food groups. I rely on simple, good quality foods.'

Supplementation

Like any good athlete, Mel tries to get everything she needs primarily from food, especially fruit, vegetables, meat and fish, but she regularly takes vitamins and mineral supplements to aid her recovery and ensure she keeps illness and injury at bay.

She takes Maxifuel BCAAs before and after exercise, the aim being to reduce muscle degradation for fuel once carbohydrate has been utilised (see Chapter 3). During a race or session of considerable length she'll have a mix of energy in powdered drink form, like Viper by Maxifuel, or energy gels. Both provide carbohydrate-loaded fuel to stop the muscles failing through lack of energy. The powdered forms are also isotonic, meaning they'll help with hydration. Mel always takes a recovery shake on finishing a race or hard session. She uses Recovermax by Maxifuel, which is loaded with proteins, carbs and other minerals and macros for all the support needed to replace glycogen stores, refuel and start repairing after a session.

Something Mel has learnt to do is to find out what energy supplements are available on a course, and either train with them for a few days to make sure she can stomach them, or, if she can't, she has to rely on putting her own supplements in a bag and ask someone to hand them to her. This is not particularly reliable. She advises triathletes to be prepared to use what's on course, so to train with it and get used to it beforehand. The last thing you want is to be sick mid-race!

On one occasion, racing in Holland, Mel did her normal routine and found out which supplements were going to be used on the course, and to her surprise it wasn't a regular provider. She tried a sample in advance. She couldn't stomach it and the thought of having to endure it or to go without anything for an entire race meant she had no choice but to take her own supplements. That pre-planning saved her a horrible race experience.

When racing an ironman most people are on the bike for an average of six hours. You only need your energy drinks for that length of time, not your water, as this can always be picked up en route. Mel explains that the pros take three or four bottles of super-concentrated energy powder. To ingest it they take a swig and wash it down with water, which mixes it in the mouth and stomach. The same routine is used for energy gels: rather than tape them to the bike (something a lot of amateur athletes do), the pros put all their energy gels into one bottle. This is far easier than opening wrappers.

💟 Personal experience...

On one Marines course I undertook we were taught that looking professional and slick puts the enemy off 'having a go', and that if you look 'a bag of sh!t', chances are that you are. The same is true when psyching out you triathlon opponents. Look slick, prepared and at ease – it'll make them feel like you've already won. Having bits taped to your bike and wrappers all around you, you'll look a joke and be treated as such.

Glossary

ADP – Adenosine diphosphate.

AT – Anaerobic threshold.

ATP – Adenosine triphosphate.

BCAAs – Branch chain amino acids.

BLABT – Swimming acronym for 'body, legs, arms, breathing, timing'.

bpm – Beats per minute.

Brick – Two or more disciplines trained in one session (usually swim to bike or bike to run).

Carbs – Carbohydrates.

DOMS – Delayed onset muscle soreness.

Duathletes – Competitors in run/bike/ run or bike/run events.

EMHR – Estimated maximum heart rate.

FITT – Acronym for 'frequency, intensity, time, type'.

Gibala interval – A type of interval training.

Glycolysis system – Part of the energy-providing pathways.

HR – Heart rate.

HRM – Heart-rate monitor.

HRR – Heart-rate reserve.

Hypoxic – Without oxygen.

ITU – International Triathlete Union.

LT – Lactate threshold.

MMHR – Measured maximum heart rate.

MRHR – Measured resting heart rate.

NSAID – Non-steroidal anti- inflammatory drugs.

PCr – Creatine phosphate system.

PE – Perceived effort.

PNF – Proprioceptive neuromuscular facilitation.

Prehab – Exercises performed to prevent injury or re-injury.

PRIA – Acronym for 'protection, rest, ice, anti-inflammatories'.

PRICE and PRICE(A) – Acronyms for 'protect, rest, ice, compress, elevate', plus anti-inflammatory medication ('A') when required.

REST – Acronym for 'recovery equals successful training'.

SMART – Acronym for 'specific, measurable, achievable, realistic, timed'.

SPORTP – Acronym for 'specificity, progression, overload, reversibility, tedium, periodisation'.

Tabata interval – A type of interval training.

Tapering – Easing off training before an event.

WHR – Working heart rate.

WTC – World triathlon corporation.

Author acknowledgments

- Huge thanks go to Exeter University, Zoggs, Zoot, TCL, Maxifuel and Ronhill for supplying kit and equipment.
- Thanks to Guy Harrop for being inspired by the idea of shooting a triathlon book and producing some truly amazing images.
- To Kate Braithwaite, Melissa Brand and Mhairi Muir for being such great models.
- Thanks yet again to the amazing Team Haynes: Louise McIntyre, Ian Heath and Rod Teasdale – for turning my black and white mumblings into this beautiful book.
- A second thanks to Melissa Brand, who's dedication to and knowledge of triathlon has hopefully been passed on to you in these pages.
- Thanks to Gill Lerwill for helping me get where I am today and believing in my ever-so-slightly irregular path!
- Thanks to Judith for proof reading my (often) coffee-fueled ramblings, and last, but by no means least, an enormous thank you to Kate Braithwaite, mainly for putting up with me when a deadline was nearing and refusing to count my words!
- Yet again, thank you to the Royal Marine Commandos past, preset and future for giving me the foot in the door, and for the sacrifices each of you make and will continue to make.

Index